I0813993

Nebraska State
HISTORICAL SOCIETY

An American Corner of the World

DAVID J. WISHART

Nebraska State Historical Society | Lincoln

ISBN 978-0-933307-43-8
Library of Congress Control Number: 2025930228
Manufactured in the United States of America

Book design by Anna Hayden-Roy

Nebraska State Historical Society
history.nebraska.gov

Contents

List of Figures

Prologue

This book is a deep geography of an American place, Richardson County, in the far southeastern corner of Nebraska, in the heart of the country. It tells the story of the changing patterns and rhythms of life there, from the first occupants, hunters and gatherers thousands of years ago, right through almost to the present. In one sense, it is a county history, though more analytical than traditional county histories, which tended to focus on notable events and prominent people. Here the focus is more on how ordinary people have lived in, and shaped, the land over time (although notable events are, of course, included). In another sense, the book is a case-study, representative of innumerable rural counties throughout the Midwest and Great Plains that experienced similar stages of initial rapid population growth and subsequent sustained population decline. These counties are all local expressions of national controls and trends – political, economic, cultural, even climatic; their stories share common themes, but are distinctive in their details.

Why then select Richardson County when so many other suitable case-studies could have been chosen? The answer lies in the enduring presence there of Native Americans, with the Iowa and Sac and Fox reservations still occupying the southern reaches of the county. Their experiences over time are also representative of those of other Native American nations across the country, though again expressed locally in distinctive ways. This juxtaposition of accounts of Native American dispossession and American succession allows a fuller story to be told than if only one side were related, and identifies Richardson County as an intrinsically American corner of the world.

An American Corner of the World

Chapter 1

Antecedents, Before 1854

The corner in southeastern Nebraska that became Richardson County in 1854 already had a deep history, evidence of which has survived on the maps and on the landscape right through to the present. Half-Breed Creek, for example, a small incised stream just to the east of Falls City, the county seat, is a reminder of the time between 1830 and 1861 when the area was set aside as a homeland for Indians of mixed descent from the Otoe-Missouria, Omaha, Iowa, Yankton, and Santee Sioux tribes. At one point the creek is reached by an unimproved road, and crossed by an old wooden bridge with a bullet-ridden sign to mark the derogatory name.

The human presence in Richardson County goes much deeper. Just to the east of Half-Breed Creek lies a sloping cornfield where a farmer's plow unearthed a cache of notched and polished stone blades in the 1980s that had been made by anonymous men and women about five thousand years ago. All over the county, bones and tools keep rising from the earth, bringing the past right back into the present.[1]

THE ORIGINAL INHABITANTS

On July 12, 1804, the Lewis and Clark expedition, on its way up the Missouri River in the early stages of its journey to the Pacific, camped on a willow-covered sandbar across from the mouth of the Big Nemaha River. The boatmen were exhausted from poling their large keelboat upstream, generally making less than ten miles a day. There was also the matter of punishing a crew member, Alexander Willard, who was accused of falling asleep on duty. He was found guilty and sentenced to "one hundred lashes on his bear back." [2]

During the stopover, William Clark, always curious about his surroundings, paddled a canoe a few miles up the Big Nemaha. Climbing a hill to the south of the winding river, Clark looked out over "one of the most pleasing prospects" he had ever seen: "a Butifull River of Clear Water" meandering through an "extensive Meadow of tall grass," interspersed with "fine Trees and Shrubs" that were draped with ripening grape vines. This was a typical reaction of explorers who encountered the tallgrass prairie in all its natural splendor.

Clark walked on up the hillside and quickly realized that he, the first known American to cast eyes on the country that would become Richardson County, was actually a newcomer to the place. He saw that the bluffs were "toped by Mounds or antent Graves" and he took this to be "Strong evidence of this country having been thickly Settled" at a previous time. He found more evidence of an earlier human presence on his way back down the Big Nemaha, a large rock that "jucted over the water" and was covered with Indian drawings of animals and a boat. Clark scraped his own name on the rock, adding to the pictorial history.

The people who built the burial mounds were farmers who lived in an earth lodge village situated on a terrace of the Big Nemaha. They grew corn, beans, and squash in the fertile alluvial soil and collected a wide array of wild foods, from yellow lotus tubers to shellfish. Archaeologists have identified the village as one of the most westerly extensions of the Oneota culture, farming peoples who occupied central and northern Iowa from about 1000 CE to 1650 CE. This projection of farming to the west had been enabled by a period of benign climate, warmer and wetter than usual. The archeologists named the village the Leary site, after a local landowner, Ed. F. Leary, who permitted the first systematic excavations in 1935.[3]

The archeologists were not able to exhume the graves at the Leary site because they lie within the Iowa reservation and the Indians had continued to bury their dead there and did not want them disturbed. But they did excavate some of the earth lodges and found them to be square, except for rounded corners, with a fireplace at the center, and a long passageway to an entrance on the west. They discovered human skeletons there too, though they may have been interred after the earth lodges were abandoned. Caches, or storage pits, had been dug in the floors of the earth lodges, and hundreds more pocked the slopes of the bluffs in carefully selected areas of well-drained soils. The caches had initially been used for storing food, then as places to dispose of garbage. The archaeologists also found graves scattered over the slopes, which they described as "overflow from the higher cemetery."

Pottery shards were strewn all over the 125-acre site, and it was mainly the style of pottery (shell-tempered, meaning that ground shells were added to the clay in the firing process) that connected the village to the Oneota complex. Stone artifacts were also abundant, including large granite anvils for grinding cherry and plum pits and pounding meat, scrapers for cleaning bison hides, arrowheads, and knives. Hoes and spades made of bison scapulae were common, as were bone awls used for skin work. Fish spines, which served as perforators, were also found, and there was a single bird bone with a flattened tip which may have been used to shape designs on pottery. The presence of bison bones all over the site proved the importance of this staple, but there was also much evidence of elk, deer, turkeys, and fish, all showing that these early farmers drew from a wide spectrum of the environment for their subsistence.

Like Clark, however, the Oneota peoples were also newcomers to the area. There are five much older archaeological sites in Richardson County, all located on river terraces, particularly along the South Fork of the Big Nemaha. The relics at these sites have been exposed by cultivation and wind erosion, or washed out in river beds – large stone blades, a grooved ax fragment, stemmed projection points, and a fire-cracked rock from some ancient hearth. The artifacts have been dated as Middle and Late Archaic, which means that there has been a human presence in Richardson County for at least 5,000 years. There are another twenty or so archaeological sites in the county that have not yet been thoroughly studied, but if they were it might be shown that human roots go much deeper in this place.[4]

The people who left behind this legacy of stone and bone were small groups of hunters and gatherers who set up winter camps in the sheltered river valleys, with wood, water, and food resources at hand. Similar sites in adjacent Missouri and Kansas reveal that these Archaic hunters relied on deer especially, but also killed other animals, including bison, raccoon, water rat, turkeys, waterfowl, turtles, and fish. Vegetal matter that was used for food has long since decomposed (except for time-defiant carbonized walnut shells), but the people would certainly have collected a wide variety of roots (Indian potatoes, for example), fruits (crabapples grew in abundance), and plants for many purposes, including medicine and adornment. Acorns were a staple in the fall, with those from bur oaks the largest and sweetest.[5] These distant peoples, living their unrecorded lives, occupied the area that became Richardson County thinly and intermittently for nearly all of its human history, making everyone else who followed a newcomer.

At the time of Lewis and Clark the Otoe were the local Indians in southeastern Nebraska. They had been in that vicinity for about a century. In 1798 they were joined by their relatives, the Missouria, who had been pressured west by smallpox and the expanding Sac (Sauk) and Fox. Clark claimed that the Otoe regarded the Missouria as "their inferiors," and it is true that this remained a division in the united society, but the relationship is still intact today in the Otoe-Missouria Tribe of Oklahoma.[6]

In 1804, the Otoe-Missouria (about 1,000 people in all) were living in a single, large earth lodge village on a terrace of the Platte, about a day's journey from its confluence with the Missouri. Lewis and Clark did not make the detour to see it, but six years later the English naturalist, John Bradbury, visited the settlement. The village was empty because the Otoe-Missouria were out on their summer hunt. Bradbury counted "fifty four lodges of a circular form, each about forty feet in diameter." The entrances of the earth lodges were latticed by sticks arranged in precise order, so that any intrusion would be noticed. Finding one open, Bradbury walked into the sunken interior. He counted eighteen posts around the circumference, each about seven feet high, and forked at the top to hold the rafters. Four "strong posts," each about twenty feet high, supported the center of the structure. Smaller branches were laid across the rafters, then a covering of sod and earth. A small hole was left in the roof to allow smoke to escape.[7]

This earth lodge village had been there, or close by (villages were shifted locally when the timber gave out, or the site became polluted with an accumulation of waste), since about 1714. This was the center of Otoe-Missouria life. It was where the Indians performed their most important ceremonies and where they grew their multi-colored crops of corn, beans, squash, and pumpkins. From this center they fanned out for their summer and winter hunts along the Boyer and Nishnabotna rivers in southwestern Iowa and the Big and Little Nemaha rivers in southeastern Nebraska. Before the Otoe-Missouria acquired horses, at some momentous point in the early eighteenth century, they hunted locally in small family groups. After the advent of horses they turned their sights more to the west, to the bison range along the Saline River in Kansas, and they hunted as a village. Horses changed everything, the distance that could be covered, the amount of meat and robes that could be carried back, the way the sick and dying could now be transported instead of being left behind, the fact that you now became a target for other Indians who coveted your prize possession.

Most of the knowledge of age-old Otoe-Missouria life has dwindled away with the passage of time, and as a direct result of an American policy aimed at suppressing Indian traditions and taking their homelands. When the anthropologist William Whitman spent the summer of 1935 with the Otoe-Missouria at Red Rock, Oklahoma (they were squeezed out of Nebraska in 1876 and 1881 to what was then Indian Territory), he found "a complete breakdown of the old culture," and he initially concluded that there was "nothing for an anthropologist to observe." But then he found a handful of elderly men and women who remembered the old ways, and he had them tell their stories, which evoke a richly variegated society.[8]

The elders told Whitman that the Otoe-Missouria were not a tribe, but a close confederation of families; it was the family that people identified with first, not the society as a whole. There were ten such extended families, each of which had its own rituals and responsibilities (and distinguishing haircut, first given to boys at age six). Some of the families were more respected than others – for their insights, or their bravery, and especially their generosity. Whitman learned that this was a class society, with hereditary chiefs at the top, followed by renowned warriors and men with sacred knowledge, and then by the mass of the common people. The elderly informants explained that women were subordinate to men, only eating after the men were finished, and never walking in front of them. But elsewhere in their stories they emphasized that women had power, especially in the fields, where they owned the crops they grew, and in the lodges, where they made the day-to-day decisions. The women were also described as the foundations of loving families. Children were desired and affectionately nurtured. Marriages were generally stable, but if not, divorce was an option. The main conflicts in society stemmed from jealousy and adultery, and retributive punishment could be severe, including maiming or even murdering the offending man or woman. The old people also spoke of the rules and procedures for minimizing conflict, such as sharing a peace pipe to make up for a transgression, giving gifts to earn forgiveness, and the taboo that forbade speaking between a mother-in-law and a son-in-law in the lodge.

They explained to Whitman that their names for the months were not abstract like ours, but place-specific, describing the turning of the year as manifested in the environment and their lives in it. September, for example, was "the month when the deer having laid down walk away leaving a frosted form," and March the "no-account moon," when there was little to do between the end of the bison hunt and the beginning of the farming cycle. And Whitman's informants described time-honored customs like burying a dead man's horse next to his grave, so that he could be carried to the spirit world, a better place that lay across a river to the north. This is some of how they lived in this small corner of the world, and it must have worked, because it lasted a long time.

The Indians' enduring world had already drastically changed by the time of Lewis and Clark. The outside world appeared, as if from nowhere, the far fringes of competing global empires: French fur traders filtered into Otoe-Missouria country from the east, sometimes marrying into the tribe; Spaniards, reacting to the French expansion, came in from the southwest in the form of the Villasur expedition of 1720 which ended in abject defeat at the hands of a combined Pawnee and Otoe force on the lower Platte. That same year Otoe raided west towards Santa Fe, killing twenty Spaniards.[9]

Contact with Europeans brought, in addition to the beneficial horse, guns that escalated the scale and carnage of war, alcohol, which tore individuals and societies apart, and disease, especially smallpox, which could hollow out an uncomprehending people in a matter of weeks. Although no historical record exists to directly attest to this, the Otoe and Missouria (still living separately at this point) were surely devastated by the 1779-82 smallpox pandemic, which played havoc with Indigenous life from Mexico City to Hudson's Bay. They definitely were struck by the 1802 epidemic, which worked its brutal way up the Missouri and out onto the Plains. Lewis and Clark encountered evidence of its toll all the way up the river in the summer and fall of 1804.[10]

These traumas intensified after the United States took over in 1803, but Americans added a new dimension of change: they wanted Indian lands. Even by 1800, American settlers had crossed the Appalachians and moved into Kentucky, Ohio, and southern Indiana and Illinois, compressing Indian space as they went. They brought death and dislocation to the Indians, whether they meant to or not, because settlers wiped out the game that the Indians depended upon, causing widespread starvation.

The young, perceptive French traveler and political philosopher, Alexis de Tocqueville, witnessed this destruction in the winter of 1831-1832, as he moved through New York to the extremity of American settlement at Saginaw, Michigan Territory. He was appalled by what he saw and perplexed that a self-proclaimed enlightened society could allow such horrors to occur. As he later wrote, "I have witnessed afflictions beyond my power to portray." [11]

Tocqueville understood exactly what was happening. As Americans moved west, they "scattered the Indian tribes far into the wilderness," either through treaty agreements or simply by displacement. This broke the Indians' "chain of memory," forcing them to leave their homelands and the graves of their ancestors behind. This wasn't necessarily accomplished by warfare, Tocqueville sarcastically explained, but effected "with wonderful ease, quietly, legally, and philanthropically, without spilling blood and without violating a single one of the principles of morality." To Americans this was a pre-ordained succession, a triumph of "civilization over savagery." Tocqueville summarized the tragic process in a single, chilling sentence: "It is impossible to destroy men with more respect to the laws of humanity."

As the Indians retreated westward, across the Mississippi and on towards the Missouri, they entered the lands of their enemies and fought with them over the diminishing game. As Tocqueville put it, there was "famine behind them, war in front, and misery everywhere."

By 1830, this zone of dislocation and death was centered over western Iowa, a hunting range that the Otoe-Missouria had traditionally claimed as their own. Dislodged Midwestern tribes such as the Potawatomi, Iowa, and Sac and Fox, together with the Yankton and Santee Sioux from the north, fought with the Otoe-Missouria and with each other over what was left of the wildlife. This was the dire context for the Otoe-Missouria's first sale of land to the United States, on July 15, 1830 at the Treaty of Prairie du Chien. (Fig. 1)

The consequences of this treaty were still unfolding in the newly created Richardson County in the 1850s, and in a sense are still unfolding now, in the controversial place-name, Half-Breed Creek.

THE NEMAHA HALF-BREED TRACT

The immediate purpose of the Treaty of Prairie du Chien, as far as the United States was concerned, was to separate the warring tribes into hunting zones of their own, in order to stop the conflict. Another short-term goal was to get the treaty participants – Omaha, Otoe-Missouria, Iowa,

Sac and Fox, and Yankton and Santee Sioux – to "cede and relinquish" their claims to western Iowa so that dislocated Midwestern Indians could be resettled there. The long-term goal was to free up more land for American settlers, who had already advanced into what would become Iowa Territory in 1838.

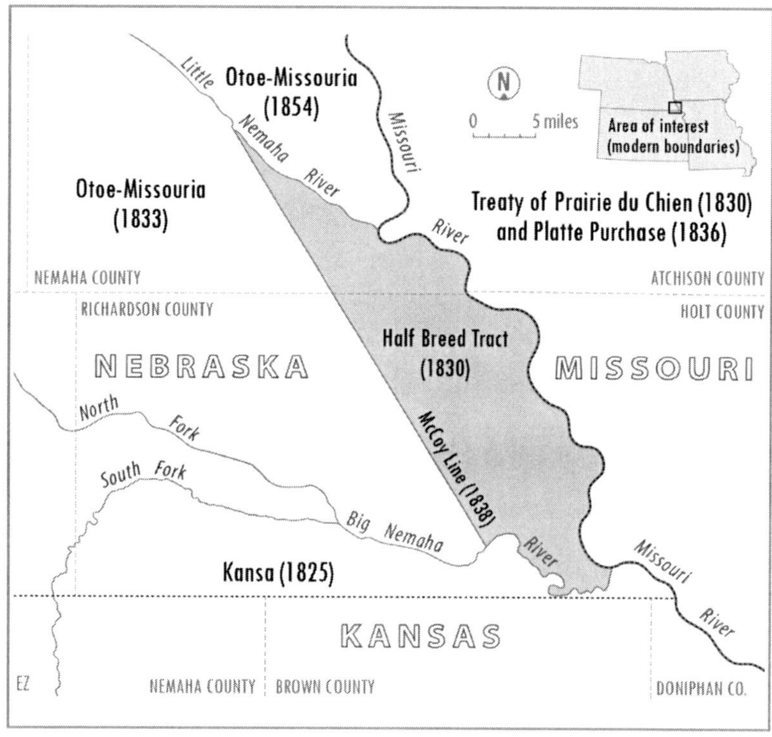

1. Original Indian Cessions

The purpose of the treaty, as far as the Otoe-Missouria and the other Indians were concerned, was to get the United States to provide them with support, because as the game disappeared in this war-torn space they could no longer support themselves. This was the recurring process of obtaining Indian lands all the way across the United States: destitute

Indians selling their only remaining asset, land, for a poor living on government annuities. Tocqueville observed and understood this too, and he wrote: "In this way Americans acquire whole provinces." [12]

After a week of speeches (hardly negotiations, because the United States had already decided the outcome), the assembled Indians agreed to the terms offered by the government's chief negotiator, William Clark (by this time Superintendent of Indian Affairs), and sold an estimated 16 million acres for $317,732. The probable fair market value for land at the time was $20 million. Clark had assured the Indians that "we don't purchase those lands with a view to settling white people on them," yet just a week later he wrote to the Commissioner of Indian Affairs, Thomas McKenney, boasting that he had obtained "a disposable country of the best lands on the Missouri." Potawatomi, Chippewa, and Ottawa were settled in the ceded lands until they, in turn, were moved out in 1846 to make room for Americans.[13]

The Otoe-Missouria's share of the proceeds for the relinquishment of their hunting grounds on the east side of the Missouri River was an annual payment of $2,500 for ten years, in money, domestic animals, and supplies. They were also to be provided with a blacksmith and $500 worth of agricultural implements. The objective was to get the Indians individualized by settling them on small plots of land, or allotments. Once settled on their allotments, with the Indian men farming, rather than hunting and raiding, the Indians would be declared assimilated, and all their remaining lands – "surplus lands," in the language of the time – would be available for Americans. This was standard federal Indian policy for the entire nineteenth century, as much a part of the American story as the Homestead Act.

One section in the 1830 treaty, Article X, related specifically to the Otoe-Missouria, and it produced the Nemaha Half-Breed Tract.

Apparently, the Omaha, Iowa, Otoe-Missouria, and Yankton and Santee Sioux had "earnestly requested" that their "half-breeds" be provided with a reservation. Moreover, they had a definite idea where this "tract of country" should be located: in a triangle of land lying between the Missouri and the Big and Little Nemaha rivers in southeastern Nebraska, with its base in the future Richardson County and its apex to the north in Nemaha County. Specifically, the boundaries traced the Little Nemaha to a point ten miles from its mouth, then struck out on a "direct line" for twenty miles to the Big Nemaha, which was followed down to its junction with the Missouri. The meandering Missouri marked the eastern boundary[14] (Fig. 1).

The twenty-mile-long "direct line" was the first straight line ever used to organize space in the area that would become Richardson County, the first of many to come.

As compensation for the cession of the Half-Breed Tract, the Otoe-Missouria would be paid $300 a year for ten years, the money coming not from the United States, but from the newly established annuities of the Omaha, Iowa, Yankton and Santee Sioux. The mixed-bloods would occupy the Tract in communal Indian fashion, but Article X also raised the possibility of assigning 640 acres of land to each individual, an early iteration of the allotment policy, the putative Indian disappearing act.

It is not clear why the mixed-bloods were singled out for such special treatment, but there are at least two feasible explanations.[15] The first is ideological: mixed-bloods, having Euro-American fathers (mainly French) were seen as "more susceptible to improvement," more likely to become Americanized and settled down to farming on allotments. As Tocqueville wrote, in the harsh language of the time, "the half-caste forms the natural link between civilization and barbarism," and he went on to claim that "everywhere the half-castes have multiplied, the savages have gradually changed their social condition and their mores."[16] The expectation was that the mixed-bloods would furnish an example for other Indians to follow along the path to assimilation.

The second possible reason for setting this land aside for mixed-bloods is more pragmatic: the Nemaha Half-Breed Tract may have been a reward to the mixed-bloods for getting their various tribes to agree to the terms of the Treaty of Prairie du Chien. They may have planned to receive the titles to their 640-acre allotments, then sell them to advancing American settlers and speculators. As it turns out, that didn't happen until 1860. Meanwhile, the Nemaha Half-Breed Tract, the first reservation in Nebraska, was a land in limbo, largely unoccupied by the mixed-bloods it was intended for, unclear as to its boundaries, and uncertain in its legal status.

It seems that the Tract was unoccupied until the early 1850s, except by Otoe-Missouria who continued to hunt there from their villages on the lower Platte. In 1833, Maximilian, Prince of Wied, the distinguished German naturalist, recorded in his journal that 150-200 mixed-bloods were eligible to settle there (a "beautiful romantic country," in his opinion), but none had done so. The parent tribes themselves, in a petition to Superintendent Clark in 1836 asking that the mixed-bloods be assigned their allotments, described the Tract as "unsurveyed and unoccupied."

In 1838, John Dougherty, Indian agent at the Upper Missouri Agency, recommended that the United States should buy out the mixed-bloods' interests in the Tract for $1 an acre, so that removed Potawatomi could be placed there. Dougherty bolstered his argument by noting that the Tract – "as good a land in any respect as can be found in the whole Missouri country" – had never been occupied by the mixed-bloods. Two years later, Isaac McCoy, Baptist minister and fervent advocate of moving eastern Indians to beyond the Missouri River, away from the corrupting influence of Americans, wrote that the mixed-bloods (whom he characterized as "more of white blood than of Indian") had "never resided on the land, or expected to do so." Like Dougherty, McCoy wanted to buy out the mixed-bloods' rights to the Tract (for $300 each) and settle other Indians there. McCoy rightly feared that if they were each given their 640 acres, then these allotments would quickly fall into the hands of speculating Americans, and the "permanent Indian frontier" on the Great Plains would be breached.[17]

In the 1840s, government plans for the Nemaha Half-Breed Tract vacillated between allocating the 640-acre allotments promised in the 1830 treaty, and purchasing the mixed-bloods' interest in the land. Mostly, it seems, the government just ignored the issue. By the end of the decade, as Americans settled Iowa and Missouri to their western borders and looked longingly across the Missouri River to boundless land, solving the issue became more imperative. In 1849, Superintendent of Indian Affairs David D. Mitchell urged that the Tract be bought back because no mixed-bloods wanted to live there. Mitchell was worried that the cost of buying the land would only increase as Americans approached from the east. The mixed-bloods were well aware of this too, and they began to occupy the area. By 1853, according to Daniel Vanderslice, Indian agent at the Great Nemaha Agency, sixty mixed-bloods were living there, along the Missouri bottoms, making "some advances towards civilization," with "comfortable houses," and "large fields under good fences." Vanderslice wanted to assign each eligible adult 640 acres, with 320 acres going to each of their children. With the Kansas-Nebraska Act and the opening of Nebraska Territory to American settlers only a year away, something had to be done about the Nemaha Half-Breed Tract.[18]

The dilemma was bequeathed to Richardson and Nemaha counties after 1854. The situation was further complicated by the chaotic process of surveying the Tract boundaries. The first survey was made under the auspices of Isaac McCoy in 1837. McCoy delegated the job to his son,

John Calvin McCoy, who started by surveying the meanders of the Big Nemaha river. But his work was soon interrupted by a death in the family, and he returned home to Westport, Missouri. The younger McCoy handed responsibilities over to a J.W. Polke, who had no surveying experience, but was nevertheless, in McCoy's opinion, "a highly intelligent young man." Polke completed the survey of the Missouri River boundary. The following year, Isaac McCoy appointed a certain Mr. Donohoe to complete the survey, which apparently he did. At some point thereafter, John Calvin McCoy discovered that the location of the straight line western boundary was wrong, so he took out a surveying party and corrected it.

This convoluted process of patchwork surveys resulted in substantial errors in the location and size of the Tract. Islands in the Missouri which should have been included were not, and the river, snaking across the wide floodplain dropping meanders like skins, was itself an unreliable boundary. As a result of the shifting course of the river, and of ongoing river erosion, the southern boundary of the Tract only extended eight miles up the Big Nemaha, instead of the ten miles stipulated in Article X of the 1830 treaty. This displaced the western boundary considerably. The size of the incorrectly surveyed Tract was given as 143,647.33 acres by Isaac McCoy in 1838 [19] (Fig. 2).

At the time, these errors were unimportant, because the area was unoccupied, and no real action was being taken to allot it or to sell it on the mixed-bloods' behalf. But after May 30, 1854, when the Kansas-Nebraska Act opened the floodgates and Americans poured in, the exact location of this choice piece of land became a matter of paramount importance.

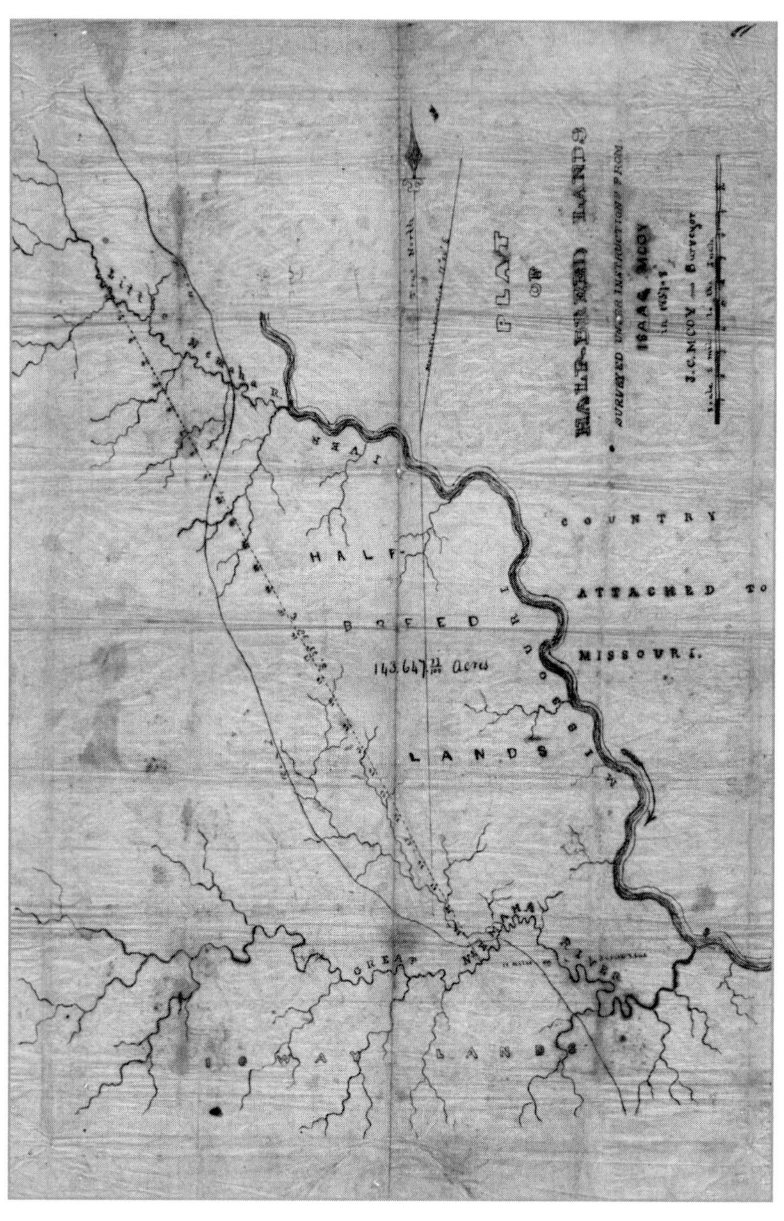

2. "Plat of Half-Breed Lands" 1837-8.
Courtesy Nebraska State Historical Society. Folder RG0726.

EMIGRANT INDIANS

In the 1830s, southeastern and northeastern Kansas became a resettlement zone for fragmented Midwestern tribes whose pieces had been scattered to the four winds. This meant that the resident Indians, the Otoe-Missouria and, to their south, the Kansa, were obliged (by poverty, famine, and government persuasion) to sell vast portions of their homelands so that the uprooted Indians could be moved in.

The first cession was made by the Kansa in 1825, an expanse of rolling grasslands in northern Kansas and southern Nebraska, 18 million acres in all, for which the Indians were paid one-half cent an acre.[20] The Big Nemaha River formed the northeastern boundary of this cession, so effectively in 1825 the United States acquired title to much of the southern half of the future Richardson County.

The remainder of the area that would become that county, outside of the already-ceded Nemaha Half-Breed Tract, was sold by the Otoe-Missouria in 1833 for 4.1 cents an acre, in yet another treaty negotiated by William Clark (he may well have acquired more Indian land for the United States than any other American). Again, the purpose of the treaty was to clear the resident Indians' title to the land to make room for displaced Indians. The cession was vaguely described as beginning at the northwest corner of the Half-Breed Tract and extending as far west "as said Otoe and Missouria have, or pretend to have any claim." [21] The Otoe-Missouria, splintered and destitute, settled in four villages to the south of the lower Platte, where they continued to starve and die.

No emigrant Indians were ever moved into relinquished Otoe-Missouria lands, but on September 17, 1836, through the "Platte Purchase," portions of the Iowa and Sac and Fox relinquished their claims to the increasingly populated and contested country to the east of the Missouri

River (what is now the northwestern corner of the state of Missouri) and accepted reservations bounded on the north by the Nemaha River and reaching down to the recently established (1832) Kickapoo reservation in northwestern Kansas. Specifically, they were given in total 400 sections of land, reaching from the floodplain of the Big Nemaha, up over the same bluffs where William Clark had found the burial mounds of ancient peoples, and south over the dissected uplands of northeastern Kansas. To the east, the reservation lands descended more than 200 feet down gullied, wooded slopes to the wide floodplain of the Missouri. The Iowa were allocated the northern half of the 400 sections, with the Sac and Fox located below.[22] The specific extent of the reservations in this unsurveyed area was obscure. Isaac McCoy simply separated the two tribes with a boundary after the fact in 1837, according to where they had located their villages (Fig. 3).

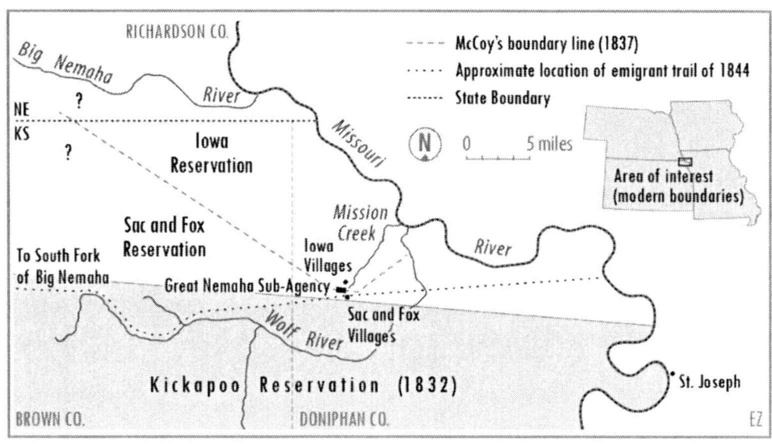

3. Iowa and Sac and Fox Villages, 1837-1854.

The Iowa and Sac and Fox were each paid $7,500 for their Missouri cession, given the services of blacksmiths, farmers, and teachers, provided with agricultural implements, cows and hogs, and furnished with ferry boats to get them across the Missouri. The United States also promised to provide each tribe with "five comfortable houses" and to plow and fence 200 acres, once they had selected sites for their villages. The boundaries of these reservations have since been changed many times, but the Iowa and Sac and Fox reservations are still there in the twenty-first century, straddling the Kansas-Nebraska line.

The transition to the new reservations was not an easy one. Back in their villages to the east of the Missouri, they were overrun by Americans, especially after the 1836 treaty was signed and it was confirmed that the Indians would soon be gone. Settlers were crowding into these "new lands," the Iowa sub-agent Andrew Hughes reported to William Clark, keeping the Indians "constantly drunk" as they traded their horses, guns, and blankets for whiskey. Hughes explained that starving Indians had been killing the settlers' cattle and hogs, and he warned of a "cloud of danger approaching." The 1836 treaty had anticipated such conflict in justifying the removal of the Iowa and Sac and Fox, stating that the Indians' continued presence to the east of the Missouri would "inevitably lead to collisions with the citizens of the United States." [23] It was the familiar story of Indian dispossession and removal, rolling out westward.

So the Iowa and Sac and Fox, again uprooted, made the trek across the Missouri River, which they hoped would put some distance and a barrier between them and the advancing tide of American settlement. The crossing of the river by more than 1,000 Indians would have been a challenge in itself, because at the time the ferry boats were just sawed lumber planks tied together and powered by a couple of men with poles. At best they were pulled across the Missouri by a rope tethered to a horse. The Indians were also moving during the farming season, so this foundation of the food supply would have been lost. Emergency provisions provided through the 1836 treaty (to the amount of $500 for the Iowa and $400 for the Sac and Fox) barely kept them alive.[24]

By June 1837 the move to their "new permanent home," a place that carried no sacred meaning for them and had none of their history written on the landscape, was complete. The Indians settled in bark-lodge villages, two for each tribe, in the verdant Wolf River valley, in what is now Doniphan County, Kansas.

The disruption of the migration, and the failure of the United States to deliver the promised annuities in a timely manner, left the Indians without supplies, until the local traders provided them on credit. And so began the downward spiral into indebtedness, which became an inescapable fact of life.[25] For the traders (most of them mixed-bloods) the Indians were a lucrative source of profit: at first for the skins and furs they provided, until the local wildlife was gone, and then for their annuities, which the traders took as payment for Indian debts.

What followed through to the Kansas-Nebraska Act were years of impoverishment for the Iowa and the Sac and Fox – of frequent famine, epidemics of smallpox, typhoid, cholera, and malaria, and social disintegration brought about by the deteriorating conditions of life. The harsh living conditions resulted in rapidly declining populations. Population estimates are complicated by the frequent movement of families back and forth to related bands who had retained land in Iowa, or had been moved separately to Kansas. Nevertheless, it appears that by 1854, the Iowa and Sac and Fox of the Great Nemaha sub-agency had only half the population they had brought to their new reservations in 1837.[26]

Even by 1842, when their sub-agent William Richardson made a detailed count, their populations had plummeted. Nine hundred and ninety-two Iowa and 510 Sac and Fox had initially settled on the reservations in 1837, but five years later there were only 470 of the former and 414 of the latter living there. To the north the Otoe-Missouria were experiencing a similar population collapse, from about 1,100 in 1830 to 500 in 1860.[27]

The Indian zone of death that had been centered on western Iowa in 1830 had moved west across the Missouri to envelop eastern Kansas and Nebraska.

The causes of the population decline were multiple and connected: disease rendered the Indians too weak to farm or hunt, and undernourished Indians then contracted more disease. Warfare may have also played a role, but if it had been an important factor in the Indians' population decline there would have been a significant demographic imbalance, because in warring societies (the Pawnees, for example, to the west, who were in a fight for survival with the Lakotas) there were many more women than men, because the men died in disproportionate numbers while raiding or defending against raids. As it was, according to Richardson's 1842 census, there were relatively equal numbers of adult men and women among the Iowa, and more men than women among the Sac and Fox. What does stand out from Richardson's count is that there were few people above the age of forty (66 from the total of 470 for the Iowa and 29 from 414 for the Sac and Fox).[28] Clearly, the hard conditions of life in this new country took a heavy toll on the elderly.

Famine was a perennial problem, but it was worst in late winter and early spring, after the meat from the winter hunt had been consumed, and before wild plants could be collected or crops cultivated. The year 1845 was particularly spare. The Indians' crops had failed entirely in 1844, and the 1845 harvest was not much better. Sub-agent Hugh J. McClintock reported in September that his charges were "destitute" and "nearly naked." The Otoe-Missouria fared no better during these years, and at one point were actually reduced to eating the grass thatch from their lodge roofs just to survive. The deprivation continued. In 1848 Swiss artist Rudolph Friederich Kurz, who was traveling west to study and paint Indians, came across thirty lodges of Iowas camped in the bluffs across the Missouri from the bustling frontier town of St. Joseph. They would go there to collect the "clippings and cuttings of meat" that remained after the butchering of hogs. They were reduced to this, Kurz explained, because the local animals they had depended upon were "well-nigh exterminated," and bison and elk had "retreated long since to regions farther west."[29]

Even when a large store of dried meat was brought in (as the Iowa did in 1839), or the crops were successful (which was the case at Sac and Fox villages in 1843), there might still not be enough food to suffice because they would share what they had with less fortunate Indians. In 1843, for example, starving Kansa and Otoe-Missouria converged on the Iowa and Sac and Fox villages, asking for food. Sub-agent Richardson reported that they did indeed share what food they had, and he commented, "they will always give as long as they have any to spare." [30] Such generosity was a hallmark of Indian life, and tellingly it was one of the targets of the assimilation policy, which sought to undermine the communality of the Indians and make them competitive with each other.

Epidemic diseases, another cause of population decline, could alter the demography of an Indian nation overnight. Despite vaccination efforts by the government, which were started in the 1830s, focusing on Indian children, smallpox remained a terrifying threat. In 1851, for example, Richardson reported that the Sac and Fox had "suffered severely" from smallpox in the spring, losing about one-fifth of their people. The Iowa were spared by an emergency vaccination effort, but 300 Winnebago who were camped north of the mouth of the Big Nemaha (they were seeking to join the Iowa, with whom they were considerably inter-married) were hit badly, leaving them "desperate and forlorn." [31]

The Missouri River had been a diffusion route for exogenous diseases ever since French and Spanish fur traders had begun moving upstream in numbers from St. Louis in the second half of the eighteenth century. Then, starting in 1844, disease found a new way into Plains Indians' lives, as thousands of Americans left from just north of St. Joseph each year, heading up the Wolf River valley to the South Fork of the Nemaha, then up the Big Blue to the Platte, and on to South Pass, leapfrogging the Indians all the way to the fields of the Willamette and, after 1849, to the goldfields of northern California. These American migrants, with their caravans of wagons and livestock, passed within a stone's throw of the Iowa and Sac and Fox villages. In addition to importing disease (including cholera), the migrants cut the Indians' timber, depleted the forage, and killed what little game was left. They also brought alcohol right to the doors of the Indians' lodges: by 1844 the five "comfortable houses" (log cabins) provided in the 1836 treaty had been stripped of their doors, windows, and hardware, anything that could be traded for liquor.[32]

While these deprivations and encroachments were occurring, the Indians were being put under constant pressure from Indian agents to individualize, to reject all they had known and completely change their ways of living. From 1837 to 1851 the Iowa and Sac and Fox were administered by the Great Nemaha Sub-Agency, which was part of the Council Bluffs Agency. Thereafter, they were given their own agency, the Great Nemaha Agency, located at Noharts, in what would soon be Richardson County.[33]

The agents and sub-agents had very little success in transforming Indian lives. This was partly because of their inefficiency and rapid turnover (there were six different sub-agents from 1840 to 1851), but it was mainly to do with the Indians' continuing attachment to the old ways. The men had no desire to give up the excitement of hunting and raiding to do what they regarded as women's work in the fields. Even in 1854 they were all still living in communal villages, rather than in individual homes on separate plots of land. As Richardson acknowledged in 1852, "they are remarkable for their tenacious adherence to their aboriginal customs." This was clearly demonstrated in 1854 when they spent their annuity money on horses – not sturdy work horses for the fields, however, but small fast horses for the hunt.[34]

The assimilation program was also promoted by Presbyterian missionaries, who opened a boarding school in 1846 (which still stands today, reduced in size and renovated, in a glade off a side road just east of Highland, Kansas). Their strategy was to change Indian children at an early age by preaching the Bible and giving them practical skills so that they could become self-sufficient farmers on their own allotments. The school had a capacity of 100, but there were rarely more than thirty students in attendance at any one time; most left to fulfill the traditional roles of Indian men and women by the age of twelve. The missionaries also gave sermons to the adults, but at best they were just tolerated because their teachings seemed to be of no practical value to the Indians.[35]

Despite the tightening grip of American power, the Indians were still the main authors of their own story, charting their own road through this new world that had been thrust upon them. The remarkable year-long tour of England, Ireland, and France by fourteen Iowa men, women, and children (including their head chief, White Cloud) in 1844-45 shows this independence and their abiding confidence in their own way of life.[36]

The Iowa were recruited by an entrepreneur, George Henry Curzon Melody, to visit Europe and perform their dances and ceremonies to a distant audience. The noted American artist and explorer George Catlin, who had visited the Iowa in the early 1830s, lent his assistance. White Cloud saw this venture as a way to make money and repay their traders' debts. It is also likely that they were just curious about this outside world that they were supposed to emulate: Indians could be explorers too.

The Iowa performed their Scalp Dance, War Dance, and Wolf Dance, and other ceremonies before rapt audiences who had come to see, in their eyes, the dying embers of a society about to become extinct. They performed before royalty, and at the famous Lord's cricket ground, and were invited to breakfast with Prime Minister Benjamin Disraeli. Everywhere they traveled, they were deluged by religious leaders from a wide array of Christian denominations (the Iowa were surprised, and amused, that white people had more than one religion) who sought to convert them. The Iowa were polite in response, but steadfast in their belief that the Great Spirit had given them their own particular religion.

As they traveled to London, Dublin, Paris, and the grimy coalfields of North East England, they keenly observed, and even kept a record of, the landscapes and life in these (to them) exotic places. They were impressed by the accumulation of wealth in these newly industrializing societies, as expressed in grand buildings like York Minster and Westminster Abbey. But they mainly saw the ubiquitous gin palaces and the manifest Dickensian poverty. In North East England, for example, they witnessed women and children dragging coal trucks by means of a harness around their waists, their knees and fingers bleeding from the effort. They could hardly credit that self-proclaimed enlightened societies would put debtors in prison and animals in prison-like zoos. If this was civilized Christian life, then they wanted nothing to do with it. And, of course, they failed to make any money, because expenses consumed earnings, and besides, they gave much of what they did earn to beggars who swarmed them wherever they went. The Iowa returned home in July 1845, filled with stories, and perhaps with an understanding that change was imminent and inevitable, but in no sense shaken in the rightness of their deepest beliefs.

It is hardly surprising that time-honored ways which had worked for generations would not be jettisoned just because strangers wanted them to change. Even in 1859, by which time the land around them was filling up with American settlers, their agent A. B. Greenwood was obliged to admit the Indians still harbored "prejudices against labor which are so deeply fixed in their minds during childhood by the recital in their wigwams of the traditions, tales, and fabulous accounts of chiefs and braves."

Inspired by such oral histories, Greenwood continued, the male child saw his "route to success" through war and the hunt, and the young female, impressed by the intended heroics, encouraged "with her smiles and admiration" the aspiring warriors and hunters.[37] In later years, following the Kansas-Nebraska Act, the Indians would move out of the villages and onto allotments, but only because they were forced to, or because they saw it in their own interests to do so.

So in the years leading up to 1854, the Iowa and Sac and Fox continued to follow their traditional rhythms of life, albeit in increasingly strained circumstances. Even though the agents insinuated themselves into the Indians' world, bypassing the chiefs in the distribution of annuities, for example (so undermining their status), and persistently urging the Indians to disband their communal villages and lifestyles, they remained in 1854 a "roving people," living as they always had done.[38]

Each year, the Indians would go out on summer and winter hunts, sometimes just dispersing along the Missouri valley, but also moving far to the west, to a bison range contested by the Pawnee, Cheyenne, Arapahoe, and Osage. In total, they might be absent on hunts for six months of the year, living in tipis or small bark-lodges in cloistered river valleys.

They returned from their winter hunts to their villages in April, the month the Otoe-Missouria called "the time they dig the earth."[39] They began their year anew with a major planting ceremony supervised by the chiefs of the Buffalo clan. The women then commenced clearing the fields and interplanting corn, beans, pumpkins, and squash in their garden plots. Periodically, men would slip away in war parties to raid the Omaha, Pawnee, Kansa, and Osage; if successful, they would return with trophies of scalps attached to the tops of their lances. They would then perform the Scalp Dance for fifteen nights, recounting their feats of courage.

One such incident occurred in July of 1854. The Sac and Fox were out on their summer bison hunt on the plains of central Kansas when they were attacked by a combined force of Comanche, Arapahoe, and Osage, leaving at least one Sac and Fox dead. Soon after, a brother of the murdered man took it upon himself to seek revenge and he confronted two Osage men on the range. He shot one of them and scalped him, but he spared the other so that he could take the bad news back to the Osage camp. The brother waited near the camp until he heard the "cries and lamentations" of the Osage, then, his debt satisfied, he left for home with the scalp. B. A. James, in control of the Great Nemaha Agency at the time, recounted that the entire Sac and Fox nation celebrated the returning hero by "dancing with joy and triumph over the trophy brought back in this warlike achievement to them." [40]

The Indians also continued to visit other tribes, especially relatives like the Otoe-Missouria and Winnebego, but also their erstwhile enemies, the Pawnee and Omaha, establishing temporary peace for the duration of the stay by creating short-term family relations. Such visits might last for months, intertribal celebrations where dances were performed, stories related, ideas exchanged, alliances strengthened, marriages made. Visiting was an emancipation, an escape from the fixity of the reservation and the relentless assault on their traditions by agents and missionaries. Even in the early twentieth century the Office of Indian Affairs continued to rail about the practice of visiting, which, it claimed, led to idleness.

The Indians' landscapes still evoked the deep past rather than a transformed present. Their main villages in the Wolf River Valley were comprised of bark lodges, each about thirty by twenty feet in size, and each housing a large extended family. The lodges had split elm or walnut bark slabs for sides, and roofs of bark laid on a frame of poles tied together by bark strips. A large bark shield served as a door. Sleeping platforms, and altars that held sacred bundles and pipes, lined the walls. Outside, raised platforms were draped with the wrapped bodies of the dead, along with tobacco and other gifts that would see the deceased comfortably into the hereafter. The Indians continued to wear their traditional clothing – bison robes and wolf and deer skins, and, for decoration, elaborate bear claw necklaces and shell ornaments – not the "citizens dress" of shirts, suits, and shoes that the agents tried to impose upon them. Prominent men and women were tattooed with "dots, diamonds, stars, lines, and feathers." Warriors had lines tattooed on the wrists, indicating the number of scalps they had taken.[41] This was the prevailing human geography of this place as Americans, who saw the world very differently, crowded in all around after 1854.

THE KANSAS-NEBRASKA ACT

The Kansas-Nebraska Act, which opened up Kansas and Nebraska Territories to American settlers, was signed into law by President Franklin Pierce on May 30, 1854. The two territories were divided at the 40° North line of latitude; both stretched west to the Rocky Mountains, and Nebraska Territory reached all the way to Canada.[42]

The Act had been a long time coming. Its main architect, Stephen Douglas, initially a Congressman from Illinois, first introduced a bill to organize Nebraska Territory in Congress in 1844, where it was defeated, not least because of southern opposition: the Missouri Compromise of 1820 had excluded slavery from those parts of Louisiana Territory north of the 36°30' line of latitude (a western extension of the southern boundary of Missouri).

Douglas had a continental vision: he wanted railroads to be built from the Mississippi valley to the Pacific, and he particularly favored a route that would extend westward from his home state. In order for this to occur, Douglas reasoned, a new territory had to be organized so that American settlement could be projected in a band, a linear railroad land grant, all the way to the Pacific. The plan was delayed for a decade for three main reasons: the extension of slavery into the West; the choice of a route for the transcontinental railroad; and the "permanent Indian barrier" to the west of the Missouri, which stood in the way of such an American expansion.[43]

The slavery issue was temporarily overcome by yet another compromise. In 1850, Utah and New Mexico Territories were organized under the rule of popular sovereignty; the people themselves would decide whether to be slave or free. In 1853, Douglas, by this time a Senator, applied this rule to the proposed Nebraska Territory, which was now divided into Kansas and Nebraska Territories. Each would be given the right to choose its own destiny by popular sovereignty: the expectation was that Nebraska would become a free state, whereas Kansas would become a slave state, a natural extension of Missouri. The southern congressmen who had been opposed to the spatial limits on slavery set by the Missouri Compromise accepted the new proposition and decisively supported the Kansas-Nebraska Act.

With the political framework now in place, Douglas could go ahead with his plan to organize a railroad from Chicago to Council Bluffs, and on to San Francisco. In his mind, the Mississippi and Missouri valleys were no longer the periphery of the United States, but the center, the heartland of a continental empire, bound together by the transportation revolution that was taking place. A potential Midwestern competitor, a line built west from St. Louis, never had a chance: Chicago was rapidly becoming the railroad hub of the country, while St. Louis remained anchored to water transportation, looking to the past rather than the future.[44]

In both 1844 and 1854, Douglas argued that in order to realize his vision – "a continuous line of settlements from the Mississippi to the Pacific" [45] – the permanent Indian barrier on the Great Plains needed to be breached. This entailed creating a positive image of the newly created territories to entice Americans. When the Great Plains had been a place to put the Indians in order to open up the eastern half of the United States to settlers, the region had been maligned as sterile, a desert even, and in no way suitable for Americans. But now that Americans stood at the doorstep of the Plains, and new land was needed, the country was recast as beautiful and fertile, a garden. And whereas Native Americans had been castigated as savages, anachronisms in a new age of progress, as justification for dispossessing them in the East and Midwest, the same Indians, relocated across the Missouri, were now praised as "advancing" and eager to settle on allotments, leaving Americans to fill the remainder of their lands. The buoyant mood was captured in an editorial in the *St. Joseph Gazette* a month before the passage of the Kansas-Nebraska Act: "the onward march of the Anglo-Saxon race, towards the setting sun, Nebraska! To Nebraska is now the rallying call of thousands on our borders." [46]

In order for this "onward march" to proceed, across the Missouri and on into the West, the United States first had to obtain the land from the Indians. Accordingly, in March of 1854, two months before the Kansas-Nebraska Act, the long-established resident Indians of eastern Nebraska, the Otoe-Missouria and Omaha, sold their remaining homelands to the United States, retaining small reservations where, in the following decades, they were pressured to assimilate and merge into American society.[47]

As part of this clearing-out of the land, the Iowa and Sac and Fox reservations were reduced in size and altered in location to make room for settlers. On May 17, 1854, an Iowa delegation met with George M. Manypenny, Commissioner of Indian Affairs, in Washington D.C. and agreed to accept a new, diminished "permanent home" (fifty square miles) below the Big Nemaha in Nebraska and extending a few miles down into Kansas. This was about one-quarter the size of their previous reservation.

The following day, the Sac and Fox delegation also consented to the sale of their 1836 reservation and committed to settle on a fifty-square-mile tract of land immediately to the west of the Iowa, lying almost entirely in what would soon become Richardson County (Fig. 4).[48]

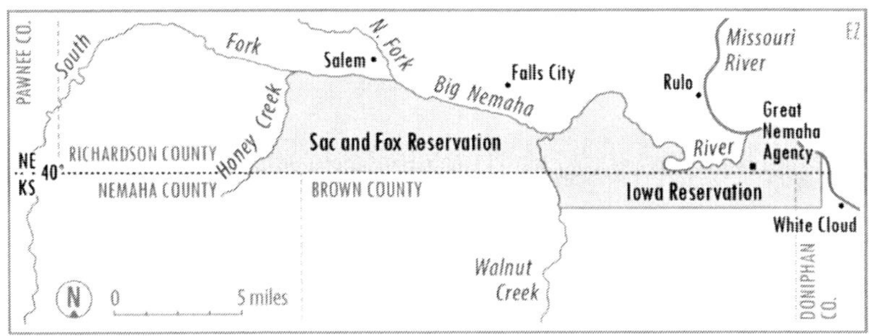

4. Iowa and Sac and Fox Reservations, 1854-61.

The terms of the treaties again reflected the persistent American policy to assimilate the Indians. Their ceded lands were to be surveyed and sold at auction to prospective settlers. In return, the Indians were given graduated annual payments, in money, or translated into services – in the case of the Sac and Fox, $10,000 in 1854 and 1855, and $9,000 in 1856 and 1857 – the idea being that as the Indians became self-sufficient on their allotments they would no longer need government support. The Indians were given six months to vacate their villages and move to the new reservations.[49]

It was distinctly specified in the treaties that no settlers would be allowed to locate on the ceded lands until they had been surveyed. This was all done, it was claimed, in the "interests of the Indians" and the "speedy settlement of the country." It was the latter that had priority, however, because even before the treaty was signed, Americans were lined up in their thousands on the east bank of the Missouri and spilling over onto the unsurveyed land on the other side.

Squatters were staking out their metes and bounds claims, marked by rocks, trees, and streams, on the ceded Iowa and Sac and Fox lands long before the surveyors moved through. By June of 1854, nearly all the country twenty miles deep into Doniphan County had been claimed. Squatting was such an integral part of the frontier process that the government had even devised a law to legitimize it: The Preemption Act of 1841 allowed settlers who were heads of households, single males over the age of twenty-one, and widows (all of whom had to be citizens, or in the process of becoming citizens) to locate on up to 160 acres before they were surveyed. These precipitant settlers were given priority to the claim after the survey was completed, and they could receive title to the land after living on and improving it for twelve months and paying $1.25 an acre.[50] This law was candid recognition that the United States could not contain its footloose citizens within legal boundaries.

The illicit settlers established local associations to protect their claims from other squatters until they could be preempted. Such grassroots organizations had also been part of frontier life across the entire eastern United States. Northern Doniphan County and southern Richardson County were regulated by the Squatter Association of the Whitehead District.[51]

The Whitehead Association was organized on June 24, 1854, a month after the Kansas-Nebraska Act, but almost a year before the land surveys were made and approved. Its members included Daniel Vanderslice and William P. Richardson, both of whom served at various times as agents or sub-agents of the Great Nemaha Agency. The Association worked to secure the claims of its members, to "settle all disputes" arising from contested claims, and to "expel intruders" by any means necessary. They established a "Vigilance Committee" to enforce their agenda. Both Vanderslice and Richardson had disputed claims settled in their favor by their colleagues in the Association. Vanderslice's claim (made as early as May 26, 1853) was strategically located along the trail from St. Joseph to the Great Nemaha Agency: it paid to be first in on the frontier, getting the choice of the best land.

After the land had been officially surveyed into the grid, the Association helped members reshape their irregular claims into squared-off preemptions. If lands were sold at auction, like the ceded Iowa and Sac and Fox reservations, then Association members swarmed the sale and bid in their friends at minimum price, while at the same time intimidating their rivals. Speculation, capitalizing on rapidly rising land values, was rampant: fewer than half of the members of the Whitehead Squatter Association were still on their claims three years later.[52]

In the midst of this rapidly changing scene, Richardson County was established in the southeastern corner of the vast Nebraska Territory on November 23, 1854, one of the eight original counties. Over the course of the next few months its boundaries were redrawn as surrounding counties – Pawnee, Nemaha, and Johnson – were created, leaving Richardson County with an area of 555 square miles of river bottomlands, steep wooded bluffs, and extensive rolling prairies, a dimension it retains today.[53]

Chapter 2

Beginnings, 1854-67

The Americans (and Europeans on their way to becoming Americans) who settled in Richardson County during Nebraska's territorial period, from 1854 to 1867, were clearly just the latest in a long line of immigrants. They came into a land that had already been surveyed into squares, a pre-arranged grid into which they fitted their lives; they came to a land where there were already two long-established Indian reservations and the still-disputed Nemaha Half-Breed Tract; they came as settlers and speculators, two categories that overlapped considerably; and they came to make a life on the farms and in the small towns that was better than the one they had left behind.

COMING IN

The first wave of American settlers into Richardson County in the 1850s came mainly from the Upper South, that band of mountains, basins, and valleys reaching back from Missouri to Kentucky and Tennessee, and ultimately to Virginia and North Carolina. One hundred and seven of the 185 heads of household counted in the 1854 Territorial Census came from that region: Kentucky was the main state of origin, with Missouri and Tennessee not far behind.[1] Perhaps this was the most northwesterly contiguous extension of the South.

Most settlers made the journey west by land, crossing Iowa or Missouri in the travel season that began after the winter thaws and spring rains (which turned the earth into gumbo, more slippery than ice) and ended in

November or December, when the roads were closed by snow and cold. They traveled in aptly named "mud wagons," whose thick wheels provided some stability on rutted and mired roads. The wagons were pulled by horses or oxen that often became immobilized in the mud, there were difficult fords to cross, and passengers did as much walking (to lighten the load) as riding. Ten miles gained was a good day.[2]

The rudimentary roads pointing west converged on the Missouri River ferries. Early on, the most frequented ferry to Richardson County crossed at St. Stephens, later, in 1858, renamed Arago. The rates for the crossing on the Arago ferry were spelled out in precise detail in 1862: seventy-five cents for a wagon and two oxen, or two horses, or two mules; fifty cents for each led horse or mule; five cents each for hogs and sheep "under the number of ten," and for more than ten but fewer than fifty, "each three cents;" ten cents for each passenger on foot; five cents for each crate of freight; and one dollar for 100 feet of lumber.[3] Once across the river, the emigrants could go about the business of settling in.

Sarah Crook, who was six years old when she took the St. Stephens ferry into Richardson County in 1855, personifies this migration flow from the Upper South. In 1919, Sarah recalled her childhood pioneer experience in an interview for a special supplement to the *Falls City Journal* celebrating the county's past. At that time she was seventy-one, her hair "tinged with gray," but her mind still "clear and vigorous." She was interviewed in her "cozy and substantial" house in Falls City, a "living witness" to history.[4]

Sarah was born in the Cumberland Mountains of eastern Tennessee in 1849. Her parents, Jesse and Eliza Crook, were hill farmers. Together with neighboring families from the Cumberlands (such a group migration was common), they struck out for an initial destination of Fillmore, Missouri, a small town situated on the bluffs north of St. Joseph, facing west to Richardson County.

The Crooks traveled in two wagons packed with clothing, bedding, and utensils, each drawn by a yoke of oxen. They also brought along two cows and twenty-five chickens. On slopes the men had to hold on to the wagon beds to prevent them sliding onto the oxen. The travelers lived off the land, hunting prairie chickens, quail, wild turkeys, squirrels, and deer. Sarah recalled that roads barely existed, but still she remembered a "wonderful trip" through blooming tall-grass prairies that were "a riot of beauty."

In a typical settlement sequence, the family stayed in Fillmore while Jesse crossed the Missouri to St. Stephens on August 4, 1854 and selected a place to live – beyond the off-limits Half-Breed Tract on Muddy Creek, about one mile north of soon-to-be Falls City. There he built a one-room log cabin with a puncheon (split-log) floor and a clapboard roof that had a wattle and daub chimney at one end. Once established, Jesse returned to Fillmore for the winter. He brought his family out to their new home on April 17, 1855, in time for spring planting. The forty-two acres that he cultivated that spring (mainly for corn) were reputedly the first ground broken by Americans in Richardson County.

Many other settlers came into Richardson County by steamboat up the Missouri River. Before the railroads conquered distance, and despite the dangers of grounding out on sand bars, catching on snags, and capsizing in thundery squalls on an unruly river, steamboats were an easier way to travel than laboriously inching across land. If emigrants from the Upper South had the means, they could travel by steamboat all the way to Richardson County – down the Ohio River to Cairo, up the Mississippi to St. Louis, then up the Missouri to complete the journey.

Steamboats had plied the lower Missouri since the 1820s, and in the 1830s they took over transportation in the fur trade, reaching even to Fort Union at the mouth of the Yellowstone. The traffic grew exponentially in the 1840s and 1850s, when the Missouri River became a thoroughfare for steamboating. The port of Rulo, for example, saw 114 steamboat arrivals, going up and down the river, from March 19 to July 30, 1858. The passage from St. Louis took about seven days and cost about twenty dollars, meals included.[5]

Like travel over land, Missouri River traffic was seasonal. The season began in March or April when the ice broke up and the river swelled with spring rains and snowmelt on the northern Great Plains. There was a second, more sustained rise in June, fed by Rocky Mountain snow melt, which allowed the larger steamboats to operate. The season closed in late November and early December, as ice once again gripped the river and water levels fell with the onset of the winter dry season. In 1860, for example, the steamboats stopped running on November 20, and stranded freight lined the docks along the Missouri. "Bring on the railroads" was the call in the Falls City *Broad Axe*, a form of transportation less governed by the seasons.[6] The citizens of Richardson County would have to wait another decade for that innovation.

Steamboats came in various sizes and served various functions. Small "packets" carried the mail, some freight, and a few passengers, and stopped at multiple river towns, whereas larger boats ran an express service between major ports like St. Louis, St. Joseph, and Omaha. The largest steamboats were more than 200 feet in length by 35 feet wide, and could carry 1,000 passengers and 500 tons of freight, while drawing only fifty inches of water. The crew, from captain to pilots, engineers to cooks, and barbers to bartenders, might number 100.[7] For some of the passengers the lower Missouri was only the beginning of a trek that would take them across the Great Plains to the gold mines of Colorado and California, the fertile fields of the Willamette, and the Mormon oasis in Utah; for others the dock at Rulo or St. Stephens was the end of their journey.

The completion of the first railroad to the Missouri in 1859, linking Hannibal on the Mississippi to St. Joseph, added impetus to the steamboat traffic on the Missouri, while also changing the orientation of Richardson County's settlement. The Hannibal and St. Joseph Railroad, a company formed by Boston investors and funded by sales from a 600,000-acre land grant from Congress, as well as by bonds from counties and towns along its route, reduced the travel time across northern Missouri to twelve hours. At Hannibal, the railroad connected to a splaying grid of lines across the Midwest to the East Coast. The railroad advertised its services in local Richardson County newspapers like the *Broad Axe*, promoting the "New Short Route" to Chicago and "All Eastern, Northern and Southern Cities" [8] (Fig. 5). Richardson County was no longer so far away.

This new transportation geography channeled settlers from the Midwest rather than the Upper South. This revised demography was evident in the 1860 Territorial Census: Missouri, with its advantage of proximity, was the leading state of origin for Richardson County's settlers, but Ohio, Indiana, and Illinois were not far behind, moving ahead of Kentucky and Tennessee. This more-or-less latitudinal migration would continue in subsequent decades, with Midwesterners submerging the few who had come first from the Upper South.[9]

The railroads, by collapsing travel time, also allowed settlers to come more easily from afar: by 1860, 409 of Richardson County's 2,828 people were immigrants from Europe, a category almost non-existent in the 1854 census. Arago, for example, was founded in 1858 by a colony of Germans from Buffalo, and it quickly absorbed St. Stephens and took over its river trade and ferry. Settlers of Swiss origin moved into Speiser precinct in the far southwest of the county, settling along the South Fork of the Big Nemaha and its wooded tributaries.[10]

NEW SHORT ROUTE
TO ALL
Eastern, Northern and Southern Cities,
VIA
HANNIBAS AND ST. JOSEPH
RAIL ROAD.

Two daily Trains leave St. Joseph as follows, (Sundays excepted:)

☞ First Express Train at 6 o'clock, a. m.

☞ Second, accommodation, at 5 o'clock, p. m.

Connecting at Hannibal with the Chicago, Burlington and Quincy, Toledo, Wabash and Western Railroads, for Chicago, Milwaukie, Detroit, Toledo and all Eastern and Northern Cities; also connecting with the Hannibal and St. Louis Packet Line. Connecting at St. Louis with the Ohio and Mississippi, St. Louis and Terre Haute, and St. Louis, Alton and Chicago Railroads, which connect with the Illinois Central, and all Eastern and Southern Railroads.

Through Tickets for St. Louis, Chicago, Detroit, Cleveland, Buffalo, Niagara Falls, Toledo, Cincinnati, Louisville, Vincennes, Terre Haute, Boston, New York, Philadelphia, Baltimore, Richmond, Washington City, and all other principal cities of the United States and Canada's, for sale at the ticket office of the Hannibal and St. Joseph Railroad, S. W. corner of Second and Felix Streets, St. Joseph.

Baggage Checked Through.

☞ Time to Saint Louis, 22 hours; time to Chicago, 24 hours.

N. B.—If you wish to secure speed and comfort, take this route, and save one week's time of tedious travel on the Missouri River.

J. T. K. HAYWARD, Gen'l Sup't.
P. B. GROAT, Gen. Ticket Agent. 2:6

5. "New Short Route." Falls City *Broad Axe*, Jan. 1, 1861.

There must have been a sense of the world getting smaller: on June 18, 1858, for example, the *Rulo Western Guide* reported that one James Bowker had left Liverpool on May 12 and arrived in Rulo on June 3, the "quickest time on record." If the days that Bowker spent sightseeing in New York, Niagara Falls, Chicago, and St. Louis are subtracted, then he made the long journey in only eighteen days and seven hours.[11] With the completion of the Hannibal to St. Joseph Railroad, this record no doubt was soon broken.

The movement of settlers into Richardson County was not a steady flow, but rather a pulsation modulated by local and national conditions. Locally, environmental setbacks soured Richardson County's reputation as a land of milk and honey and deflected potential settlers elsewhere. There were severe droughts in 1854 and 1860, which desiccated the crops of American settlers and Indians alike. The winter of 1855-6 was so severe that the ground was frozen hard and the dead could not be buried. Following that hard winter, hailstorms destroyed the spring crops, and then grasshoppers ate what remained. And in July of 1858, after twelve successive days of torrential rain, the Big Nemaha overflowed its banks, bridges were washed out, farms inundated, and Falls City was left stranded. William Dorrington, an eyewitness to the flood, described the country as being "full of distress," its inhabitants "naked and starving." The effects lingered on as contaminated stagnant water resulted in "much sickness and death" over the course of the year.[12]

National crises, especially the financial "panic" of 1857 and the Civil War, also affected the flow of migrants into Richardson County. The panic of 1857 was exactly that, a contagious loss of confidence in the nation's banks and the country's economic health. It was brought on by a concurrence of events, some of them international (including a similar panic in Britain), but a primary cause was the runaway speculation by absentee eastern investors in railroads, paper towns that came to nothing, and cheap lands in newly settled areas like Richardson County. The failure of the New York City branch of the Ohio Life Insurance and Trust Company on August 24 prompted the panic, as anxious depositors tried to extract their money from banks, which then suspended convertibility to protect their assets. Many banks failed, railroad stocks tumbled, land prices plunged, farmers defaulted on their mortgages, credit and growth dried up. A catastrophic fall in wheat prices contributed to the distress. The panic subsided by 1859, but for at least a year migration to frontier areas like Richardson County was curtailed.[13]

It's difficult to say decisively what effect the Civil War and its violent prelude in "Bleeding Kansas" had on migration to Richardson County: there are no census records for 1865 to show the population changes from 1860. On the one hand, Richardson County, and Nebraska Territory in general, may have become a more attractive destination by comparison, because Kansas was in turmoil from 1855 on as proslavery and antislavery forces fought for control of the Territory. Far from solving the sectional differences over slavery, the Kansas-Nebraska Act had only hardened the opposing sides and set the stage for the Civil War. The lawlessness occasionally spilled over into Richardson County in the form of "jayhawkers," armed bands of men supporting one side or the other (or just themselves). Richardson County newspapers seemed to treat them more with amusement than concern, and little harm was done.

According to the 1860 census, there were no slaves in Richardson County, but there were 300 slaves just across the Missouri in Holt County, Missouri. Richardson County became an escape route crossed by a leg of the Underground Railroad, which ran through Falls City and channeled fugitive slaves north to Iowa, often with their owners in close pursuit. Falls City was a safe haven: many of the streets there, including the main street,

Stone Street, were named after prominent abolitionists. The Dorrington House, at 1601 Stone Street, home to David and Ann Dorrington (immigrants from England), was a particularly important refuge. The Dorringtons had a contract to carry the mail from Topeka to Rulo, and escaping slaves were surreptitiously carried north in their wagon, housed in their barn, and moved on to Nebraska City and across the river to safety. The original Dorrington House is long gone, but the importance of the location was recognized on September 9, 2022, when the National Park Service identified it as a National Underground Network to Freedom Site.

For the most part, however, the ravages of the Civil War were remote for citizens of Richardson County, unless, of course, you were one of the more than 300 young men (including forty-one Iowas) who enlisted and fought, and sometimes died, on battlefields in the East and Indian wars in Minnesota and Dakota Territory.[14]

On the other hand, the Civil War definitely made it more difficult to get to Richardson County. Once the war started, steamboat traffic on the Missouri virtually ceased, as Union forces commandeered vessels for use as troop ships, gunships, and hospitals. The steamboats that did chance it upriver were sometimes shot at, and even burned, by Confederate sympathizers. The Hannibal and St. Joseph Railroad was no safer. Bridges and tracks were periodically destroyed by secessionists, most destructively on September 3, 1861, when they burned the supports of the Platte River bridge, just east of St. Joseph, causing a collapse and derailment that killed as many as twenty people and injured about 100.[15] With the disruption of the rail and water routes, overland travel to the Missouri River ferries may have become the best option again, and this tedious traveling probably resulted in fewer numbers coming into Richardson County.

Any hiatus in growth ended with the close of the war and the recommencement of railroad construction from the east, connecting Nebraska Territory to its main source area of migrants, the Midwest from Illinois to Ohio. The railroads sprinted across Iowa, with the Cedar Rapids and Missouri River line reaching Council Bluffs by 1867. By 1870, another four rail lines traversed Iowa to the Missouri, and yet another had edged up the eastern side of the river from St. Joseph to Council Bluffs, providing an alternative to the steamboat.[16] Settlers poured into Richardson County, whose population increased to 9,780 by 1870.

THE SURVEYORS' GEOGRAPHY

All but the earliest settlers (such as Sarah Crook's family) came into a country where the geography had already been laid out for them by government surveyors. This surveying of the public domain – putting down a grid of townships, each divided into thirty-six square-mile sections, then opening up land offices where the squared-off country was sold to settlers through various land laws – was the second stage of the settlement process (the first stage, of course, was getting the land from the Indians). This "rectangular survey system" prevailed over almost 70 percent of the continental United States, a brand-new geography of straight lines and rectangles thrown down like a net over previous, enduring geographies that had followed the grain of the land.[17]

Richardson County was initially surveyed in this manner from August 1855 to November 1856. The survey commenced in the southeastern corner of the county (and of Nebraska Territory). The initial point of departure was where the 40° North line of latitude met the Missouri River. This "baseline" was surveyed west for 108 miles in late 1854, where work was halted by "apprehensions of hostile interruptions from Indians." It was later, in 1859, extended to the crest of the Rocky Mountains, and it became the baseline for the survey of the entire states of Kansas and

Nebraska. At the point where they were halted in 1854, the surveyors established the Sixth Principal Meridian, the north-south line running from present-day Oklahoma to South Dakota. This became the other axis for the survey of not only Kansas and Nebraska but also most of Colorado and Wyoming. Richardson County's portion of the grid fell within ranges 13 to 18 east of the Sixth Principal Meridian and townships 1 to 3 north of the baseline.

In 1854, the Surveyor General of the United States commissioned a "conspicuous and enduring monument" to be erected at the point where the 40° North baseline ran into the Missouri River. A party of men brought this pyramidal monument up from St. Joseph. There was no ferry in the immediate vicinity, so they hired an Indian with his canoe to carry it across the swollen Missouri. In deference to the wandering character of that river, they erected the monument on a nearby bluff, where, in renovated form, it still stands.[18]

Deputy Surveyor Michael McManus of St. Stephens was the man in charge for most of the central and eastern townships in the county. He led a team of three chain carriers, whose duty (detailed in their contracts) was to "level the chain on uneven ground" and "report the true distance to all notable objects," one axeman to clear the way, and a flagman and compassman to sight the direction ahead. The team surveyed the outlines of each township first, marking their corners with "monuments" (really just wooden posts in the ground, or piles of stones); then they worked around the thirty-six interior sections, marking where they intersected.[19]

The team worked quickly; they were paid by the hour. They labored across the waterlogged and mosquito-ridden floodplains of the Missouri and Big Nemaha Rivers, cutting through tall stands of reeds and sedges; they struggled up the 200-feet-high bluffs of the Missouri, through old woods of hickory, oak, and walnut, trees that had been there when Lewis and Clark passed by; they tried to keep the chains straight across steep ravines clogged with shrubs and vines, and they worked through plum, hazel, and sumac thickets that girdled the edge of the woods, and out onto the rolling bluestem prairies that stretched indefinitely to a distant low horizon in the west.

McManus, like public land surveyors everywhere, had been instructed by the Surveyor General to keep an "on the spot" accurate record in relation to "running, measuring and marking lines" section by section, and also to give "as far as possible, a full and complete topographical description of the country surveyed, as to every matter of useful information." These field notes, together with a summarizing "general description" of each township, provided the factual content for plat maps that were drafted at the General Land Office and approved as "strictly conformable" by the Surveyor General.[20] These simple but revealing maps give a glimpse of what life was like in Richardson County before surveyors like McManus imposed order on the land, (Figs. 6-8).

McManus and his fellow surveyors thought highly of Richardson County. The majority of the soils were described as "first rate," especially those derived from loess and glacial till on the rolling uplands, and the rich alluvium of the river terraces of the Big Nemaha. Most of the county was deemed "handsomely situated for cultivation." Exceptions were the steep wooded bluffs along the Missouri, the dissected sandstone and limestone hills in the southwestern part of the county, and especially the marshy soils of bottom lands such as the country south of the Big Nemaha near its mouth, which was adjudged to be completely "unfit for cultivation."

Another crucial resource, water, was readily available over much of the county, whether from perennial streams like the Big Nemaha and its forks and major tributaries, or from what the surveyors described as "springs of pure water" that issued mainly from aquifers in the alluvium of river terraces, but also from ancient buried river valleys on the uplands.[21] Also, though the surveyors could not have known this, Richardson County is the wettest place in Nebraska, with an average of thirty-four inches of precipitation annually, most of it fortuitously falling in the growing season. Droughts would occur in Richardson County, but they were not the scourge they would prove to be on the western Great Plains.

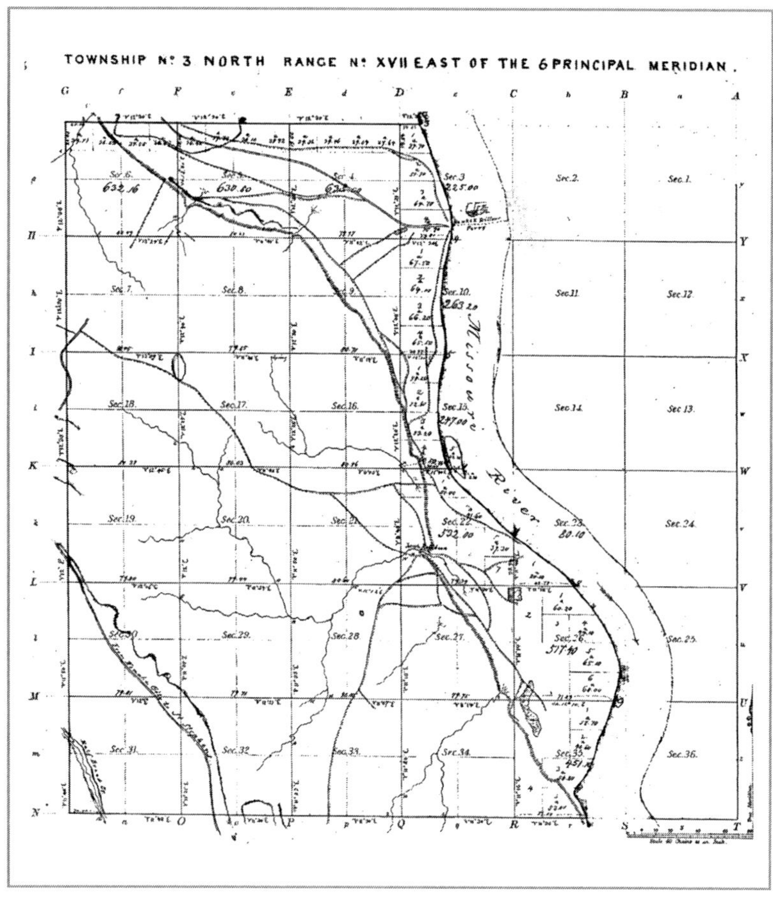

6. Surveyor's Map Showing Trails and Steam Ferry, 1857.
Source: Surveyor General's Office.

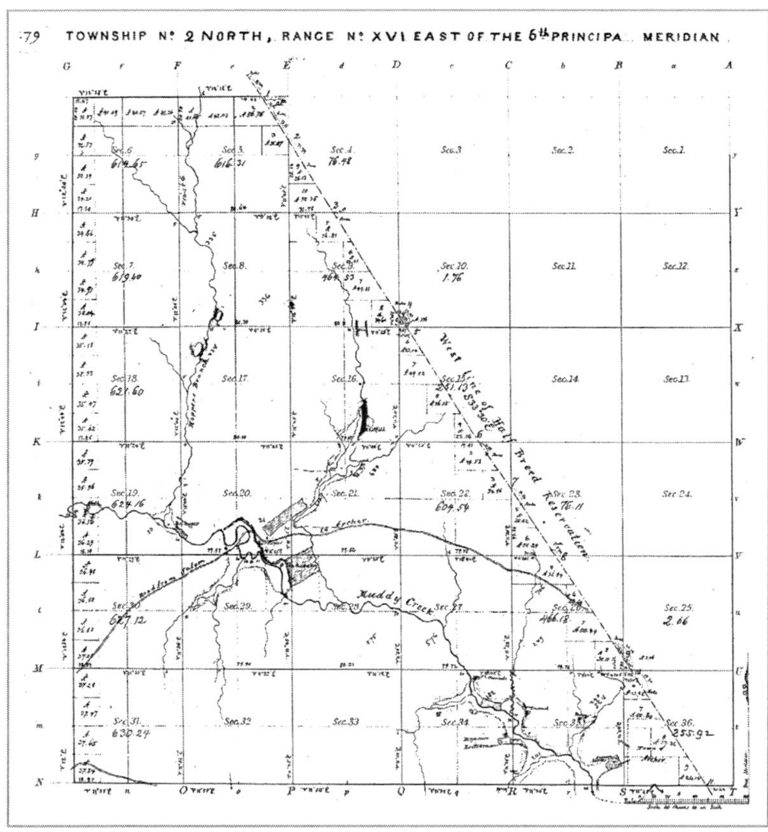

7. Surveyor's Map Showing Western Boundary of the Half-Breed Tract and Town of Archer, 1857. Source: Surveyor's General's Office.

Water was also a potential power source for sawmills and gristmills, essential enterprises in newly settled areas. McManus identified "five or six" promising sites in a single township along the Big Nemaha near Salem, and he considered them all to be "well-adapted to manufacturing." In fact, there was already a hydraulic sawmill in Salem at the time of the survey, located at the falls of the North Fork of the Big Nemaha, just above its junction with the mother stream. However, rivers and creeks, beneficial in most respects, could also pose problems for settlers: their banks were often steep, and as high as fifty feet for the Big Nemaha near Salem, and their water was "mirey," both conditions making it difficult to get a team and a wagon across.

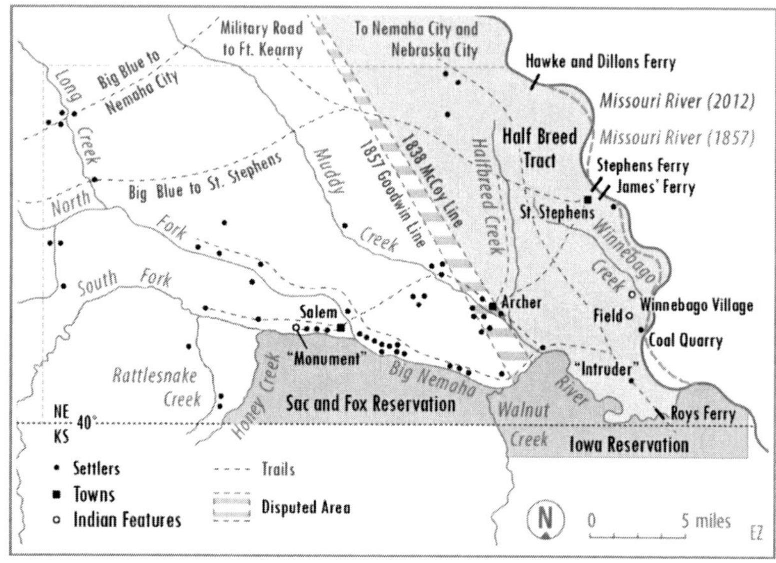

8. Surveyors' Geography of Richardson County, 1855-56.

The real limiting environmental factor noted by the surveyors was the scarcity of timber, which was immediately needed for construction, fences, fuel, furniture, wagons and wagon wheels, and much more. There was ample good timber in the Missouri bluffs and on its floodplain, although thirty years of powering steamboats had taken out the cottonwoods that grew closest to the river. But the deciduous woodlands ended above the bluffs where the prairie began, except for a narrow extension of bur oak, hickory, maple, elm, black walnut, and hackberry west along the Big Nemaha. The surveyors also found "scattered groves" of timber in places on the North Fork of the Big Nemaha and on Rattlesnake Creek in the southwestern corner of the county. But in general, trees were pinched out in the grasslands to the west: many townships there had no timber at all, and, as the surveyors pointed out, this was "sure to retard settlement."

McManus and his fellow surveyors were also instructed to make note of potentially useful geological outcrops, and particularly to look for "coal banks or beds." They found limestone and sandstone in many parts of the county, especially in the Missouri bluffs and along the North and South Forks of the Big Nemaha. Both limestone and sandstone were useful for construction, and the former also provided (once pits and kilns were in place) lime for whitewashing homes, thereby brightening them up, as well as preserving them, for sanitizing outhouses, and for counteracting acidity in soils. Coal deposits were less evident in Richardson County, though McManus did find a "coal quarry" that was "worked somewhat" in the bluffs just to the north of the newly founded town of Rulo. But as for providing an alternative source of fuel and energy in a tree-scarce place, coal was just a pipe dream.

All of the Richardson County plat maps showed the recent evidence of the beginnings of American settlement, as well as lingering evidence from the long past that preceded it. Again, the Surveyor General was explicit in his instructions, ordering the surveyors to record all "improvements" and all roads and trails "with their directions whence and whither." In Richardson County, the surveyors found and mapped locations of settlers, the beginnings of towns like Archer, Salem, and St. Stephens, a cobweb of trails heading "whence and whither," and frequent reminders of the Indian past and present.

The network of American trails – rough wagon roads across the prairie, cutting through the stands of little bluestem, needlegrass, and prairie dropseed – linked the embryonic towns to each other and to the Missouri and Big Nemaha ferries, the connections to the outside world. These trails were also a small part of a much wider network of military and emigrant routes heading west to Fort Kearny, in central Nebraska, then on to the Rocky Mountains and beyond. Richardson County was actually a little off the beaten track as far as this long distance travel was concerned: emigrants tended to pass to the south, traveling west from St. Joseph via the Big Blue and Little Blue Rivers to the Platte, or to the north, through Nebraska City or Omaha, which were major outfitting centers served by an abundance of ferries and steamboats.

The local trails crossed the uplands where they flattened out above the shoulder of the bluffs and above the heads of gullies that cut deeply into the slopes. The road from St. Stephens to Roy's Ferry on the Nemaha, for example, ran south over the interfluve between Half-Breed Creek and Winnebago Creek and dropped down to the ferry near the river's mouth. The trail continued south across the Iowa reservation to connect with roads to and from St. Joseph. Trails also converged on Roy's Ferry from the new towns of Archer and Salem, following the uplands between Muddy Creek and the Big Nemaha. The river at Roy's Ferry was fifty feet wide, deep, and swift: fifty cents was added to the price of ferriage when the river was more than "two thirds bank full."

The surveyors located fifty-five settlers' homes outside of the villages of Salem, Archer, and St. Stephens. This would probably have been an undercount, because the surveyors would have missed settlers' "improvements" in the interior of sections as they worked around the perimeters.[22] There were no American settlers, of course, on the Iowa and Sac and Fox reservations, other than Indian agents and other employees of the Indian Office, along with missionaries, all of them working to put the assimilation policy into practice. The Half-Breed Tract was also off-limits to settlers, though the surveyors did find one American squatting there, and they labeled him an "intruder."

These exclusions meant that the best options for settlers were along the north bank of the Big Nemaha, west of the Half-Breed Tract, and along the lower reaches of the Big Muddy (where Sarah Crook's family had put down roots). The surveyors' notes and maps evoke the geography of these nascent human landscapes. The settlers lived in log cabins and temporary dugouts in the shelter of the woods, with water below and trails above. They grew corn in small fields on the river terraces and at the prairie's edge. A few of the fields had rail, and more rarely, sod fences.

The towns of Salem and Archer (both were founded in 1855) emerged as service centers for nearby farmers. In 1856, when it was surveyed, Salem had a tavern, a store, a post office, and two dwellings, in addition to the sawmill. At the same time, Archer had a hotel, two general stores, and a blacksmith shop. In these early days, however, when most supplies were obtained by individual settlers walking back to Missouri, the main function of the towns was to serve as points of contact, places where settlers could congregate, socialize, and organize. Services would quickly follow.[23]

The third town in the county in 1856 was St. Stephens, with its store, hotel, and blacksmith shop. Unlike the other two towns, St. Stephens was not the focus of a cluster of rural settlements, but instead grew as a disembarkment point for emigrants crossing on the St. Stephens ferry, and heading west into Richardson County and myriad points beyond.

There were not many settlers in Richardson County outside of these small concentrations of population. A few had settled on the long-distance trails to the Big Blue and Fort Kearny, capitalizing on a market that came to them in the form of emigrants and teamsters needing food, feed, shelter, and repairs. The surveyors found no settlers at all in three of the treeless northern townships, and in the rugged township in the southwest of the county.

The entire county, but especially in, and just above, the bluffs of the Missouri, was laced with Indian trails, the comings and goings of centuries etched into the land – the surveyors made note of them in their field record, but did not map them because they were too numerous. They also found a "monument" on the bluffs to the west of Salem, a six-feet high and five-feet wide mound on the grave of a chief. And they came across a Winnebago village and cornfield located on the creek that bears their name, just above the mouth of the Big Nemaha. They had periodically lived there since they first fled their cold Minnesota reservation around 1850.

The signs of this old geography were everywhere, but they were quickly becoming superseded by the public land survey, which produced a practical and efficient way of transferring former Indian lands to American settlers and speculators. It is remarkable how the actions of a few ordinary men like Michael McManus could change the American landscape so suddenly and completely.

LAND LAWS, SPECULATION, AND SETTLEMENT

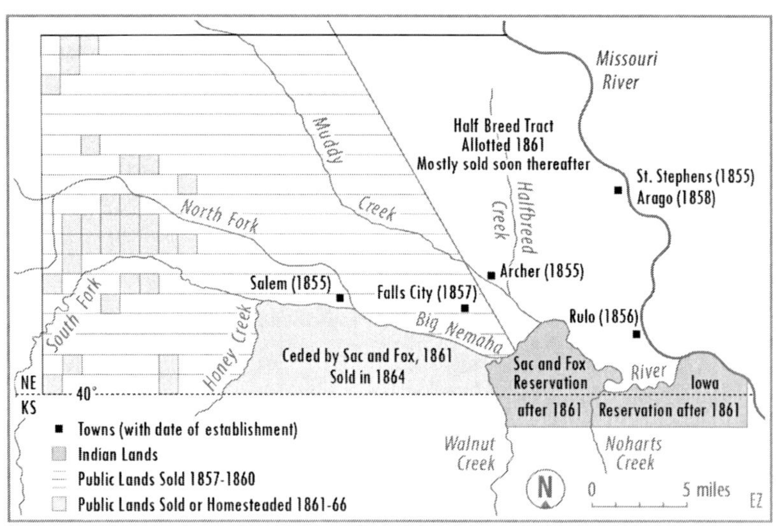

9. Early Land Sales in Richardson County, 1857-66.

The map (Fig. 9) giving the dates of the first sale of public land by section (that is, the predominant land law used in each section) shows some predictable patterns: the exclusion of Indian lands from sale, of course, and although reduced in size after 1861, the two reservations still accounted for much of Richardson County south of the Big Nemaha; and the continuation of the preference for wooded land near water, an understandable pattern already seen in the surveyors' reports in 1855-6. But the map has its surprises too, not least the extensive areas of remote, tree-scarce uplands in the northwestern quadrant of the county (much of which the surveyors had declared "unsuitable for settlement") that sold just as quickly as the wooded valleys from 1857-60. These patterns become comprehensible when the details of the prevailing land laws are understood, especially their capacity for speculation.[24]

Many of the earliest sales of land, securing the wooded valleys, were made through the Preemption Act of 1841, otherwise known as the Land Distribution Act. After 1853, this preemption privilege was extended to squatters who had settled ahead of the survey: they would be allowed to adjust their irregular metes and bounds claims, oriented to rocks, rivers, and trees, to the newly established grid and legitimize their ownership by following the conditions of the 1841 act. The philosophy was that settlers who had occupied and cultivated claims before the surveyors passed through should be rewarded for their efforts by being allowed to buy their lands at the standard rate without competition. This was in keeping with the long-standing government policy of earning money from the sale of lands, a policy that prevailed until the Homestead Act of 1862.[25]

The Preemption Act, like all government land laws to varying degrees, was subject to abuse: there was nothing preventing a would-be settler, for example, from living on his or her land free for twelve months and taking out the timber, before relinquishing the claim and walking away. In fact, the Preemption Act was eventually repealed in 1891, partly because it had been superseded by the Homestead Act, but also because of its manifest abuses. Still, most of the preemptions along the Big Nemaha and its tributaries were carried to completion and paid for within the specified twelve months. After that, of course, it was up to each settler to decide whether to make a life on the claim or sell it at a profit as surrounding land values rose like a tide.

Preemptions were important, but by far most of the public domain in Richardson County was taken through the agency of Military Bounty Land Warrants. These were certificates issued to veterans of America's wars, from the Revolutionary War through the Mexican War and various Indian wars until 1855. Warrants gave veterans, or their widows and heirs, 160 acres of public domain without cost. They were initially issued as an incentive to enlist, then as a reward for service, and finally as a massive real estate give-away, anticipating the free land of the Homestead Act.[26]

The largest issue of warrants – sixty million acres to half a million veterans – came through four congressional acts from 1847 to 1855. These warrants were the main means of claiming land not only in Richardson County, but also in all of southeastern Nebraska (including the burgeoning city of Omaha), eastern Kansas, and western Iowa. The warrants went primarily to speculators, because the Assignment Act of 1852 made them transferable: most veterans were more interested in quick cash than a hard life on a farm, so they sold their warrants at discounted prices from sixty cents to $1 an acre, the exact cost depending on time and place. Only 2 percent of warrant recipients from the Old Soldiers Act of 1855, for example, chose to settle on the land; the remainder opted to sell.[27]

Entire townships in western Richardson County were sold, but mostly not settled, from 1857 to 1860 through the use of Military Bounty Land Warrants.[28] The Panic of 1857 seemed to have no effect on the pace of land acquisition, as opposed to the pace of actual settlement. To give just one example: Richard Maloney, of Galesburg, Illinois, located 1,280 acres of warrant land in the far northwest of the county from 1858 to 1860.[29] He chose the land well: the surveyors had considered it "excellent for agricultural purposes," even given the lack of timber. In subsequent years, Maloney transferred some of the acres to his wife and children (perhaps to minimize taxes), and he frequently mortgaged his holdings when he needed money. In the early 1870s, after his land values soared when the Atchison and Nebraska Railroad built through nearby, Maloney sold two of his quarter sections, one for $1,600 and the other for $2,000, and he also sold a full section for $6,400. So within a decade and a half, lands that had cost Maloney about $1 an acre were selling for $10 an acre, or more. Clearly there was more to life in frontier America than toiling on a quarter section of land, fulfilling the ideal of the Jeffersonian yeoman farmer.

The only sections that were first sold after 1860 were in the western reaches of the county, between the North and South Forks of the Big Nemaha and down to the Kansas border. Much of this land had been characterized by the surveyors as "rocky and stony," and with second- and third-rate soils.[30] This, plus the remoteness of the area from the lifeline of the Missouri River, deterred settlers and petty speculators alike from selecting it. Most of these sections were taken from 1862 to 1867, after the passage of the Homestead Act. This act had similar eligibility requirements as the Preemption Act, with the important modification that single women over the age of twenty-one could participate. Settlers had to live on and improve up to 160 acres of land for five years and then attest to such at the local land office, before receiving title at virtually no cost. This was a much better deal for genuine settlers: it extended the right of free land that had previously been the privilege of veterans and their families to the general public at large, while presenting fewer opportunities for speculators, because homesteads required residency. The Homestead Act was indeed manipulated for gain (by commutation, for example, which allowed settlers to acquire title after six months by paying $1.25 an acre, then selling at will), but more than any other land law it conveyed land into the hands of Americans and recent immigrants, giving them a chance to make a new start as small farmers in places like Richardson County.[31]

REDUCING THE INDIANS' LANDS

With the public domain mostly taken by 1860, settlers and speculators looked for new opportunities for land in the largely unoccupied Half-Breed Tract and the seemingly underutilized Iowa and Sac and Fox reservations.

Americans within Richardson County, and in western Missouri waiting to cross over, resented that the fertile, well-watered, and substantially wooded Half-Breed Tract was being kept out of their hands, and they agitated for its opening. Settlers had already been stealing timber from the Tract and selling it to the steamboats for fuel. Moreover, there was still uncertainty as to the exact location of the Tract's western boundary, the 1838 McCoy line (Fig. 2). Certainly the boundary was no longer demarcated, the original stakes having long-since rotted into the ground, so it was not at all clear where the public domain ended and the Tract began.[32]

The mixed bloods, as they began to assert their claims to the Tract in the mid-1850s, were fortunate to have George Manypenny as Commissioner of Indian Affairs. Although a firm advocate of allotments and assimilation (and speedy American settlement), Manypenny was also an honest man who felt a sense of obligation to his Indian "wards" and had endeavored to honor the terms of their treaties. He had visited the emigrant Indians in Nebraska, and perhaps the Half-Breed Tract too, in 1853, and he negotiated the 1854 treaties with the Otoe-Missouria and Omaha, making sure that they received the reservations they wanted, not the ones they were originally assigned.[33] Manypenny set in motion the distribution of allotments to the mixed-bloods, in accordance with Article 10 of the 1830 treaty.

First, there had to be a census to identify the legitimate claimants to the Tract. On May 15, 1856, Manypenny assigned Joseph L. Sharp of Glenwood, Iowa, to organize the count. To the credit of Manypenny and the Office of Indian Affairs, Sharp was told to recognize as rightful claimants not only the mixed-bloods who had been alive when the 1830 treaty was signed, but also their offspring who had been born since that date. Sharp placed advertisements in regional newspapers requesting the relevant mixed-bloods to report to him. A list of approved claimants – 185 Yankton, 105 Otoe-Missouria, 58 Iowa, and 17 Santee – was submitted on April 24, 1857. In an act of raw racism, Sharp expunged from the list twelve claimants who were "mixed with the Africans." [34]

The next step was to assign an allotment to each mixed-blood. Manypenny chose William Stark of Xena, Ohio, to do the job. The mixed-bloods already settled in the Tract were given priority of choice. After that, in an attempt at equality, allotments were assigned to include some areas of good quality soils and a balance of woodland and prairie. The 1830 treaty had called for 640-acre allotments, but there were too many vetted claimants to honor that promise. When the allocation was completed in 1860, 389 allotments, averaging 314 acres and amounting to a total of 122,240 acres, had been assigned. The first allotment, located by the Missouri River in Nemaha County, next to the Richardson County line, went to Louis Neals, the son of an American father and a mixed-blood Omaha mother. This was the very first allotment in the United States, the beginnings of a tenacious policy that would prevail until 1934, resulting in the fragmentation of many reservations.[35]

While the allotment process was proceeding, it was discovered that some fifty to 100 American families were living inside the Tract, including in the town of Archer. By 1860 Archer was incorporated, and boasted ten houses, a sawmill and a grist mill, a double log house that served as a hotel, a subscription school (where parents paid the teacher's salary), a doctor, and an improvised nurse, Sally Dodge, who had a "good knowledge of herbs." Archer had also been proclaimed the county seat in 1855 (when it was barely an idea of a town) by pulling strings in the Nebraska Territorial Legislature. The founders of Archer (including Judge Elmer Dundy, who would go on to make the momentous decision in the celebrated case, *Standing Bear v. Crook*, in 1879) had high expectations for the town: when they platted it on July 4, 1855, they mapped 100 city blocks around a grand courthouse square.[36] These grandiose plans quickly came to nothing when the western boundary of the Tract was re-surveyed and Archer was found to be in Indian Country.[37]

The re-survey was probably instigated by rival towns like Salem, which resented Archer's instant prominence. The survey by William Goodman in 1857 established a new western boundary, two miles to the west of the McCoy line at its base and tapering all the way to the apex of the Tract. It seems that McCoy had only surveyed eight miles up the base of the Big Nemaha, instead of the stipulated ten. Possibly, the starting point for the survey, where the Big Nemaha flowed into the Missouri, had been radically altered by river erosion in the twenty years since McCoy made his survey. In any case, the new official boundary left the town of Archer and its surrounding settlers on an Indian reservation.

The settlers protested, threatening violence if attempts were made to eject them from their homes. They also lobbied Congress, which responded by reinstating the 1838 McCoy line as the western boundary, thus protecting the settlers' claims and improvements. But the Indian Office, insisting on the inviolability of all treaties, recognized that a mistake had been made in the original survey and mandated that the settlers would have to pay the mixed bloods $1.25 an acre for the lands they occupied.

The resulting revenue of $19,008 for 15,697 acres was divided among the 96 mixed-bloods who had been identified as eligible for allotments but who, for reasons of their own, had not taken them up. The uncertainty of all this condemned Archer to extinction: when longtime Richardson County settler Isham Reavis visited the site a few decades later, he found only a graveyard to mark its dying memory.[38]

As had been predicted, and perhaps even planned, the mixed-bloods' allotments quickly passed into the hands of Americans. No protections were established, no restrictions on resales imposed; some mixed-bloods were bought out even before they officially received their titles, often for a pittance. When Judge C. O. Snow of Auburn, a former real estate abstractor, made a detailed study of the allotments in the 1930s, he came to the conclusion that they were nearly all sold "at the earliest opportunity," mainly because the mixed-bloods could not afford to pay the property taxes that came into effect as soon as they owned the land. Apparently James W. Denver, Manypenny's less principled successor as Commissioner of Indian Affairs, had a hand in obtaining some of these lands.[39] And so, after thirty years of ineffectual existence, the Nemaha Half-Breed Tract disappeared as a separate geographical entity.

The same year, 1861, that the Nemaha Half-Breed Tract was allotted and quickly sold, the reservations of the Iowa and Sac and Fox were again rearranged and reduced, resulting in a loss to the Indians of 32,098 acres of land (Fig. 10).

The loss could easily have been much greater. As Americans settled around the reservations after 1854, the demand to remove all Indians entirely gained momentum. As soon as the Indians sold portions of their lands (as in 1854), their agent Daniel Vanderslice reported, "mendacious whites" began clamoring for additional cessions from the reservations. The argument here, and across the nation, was that the Indians had more land than they needed, and Americans would put it to better use. The Indians had only two options, Vanderslice argued: they could settle on individual allotments and at least secure some of their lands; otherwise, they should be "colonized in a more southern climate," meaning moved out to Indian Territory along with other dispossessed Indians from every corner of the country.[40]

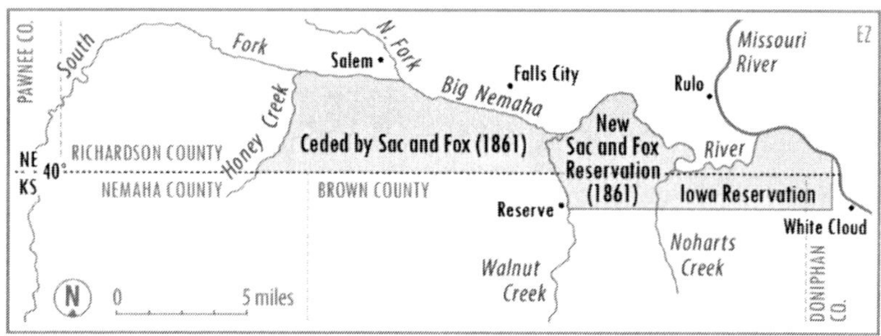

10. Iowa and Sac and Fox Reservations, 1861.

This uncertainty left the Indians steeped in "restlessness and disquiet," and torn about what to do. Chiefs of the two nations even visited Indian Territory in 1857 to talk with the Cherokees about moving there. But gradually, first the Iowa, then the Sac and Fox, began to abandon their villages and move out onto individual plots of land, laying the groundwork for future allotments and the preservation of some of their reservations.[41]

The relocation of the Great Nemaha Agency north from the Wolf River valley to Richardson County (just north of the Kansas line) also strengthened the Indians' hold on their lands. By 1858, considerable investment had been put into the new agency at Noharts (named after the Iowa chief, No Heart): a substantial log house served as the agents' home, with a portico on the front and a porch on the back, and a fenced garden attached. A schoolhouse and a teacher's house were added by 1860. The agency became the hub of Indian life, as the Iowa especially began constructing houses and fencing fields along the terraces south of the Big Nemaha.[42]

In 1861, chiefs of the Iowa and Sac and Fox met with Vanderslice and agreed to accept smaller reservations. It was a pragmatic decision; they did not want to be uprooted again. The Sac and Fox ceded the entire reservation they had been given in 1854, the land between Honey Creek and Walnut Creek. This land was to be surveyed into 160-acre squares and sold to the highest bidder (and in no case for less than $1.25 an acre). As usual, the proceeds from the sale would be held in trust by the United States and expended annually on behalf of the Sac and Fox in the form of annuities and services designed to advance the assimilation project. The Sac and Fox were moved a few miles to the east and resettled on a new reservation between Walnut Creek and Noharts Creek. This had previously been the western half of the Iowa reservation, so the Iowa had to be compensated with one-half of the returns from the sale of the Sac and Fox lands. The Iowa retained the eastern half of their former reservation. After much delay, the ceded Sac and Fox lands were sold in 1864 to American bidders who had been impatiently waiting for this new bonanza.[43]

The reduction of Indian lands in Richardson County was not over, however. The reservation boundaries set in 1861 have persisted to the present, but this did not prevent the loss of Indian control over lands within them. Nor did it quieten the Indians' fears of a wholesale removal to Indian Territory: after all, for generations removal had been their domineering fate.[44]

LIVING AND DYING

Most of the early American settlers in Richardson County lived by farming, or at least that's what they reported in the 1855 Territorial Census: of the ninety-five heads of families listed, eighty-five identified as farmers;

the few others included merchants, carpenters, a doctor, and a clergyman. It was likely, however, that they were just part-time farmers, and that as soon as they registered their claims and broke a few acres of ground, and not withstanding any residency requirements, they would take off for the bustling towns that lined the Missouri from St. Joseph to Nebraska City and Omaha. There they could find employment outfitting emigrants, and in transportation and construction. A transformed rural landscape was, therefore, slow to emerge: even in 1860 only one-fifth of the small area in farms ("small" because so much of the land was being held by speculators and was sitting idle) was "improved," meaning cultivated in some way.[45]

As the surveyors had discovered earlier, in 1860 farms lined the wooded streams, especially Muddy Creek and the Big Nemaha, the area most accessible to the Missouri River and the outside world, beyond the still-off-limits Nemaha Half-Breed Tract. More remote farms in the western half of the county, beyond effective haulage distance to the Missouri, raised livestock that could be driven to the river, "marketed on the hoof." Some farmers inhabited the settlements of Archer, Rulo, Falls City, and Salem, practicing the "Swiss system of farming," meaning they lived in town, separately from their fields.[46]

Access paths led up from each farm to connect with wagon roads fanning across the uplands. Movement was difficult and, especially in the winter, dangerous. Many stories of accidents and deaths in the early days were passed down over the years, including that of Samuel Bright, a German immigrant who was overtaken by a blizzard and fell into a creek in the hard winter of 1855-6. Bright died of exposure just after making it back home. It is said that when they pulled his boots off, his frost-bitten lower legs came off with them.[47]

Farm buildings were made of logs rather than sod, because the bunch grasses of the tallgrass prairie, despite their extensive networks of roots and rhizomes, presented a discontinuous cover that did not cohere as well as the thickly matted short-grasses of the western plains (the true "sod-house frontier"). Fields were located at the edge of the prairie: prairie sod was difficult to break, but not as arduous a job as removing trees and stumps. Only a few fields were enclosed to keep out encroaching cattle and to proclaim ownership: wood for fences was in short supply and expensive.

The sod was sliced open using a moldboard plow, with its curved iron share, pulled by a team of oxen. Oxen were preferred to horses for heavy work like initial plowing, pulling out tree stumps, and grading roads. They were more stoic than horses and, crucially, they cost less. The 1860 Territorial Census recorded 723 "working oxen" in Richardson County, compared to 565 horses, and noted that whereas a team of oxen could be bought for about $90, a team of horses might cost as much as $250, a big difference in a cash-scarce place.[48]

It is possible that by 1860 some progressive Richardson County farmers had adopted John Deere's superior plow, with its saw-steel share that, unlike its iron predecessor, shed the soil as it cut. Ten thousand of these innovative plows were being manufactured each year by that time.[49] But few Richardson County farmers had much in the way of personal assets, so the cost may have been prohibitive.

Corn was the favored "sod crop," and it yielded well on the humus-rich soils. It was sown using a hand planter, which inserted the desired number of seeds into the furrow of the newly-opened earth. *The Nebraskian*, published in Nebraska City, about fifty miles north of Richardson County, estimated (optimistically) that local corn could yield 75 bushels an acre, and explained that at the going rate of 25 cents a bushel it would take only 20 acres of cultivated corn to earn the preemption fee of $200 in one season. Irish potatoes were also grown, and small amounts of spring wheat.

Most farmers kept chickens, swine, and milch cows, and, to a lesser degree, sheep. Cows fattened well in summer on the prairie uplands, giving, it was claimed, their butter an "excellent flavor." Cut prairie hay was used for winter feed and was cheap, costing about one dollar a ton. Honey and molasses, in addition to eggs and butter, were important money-earners.[50]

Inland towns like Archer, Falls City, and Salem began as places of assembly and service centers for surrounding farmers. River towns like Rulo and St. Stephens got their start as ports of entry for emigrants coming up the Missouri, or crossing the river on ferries from Iowa and Missouri. All these towns (even ill-fated Archer for a while) quickly added services for settlers who had previously been obliged to travel back to Missouri for supplies: a sawmill and a gristmill first, then a general store to serve the farmers coming in with their corn, then a tavern, a hotel, and an accumulation of dwellings and occupations.

By 1858, for example, the *Rulo Western Guide* (towns quickly began publishing newspapers promoting themselves) was featuring advertisements for three different attorneys, a notary public, a real estate dealer, a house carpenter and builder, a merchant specializing in hides and furs, and a saloon that boasted that it was "always ready to attend to the wants of the thirsty."[51]

The 1860 Territorial Census recorded Rulo's ongoing growth and diversification: residents variously described themselves as hotel keepers, millers, carpenters (many in this category), physicians, brewers, blacksmiths, shoemakers, tailors, painters, saloon keepers (three in total), wagon makers, and ferrymen, in addition to numerous farmers and common laborers. By this time, there were seven sawmills in the vicinity of Rulo, four powered by steam, two by water, and one by a horse. Richardson County was rapidly supplying its own basic needs, and St. Joseph (whose businesses regularly advertised in the *Rulo Western Guide*) was just a brief river trip away for more sophisticated goods and services.[52]

The 1860 Territorial Census also provides insights into the demography and economic situation of Richardson County's first American settlers. Like frontier areas everywhere, this was no country for the old. The town of Rulo, for example, had a population of 240 in 1860, but only eleven were older than 50. There were more men than women, but not inordinately so. Women certainly had fewer options than men in Rulo's burgeoning economy: nearly all were listed in the census as "housekeepers" or "domestics." The exceptions (few enough to be named) were Elie Plant, who ran one of the town's saloons, Mary Thomas, a hotel landlady who had come all the way from Wales, Adie Hart, a school teacher from Ohio, and Lydia Sherman, a seamstress who was also from Ohio. Falls City and its surrounding township presented a similar picture in the census, with diversifying economic opportunities for men, and mainly work in the home for women.[53]

The fragmentary census returns also shed light on the distribution of wealth in early Richardson County. Farmers were land rich (often with more than $1,000 worth of land) and cash poor (with no personal assets or at best a few hundred dollars). Merchants like J. D. Early and E. C. Shriner were doing well: each had $6,000 in real estate, and $1,850 and $4,600 respectively in personal wealth. The richest two men in the county in 1860 were Charles Mason, from Canada, who had $10,000 invested in land and $1,000 in other assets, and who grandly described his occupation as "gentleman," and Houston Knuckolls from Virginia, who candidly called himself a "speculator," and who, at the age of twenty-three, had accumulated $30,000 worth of land, as well as $1,000 in personal assets. By contrast, farmers and laborers generally reported that they had no assets at all, as did Adie Hart and Lydia Sherman, the teacher and seamstress introduced above.[54]

One particularly revealing section of the 1860 Territorial Census listed the names and ages of those who had died over the previous year, along with the cause of death and the number of weeks they had been ill. Of the fifty-three people who died in Richardson County in the twelve months preceding June 1, 1860, only six were older than fifty, which is not surprising considering the small number of aged people overall in the county. By contrast, sixteen of the dead were children under the age of one, underlining the precarious nature of life in its early stages in frontier conditions. Most of the fifty-three deaths were attributable to fevers of various kinds – lung, brain, bilious, typhoid, intermittent, and yellow. Consumption (pulmonary tuberculosis) and whooping cough also carried away multiple children and adults. Two of the deceased fell prey to apoplexy, two were shot, and two were stabbed. Then there was Fred Plege, a two-year-old from Ohio who died of "cutting teeth" after forty-two weeks of illness. He had been ill almost all his short life.[55]

Death was always close at hand for American settlers and Indians alike. In the summer of 1860, for example, an epidemic of "bloody flux" (dysentery) spread inland from a steamboat docked at Rulo, leaving sixteen dead in a single week at Salem. That same year, following another hard winter, there were many deaths on the reservations from consumption among poorly fed and inadequately clothed Indians. And in 1868, a cholera epidemic swept through Arago and virtually depopulated the town.[56]

On the reservations, the Iowa and the Sac and Fox continued to live traditionally, especially the latter. By dint of necessity they were moving out from their villages onto their individual plots, but most still lived in the old bark-covered lodges, not the new log cabins. Their year was still calibrated to their ceremonies, such as the Green Corn Dance, which called on the Great Spirit to nurture the crops, and the Buffalo Dance, which permitted the bison hunt to proceed. These hunts still took them far to the west, but the diminishing bison range was now contested by hostile Indians like the

Cheyenne and Arapahoe, and the Osage. The Iowa and Sac and Fox still wore traditional clothing, and, despite their agents' efforts, they insisted on visiting their relatives, like the Winnebago and the Sac and Fox of the Mississippi, often for weeks at a time.[57]

The two parallel ways of life in Richardson County intersected, generally peacefully. Settlers and Indians traded with each other, as in 1865 when the Iowa exchanged large amounts of their timber, corn, and other vegetables at the American settlements, and returned home with flour, meat, coffee, and sugar. One young boy, Francis Strumbo, whose family settled at Nemaha Falls in 1854, just southwest of Falls City, was virtually adopted by Mas-sau-quit, a chief of the Sac and Fox. Strumbo was invited into their lodges, included in their ceremonies, and even taken along on a distant visit to the Otoe on the Big Blue River, which he remembered as "great sport." When Strumbo left to join the Seventh Kansas Cavalry during the Civil War, Mas-sau-quit gave him an "elaborate belt," promising that it would protect him in battle.[58] And indeed he did come back.

Relationships between two very different groups of people living side by side in Richardson County were not always so good. Some settlers – agent Vanderslice called them "evil doers" – sought to take advantage of the Indians by selling them alcohol, stealing their timber, and agitating for their lands. One violent incident in 1857, related by Vanderslice in his annual report, illustrates these tensions and underscored the reality that Indians could not expect to receive justice in American courts.

On July 12, a local settler, Michael Ferry, shot and mortally wounded an Iowa, Wah-gre-rah-qua, on the reservation. Ferry fled to St. Joseph, where he was arrested. On July 15, Ferry was taken upriver on a steamboat under police escort to be identified by the dying victim and other Indian eyewitnesses. Meanwhile, a mob of Ferry's associates had gathered on the reservation, with plans to rescue him. In this heated atmosphere, Ferry was put on trial in Troy, the county seat of Doniphan County. The judge showed no interest at all in taking testimony from the dying Wah-gre-rah-qua, or from the other Indians who had witnessed the violence. Then Ferry's friends disrupted the hearings and, as fights broke out, he escaped. He was soon recaptured and put in jail in Leavenworth County, awaiting a new trial. He quickly escaped again and was never recaptured or punished for his crime. There could be no justice for Indians, Vanderslice argued in his report, as long as their evidence was discounted, and he closed on this note of sarcasm: "a white man may kill as many Indians as he pleases, provided it is only done in the presence of Indians." [59]

Like people, towns lived and died in Richardson County. Whether they survived or not depended upon how well they competed for the trade of the countryside and for control of the inflow of emigrants. Many of them died quickly. Archer, of course, was defined out of existence by the re-survey of the western boundary of the Half-Breed Tract. Some towns, like Meonond, were no more than a post office. Others, like Springfield, didn't make it past the platting out of a townsite. More towns died than lived on.[60]

The competition between towns was on display in early June of 1858, when the citizens of White Cloud, Kansas, paraded their brand new steam ferry up around the bend of the Missouri to lord it over Rulo, which had not yet developed a ferry. Coverage of the event – by all accounts quite a party – in the town's respective newspapers, highlighted their rivalry.[61]

The *White Cloud Chief* presented its impressions of Rulo on June 10. The editorial began with reluctant concessions: yes, Rulo was "making considerable improvements in its buildings, and its town company was "energetic;" "quite possibly," it was allowed, Rulo could become a "place of some importance" in the future. Then the editorial turned to its main message, the "several disadvantages under which Rulo labored."

First, there was (at that time) all the surrounding land tied up in the Half-Breed Tract, inaccessible to Americans, and populated by mixed-bloods who, in the newspaper's opinion, were "not far in advance" of full-blooded Indians. Then there was the "low marshy bottom" that lay between Rulo and the Missouri River. Not only was this a transportation barrier, but surely it was also unhealthy, miasmatic? Moreover, it was claimed the Missouri River itself was two miles wide at Rulo and therefore "inconvenient for ferrying." Finally, in an underhanded slur, the editorial cautioned that Rulo was inhabited not by Americans, but by Frenchmen, many of them married to Indian women.

The *Rulo Western Guide*, a newspaper with the avowed goal of "developing the fertile lands of the Nemaha valley," gave its response the following week. It was indeed true that Rulo had many fine buildings – fifty, it was claimed, had recently been completed, and many more were under construction. The problematic Half-Breed Tract was about to be opened to Americans and would be settled within six months, which was an optimistic assumption, but not too far from the truth. As for the marsh, it was actually a "beautiful dry prairie" and a perfect landing for a ferry across the only half-mile-wide Missouri. Finally, the editorial proposed that the enterprising Frenchmen in Rulo were "just the right stripe to build up a city." As it turned out both towns would prosper, then decline.

Competition was particularly heated when the matter at hand was the selection of the county seat. Getting this status was almost a guarantee of success. Functions were immediately added to a county seat: the county treasurer, for example, who was responsible for tax collection (literally collecting door to door), the county clerk, who in Richardson County was also the registrar of deeds, and the sheriff and county judge. The county seat became a magnet for settlers, drawing more widely than other towns, and this extra traffic spawned new services. Just being the county seat, a place of promise, immediately raised real estate values for residents, and so attracted more population and investment. And, looking ahead, being the county seat greatly increased the chances of attracting a railroad, and after that unlimited growth.

The initial contenders for county seat in Richardson County (following the demise of Archer) were Rulo, St. Stephens, Falls City, and Salem. The town of Geneva, which was incorporated in 1857 at the exact geographic center of the county, with the express purpose of becoming the county seat, proved only to be a pretender, not least because the site had no water, even when wells were dug to a depth of seventy feet. It was really a two-town fight between Salem and Falls City, because the other two contestants were river towns, looking outward rather than inward to the heart of the county. The choice was to be decided by a vote of county residents.

The first three attempts to get a decisive vote were made in late 1858 and early 1859. They were all inconclusive, either because no town got a majority, or because the results were contested by the losing towns on various claims of fraud. In the third try, for example, the votes for the entire precinct of St. Stephens had to be discounted because of blatant improprieties in their collection. A new election was scheduled for May 22, 1860.[62]

In the tense days leading up to the election, fistfights erupted throughout the county between proponents of the various towns. Things got much worse on election day. Rulo and Salem had joined forces to oppose Falls City, and each had sent an observer there to monitor the count: H. Davis, a physician from Rulo, and another physician, referred to only as Dunn in the record, from Salem. Falls City appointed its own observer, Richard Meeks.

With town survival potentially at stake, the overwrought observers got into a fight outside the City Hotel. Meeks was "worsted" in the fight, and retreated to a nearby bank to "repair damages." Davis was also hurt, and he lay down on a bed in the hotel to recuperate. Meeks came back to the hotel with two loaded revolvers, climbed the stairs to the room where Davis was resting, and shot him several times. Davis would die a few days later. Meeks, making his escape, was confronted by Dunn on the stairs and shot through the heart. (These were the two deaths by shooting listed in the 1860 mortality census). Dunn raced out of town on his horse, under rifle-fire from Sewell Jameson, editor of the Falls City *Broad Axe.*

Dunn was never arrested, even though he paraded through Falls City with a "wagon-load of ladies" just a few days later. He was known to be a "dangerous man with a gun," and people were afraid of him, so they let him be. Richardson County was one of forty-nine counties in the Midwest (from Ohio to Nebraska) where the birth of the county seat was a baptism in blood.[63]

The May 22 vote came out decisively in Falls City's favor. One reason for the victory was that the mayor of the town had come up with an inducement for the voters, a pledge of $3,000 for the erection of a two-story brick or stone courthouse, set in the middle of a public square. And sure enough, the new county seat had a brand-new courthouse by 1863, though it was a more modest frame building, not the one that had been promised. By that time, Fall City, with a population of about 500, and with its new status and functions, had bounded ahead of Salem, which remained only a service center for surrounding farms.[64]

Together, the settlers in the towns and countryside laid the foundation of a civil society. The first school, near Archer, was built in 1855. It was made of logs, with each patron providing their share of the wood. School districts subsequently proliferated, often with women as organizers and teachers. Churches seem to have emerged more slowly (the first church in Falls City was built in 1867), though religion came in with the settlers, and services were held from the beginning in homes or under a canopy of trees. Men were elected to public office, with the first election in 1855 sending two representatives to the Nebraska Territorial Legislature. Taxes were collected, a meager total of $292.99 in 1857, drawn from a county tax, a territorial tax, and a school tax. The society was kept more or less civil by rules and laws, even by shame, as when the *Broad Axe* published the names of 144 tax delinquents on its front page, together with the amount they owed.[65] This foundation was built upon over the next seventy years of expansion, which turned out to be the halcyon years of Richardson County.

Chapter 3

Expansion, 1868-1930

The years between 1868 and 1930 were a time of population growth, economic expansion, and vibrancy for Richardson County as a whole. The county reached its maximum population ever, 19,178, in 1930, decades after the surrounding counties had already begun their long declines.

There was a more complicated demographic shift in motion, however, as revealed in the trends on the population graphs (Figs. 11-12). The rural population of Richardson County (defined in the 1910 census as farm population and places with fewer than 2,500 inhabitants) accounted for a smaller percentage of the whole as each decade went by: from 90 percent in 1880, to 75 percent in 1920, and 71 percent in 1930. As farming became more mechanized, fewer farmers were needed to do the job, and fewer farmers meant fewer customers in small town stores. Most of the county's small towns began their decline within a few decades of their start. Their glory days were all too short.

Falls City (by definition, the only urban place in the county) continued to grow until 1950, twenty years after the county's population as a whole had started to decline. As it gathered migrants from the small towns and the countryside, Falls City's share of the county's population increased: from 10 percent in 1880, to 15 percent in 1900, and 29 percent in 1930, a rural-to-urban drift that was underway nationwide.

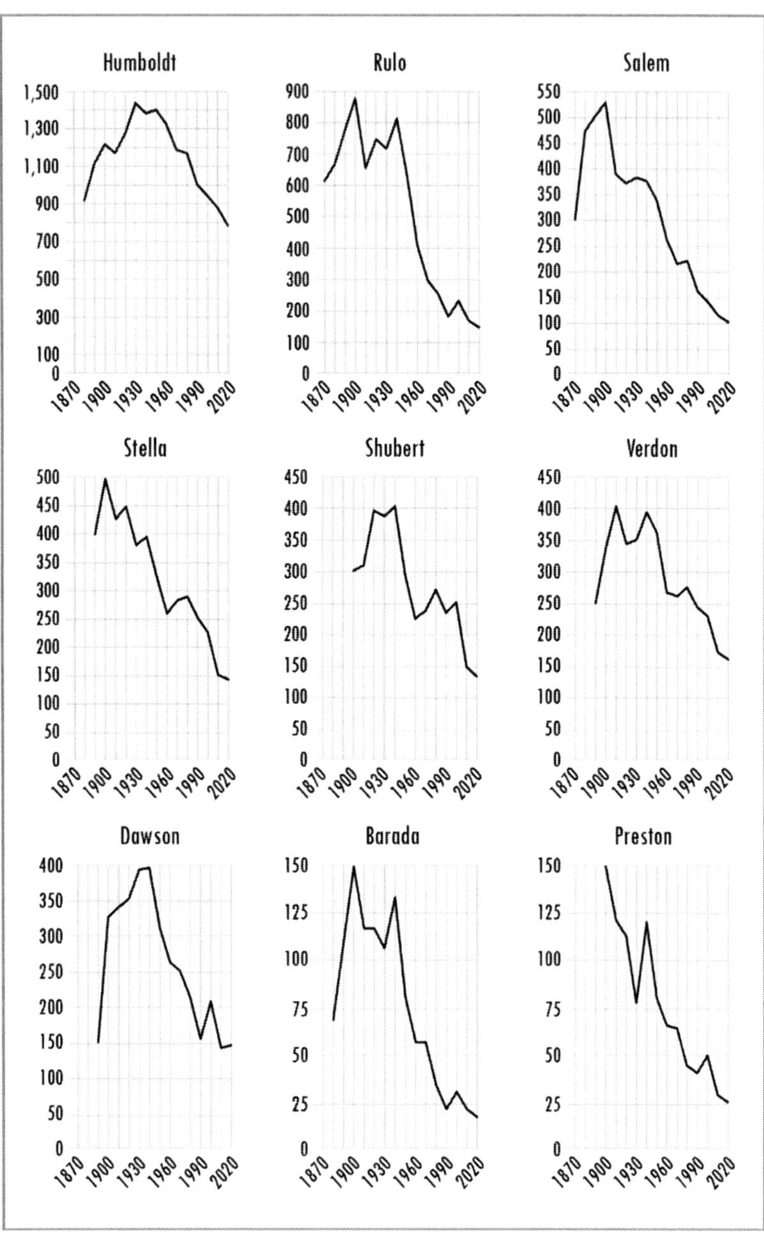

11. Richardson County Small Towns Population Graphs. Source: US Bureau of Census.

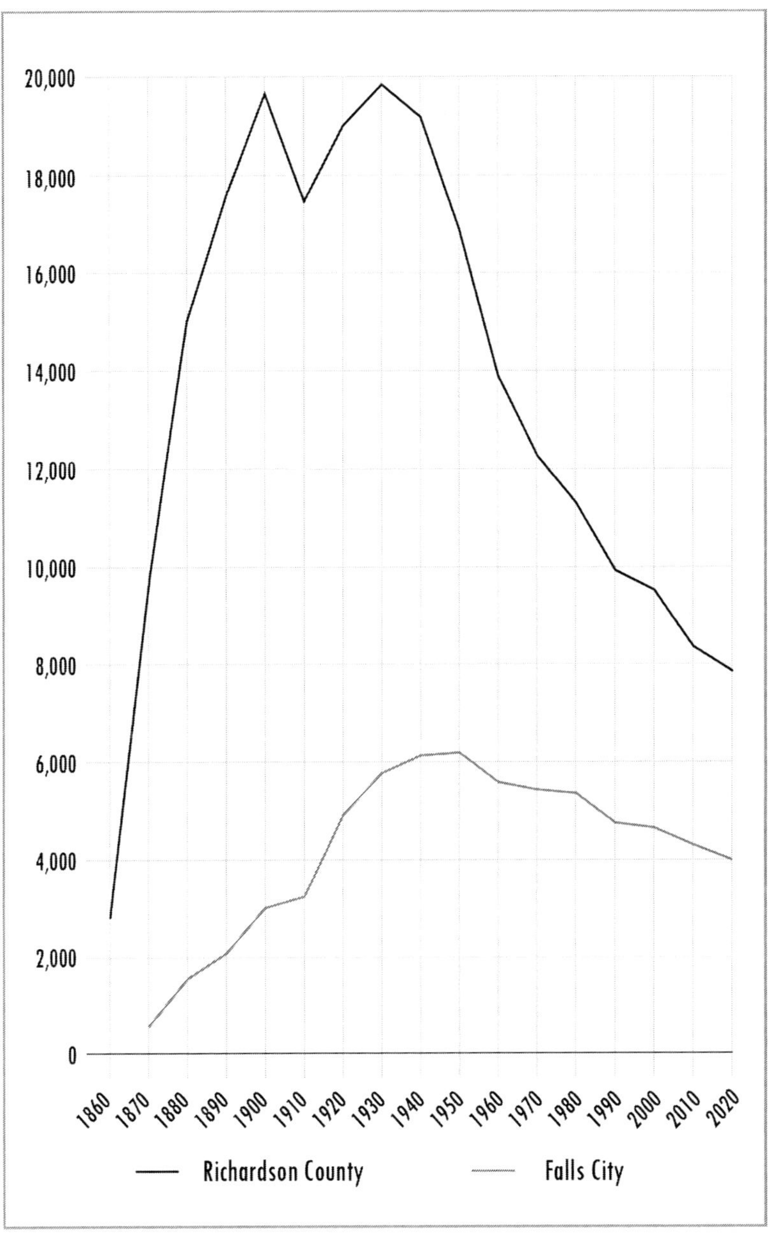

12. Richardson County and Falls City Population Graphs. Source: US Bureau of Census.

THE IMPACT OF THE RAILROADS

The extension of the railroads into Richardson County in 1871 was the primary reason for the sustained growth that prevailed until 1930 (Fig. 13). The county was incorporated into the splaying national railroad network, bringing markets and supplies within easier reach[1]: Freight rates plummeted as farmers and merchants were relieved of the effort and expense of hauling their loads to and from the steamboat termini at Arago and Rulo, or the nearest railroad, the St. Joseph and Denver City, at Hiawatha, Kansas. As a result, businesses and farms became newly profitable. The penetrating railroads opened up previously underdeveloped sections of the county, breaking settlers free from their former lifeline, the Missouri River. By 1885, only parts of the far southwest, the far northwest, and the Missouri Bluffs were more than ten miles from the tracks. The railroads also lifted the land values in their vicinity, prompting settlers like Richard Maloney to sell out at a profit to new farmers who poured into this newly accessible place from the Midwest, where they had lacked the means to buy or rent land.

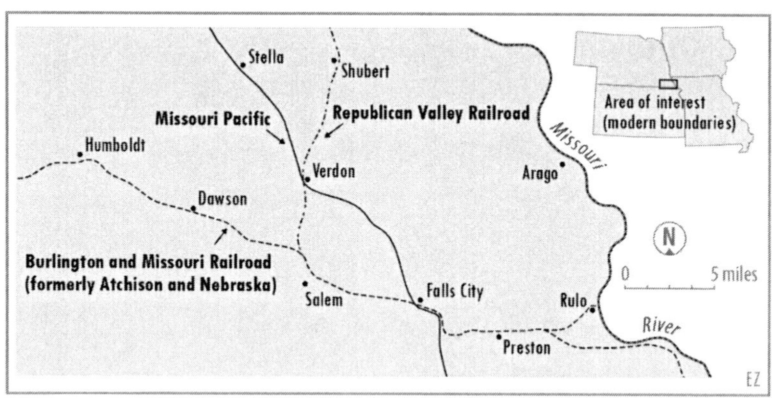

13. Richardson County Railroads, 1885.

As they built through, grading, bridging, and "ironing," the railroads confirmed existing towns like Rulo, Salem, and Falls City. Richardson County and the surrounding area of southeastern Nebraska and northeastern Kansas, adjacent to the Missouri River, was one of the few parts of the Great Plains to be settled by Americans before the railroads were in place. Elsewhere in the Great Plains, most settlers came in with, or just after, the railroads because, in a land of unnavigable rivers, railroads were the only connection across the great distances to the wider world. Most Great Plains towns, therefore, were creations of the railroads.[2] In Richardson County, these new towns included Preston, Verdon, Stella, Shubert, Dawson, and Humboldt (though Humboldt was already an embryonic village) (Fig. 14). On the other hand, the railroads condemned to death some existing towns, like Arago and Cottage Grove, as the tracks callously passed them by.

14. Humboldt in 1873. Courtesy Nebraska State Historical Society. Folder RG2457.

There were many failed speculative schemes for railroads in the late 1860s, before the Atchison and Nebraska Railroad laid the first iron rails in the county in the spring of 1871. The Kansas and Central Nebraska Railroad, for example, had been projected to run along the Missouri valley from Leavenworth through Rulo to Arago, then on north, but it never got past the planning stage. The Burlington and Southwestern did start grading south from Rulo in December of 1869, only to be bought out by the Atchison and Nebraska, which had laid its tracks north to the Kansas state line. Another prospective railroad, the Kansas and Nebraska Narrow Gauge, like many others, was just an aspiration.[3]

The Atchison and Nebraska Railroad (another venture by Boston capitalists) quickly worked its way up the Big Nemaha valley in the spring and summer of 1871, connecting with a spur to Rulo, reaching Falls City on July 4, Salem on August 24, the village of Humboldt in October, and Table Rock in adjacent Pawnee County on December 6. Construction then halted for the winter. It resumed on April 1, 1872 and reached its destination, the capital city of Lincoln, in August.[4] The railroad was not constrained by the grid, but like the rivers, cut across it at will.

The coordinated arrival of the Atchison and Nebraska at Falls City on Independence Day was the occasion of a great celebration that was covered in the town's newspaper, the *Nemaha Valley Journal*, in breathless detail.[5] Initially, there was trepidation that the line would not make it at all to Falls City, as if it were too great a dream to realize. Nevertheless, the citizens went ahead with a welcoming parade to the terminus south of town, led by the Falls City brass band in a wagon painted red, white, and blue. At 3:30 p.m., right on time, to the sound of a whistle, the train pulled into town. It was a modest affair, just an engine, a single coach filled to the brim with "excursionists" from Atchison, and a flatbed car, also packed with passengers. The band struck up a celebratory tune, and the great day closed with supper at the City Hotel, followed by a "brilliant ball" that brought the people of the two towns together, reveling in their instantaneous proximity.

The new neighbors couldn't get enough of each other. Two days later, the Atchison and Nebraska announced that it would subsidize a "grand free excursion" for Falls City residents to Atchison.[6] At 7:30 on the morning of July 8, a boisterous crowd climbed on board an enlarged train – seven coaches and two flatbed cars – and started their six-hour trip to Atchison. At 8:10 the train stopped at Rulo to take on more passengers; it was said that there were as many as 500 on board. They continued south between the high bluffs and the Missouri River, passing through what one passenger described with only some hyperbole, as the "most magnificent country in the world," and on to their final destination at Atchison.

In Atchison, a bustling river city of more than 7,000 people, the Falls City sightseers were feted with reciprocal hospitality. They were taken on a grand tour of the city and wined and dined. They were impressed with the town's "metropolitan aspect." After a brief, memorable visit, they climbed back on the train, heading home.

The revolving visits continued, though the subsidies were reduced. On July 9, "myriads of the good citizens of Atchison" thronged the train and set off to Falls City, traveling on half-price tickets. They were met at the depot by the town's leading citizens and escorted to lunch at the two hotels in "buggies, carriages, lumber wagons, and every other description of conveyances." They stayed only for lunch, then it was back on the train to Atchison.

The subsidized visits continued back and forth up the line. When the tracks were laid into Humboldt on October 6, their citizens in turn were given a free trip to Atchison. No doubt the residents of Falls City would have joined the party when the Humboldt train stopped there on its way to Atchison.

Very soon there was a set timetable for the daily mail train and the daily accommodation train. On the latter, day-trippers would leave Falls City at 7:15 in the morning and arrive in Atchison at 1:35 p.m. They would return home on the 7:30 evening train, having spent an afternoon shopping, sightseeing, and visiting in Atchison. So among the many impacts that railroads had on life in Richardson County was the beginning of a small-scale, local tourist trade.

The Atchison and Nebraska was bought out by the Burlington and Missouri Railroad in 1880. Two years later, the Missouri Pacific built south-north through the center of the county, linking Hiawatha to Omaha via Falls City. In 1884, the Burlington and Missouri built a branch line, initially called the Republican Valley Railroad, from Salem to Nebraska City, opening up the northeastern portions of the county. With this, the railroad system was just about complete: there was little incentive for additional railroads, because most of the trade and profits of the countryside had been captured.

One small, crucial extension of the network remained: on October 20, 1887, after two years of construction, a steel railroad bridge was erected across the Missouri River from Rulo, linking up with the Kansas City and Council Bluffs Railroad on the other side, and all the major markets it served (Fig. 15). This was a big boost for Rulo, but also for Falls City, just eight miles down the tracks.[7]

The railroads re-aligned the form and functions of existing towns like Salem and Falls City, glancing by the corner of the gridded towns, and quickly attracting a depot (two in the case of Falls City, one for each railroad), a freight yard, a baling house to store the hay, stockyards, and most crucially, a grain elevator, the point of connection between local farmers and their distant markets.[8]

15. Bridge Construction over Missouri River at Rulo 1887.
Courtesy Nebraska State Historical Society. Folder RG2457.

Early grain elevators, built of wood and powered by steam, were needed every eight miles or so along the tracks, because they could store only about 30,000 bushels of grain. Farmers also needed an elevator within eight or ten miles so that they could load their grain on wagons, transport it to the elevator, have it lifted and stored for future sale, socialize for a while, then return home, all in the same day.[9] Falls City was actually slow in building an elevator: the same issue of the *Nemaha Valley Journal* that heralded the first train on July 4, 1871, fretted that Rulo had got a head start by opening up an elevator and was poised to capture the trade of the rich farming country along the Big Nemaha.[10] Soon Falls City had its own elevators and its own share of the countryside.

Because there was a need for an elevator every eight miles along the tracks, and because in the early days trains had to stop every few miles to take on fuel and water, stations sprang up at regular intervals, and quickly grew into small towns. These new railroad towns included Verdon and Stella on the Missouri Pacific line.

After the Missouri Pacific acquired its right-of-way through the county in 1881, the company dispatched an agent from Omaha to locate the stations, and therefore the towns, along the line. The agent made the rounds of the farmers on the route, getting them to bid against each other for the right to host the town, thereby lowering the price the Missouri Pacific had to pay for the land. The station that became Verdon was located on property owned by John A. Hall, a prominent farmer. After the town was platted and registered, on February 22, 1882, Hall and the Missouri Pacific divvied up the city lots, each taking them in turn until they were all accounted for. The sale of these lots – small business sites along Main Street and larger residential lots beyond – yielded profits for both Hall and the railroad. The long-term profits for the railroad, however, came not from lot sales, but from the transportation of grain from the surrounding countryside, funneled through the grain elevators. Railroad towns like Verdon were founded like this throughout the Great Plains in the late nineteenth and early twentieth centuries.[11]

Verdon became a rail junction in 1884, when the Burlington and Missouri built its branch line to Nebraska City, passing just north of the town. With its two railroads, Verdon soon had two of everything: depots, elevators, feed and cream stations, and coal sheds. The well-connected town flourished: population soared to its maximum ever, 406, in 1910 (Fig.16). The number of businesses providing the town's growing population and the surrounding farmers with goods and services also soared, to thirty-eight (general merchandise stores, blacksmiths, carpenters, physicians, banks, hotels, and a flouring mill) within just five years of its founding. It was a brief time of expansion; by 1915, with its population falling, the number of businesses in town had begun to decline too.[12]

16. Photographic Postcard of the Main Street, Verdon, 1911.
Courtesy Nebraska State Historical Society. Folder RG2457.

Stella was the next station selected, six miles up the tracks from Verdon. A certain Mr. Clarke provided the site, on a rise above the Big Muddy, and in return he was given a share of the townsite sales. The town was named after Mr. Clark's daughter, a common christening practice. By the time the tracks were laid to Stella, an elevator and stockyards had already been erected. The shape of the new railroad town was similar to Verdon's, with a business district along Main Street leading away from the peripheral tracks, residential districts beyond, and new additions by 1885 to accommodate the rapidly growing population. Within a year of its founding, there were fifty buildings in town, including twenty-five businesses of all types, among them four general stores, two drug stores, two lumber yards, and a flouring mill. By 1890-1, forty-four businesses were operating in the town, including a bank, a newspaper, an opera house, and two hotels. Stella also gained a post office, a major draw (farmers collecting mail also shopped in town). The post office had been moved from Dorrington, nine and a half miles to the west, when that town was ignored by the railroad and left stranded on the prairie. Stella's period of expansion was even briefer than Verdon's: its peak population of 498 was reached in 1910, and as it began its decline, the number of businesses fell also, down to thirty-three by 1915.[13]

17. Activities in Downtown Humboldt, Nebr. ca. 1910.
Courtesy Nebraska State Historical Society. Folder RG2457.

Similar stories of Richardson County towns rising quickly from the earth under the stimulus of the railroad could be told for Preston, Dawson, and Humboldt on the Atchison and Nebraska line and Shubert on the Burlington branch line. By 1890, Humboldt (founded in 1873) had a population of 1,114 and offered seventy-eight services, including all the basics (elevator, blacksmiths, general stores, physicians, and saloons), but also more specialized enterprises such as a carriage factory, a 1,500-volume public library, and two newspapers. By 1910 Humboldt had a thriving industrial sector, including the Humboldt Brick Company, which employed thirty men and turned out 50,000 bricks each day to be marketed throughout the central and northern Great Plains (Fig. 17). Humboldt's growth was consequently more sustained, through to a maximum population of 1,435 in 1930. Nearby Dawson also experienced steady growth after the initial expansion prompted by the railroad; its maximum population of 394 came in 1940. The fact that both Humboldt and Dawson were situated in a particularly rich farming area also kept them growing.[14]

Shubert kept growing too, to a peak of 404 in 1940, perhaps because it was the only trading center on a railroad in the northeastern quadrant of the county. Preston, on the Sac and Fox reservation, had less than two decades of growth, and began declining by 1890; in 1915 there were only six services in town, including the vital grain elevator.[15]

18. Plante Mercantile House and French Settlers, Rulo.
Courtesy Nebraska State Historical Society. Folder RG2457.

Two sizable towns that preceded the railroad, Rulo and Salem, experienced the same spurt in growth when the tracks arrived, but it was brief, and over by 1910. By 1915, Rulo had only forty-seven businesses (Fig. 18), and Salem, once a contender for county seat, was down to thirty-three (Fig. 19). It may have been that these two once-prosperous towns just faded away in the shadows of burgeoning Falls City.[16]

19. Main Street, Salem, Nebr. Circa 1910.
Courtesy Nebraska State Historical Society. Folder RG2457.

The towns left by the wayside when the railroads built through became isolated "inland towns" that had little chance for success, because they had to bear additional transportation costs just to get their products to the tracks, and they had to pay more for their supplies for the same reason of distance.[17] Most, like Cottage Grove and Arago, quickly withered and died.

Cottage Grove had ambitiously been located at the crossroads of four precincts, in a vain attempt to capture enough of the precincts' votes to gain the county seat. By 1881, at the height of its prosperity, the town had twenty-five residents, a few businesses, and a post office. Like Dorrington,

Cottage Grove failed overnight when the Missouri Pacific chose to build through Verdon, two miles to the west. Verdon's population was immediately boosted when the people of rejected Cottage Grove moved in mass to the railroad tracks, bringing the post office with them.[18]

Arago's demise was a similar story of a railroad handing a town a death sentence. This Anglo-German town, the successor to St. Stephens in 1858, had flourished as a steamboat landing; it was not uncommon to see four or five steamboats docked there at any one time. Arago had the usual array of services, but also some others that set it apart. There was a large pork packing plant, processing local hogs for sale in northwestern Missouri and southeastern Nebraska, and a whiskey distillery and a wagon maker, both selling to emigrants heading west.

Then, in 1868, the St. Joseph and Council Bluffs railroad laid its tracks along the east side of the Missouri, rendering Arago's steamboat trade obsolete. It was cheaper and quicker to ship on the railroad. Many of the town's businessmen moved to Falls City, some residents bought land and took up farming, and still others moved back to Buffalo, New York, whence they had come. The town was abandoned, except for scattered dwellings in the bluffs. In time, the Missouri River finished what the railroad had started, and the remains of Arago were washed away.[19]

Nims City, in the remote and rugged southwest of the country, purposely tried to make it as an inland town, and it briefly roared before it died. The town was platted in 1903 by Betsey Nims, but it was really run by E. J. Duryea, a merchant who came down from Dawson and set up a general store. At its peak in 1906-08, Nims City had several stores, a church, and an opera house, which also served as the town hall. In addition, there was a gambling house at the edge of town, operating freely in the absence of any nearby law and order. Like all inland towns, Nims City was really just part of the countryside, a "point of contact" for surrounding settlers. There was no elevator, of course, because there were no railroad tracks; farmers had to haul their grain to Dawson on the Burlington and Missouri. The town failed with the advent of the automobile, which effectively brought Dawson, Humboldt, and Salem – larger places with cheaper prices and more choices – within reach. Duryea, who owned one of the first automobiles in the county, saw the writing on the wall and moved back to Dawson. An observer in 1917 commented that "the place has not continued to prosper as formerly," and Nims City was soon a ghost town.[20]

Barada was the only inland town in the county that survived, though only barely. Located in the verdant, rolling hills of northeastern Richardson County, the town was founded in 1858 by Antoine Barada, son of a French father and an Omaha mother, on his inherited 320-acre allotment in the Half-Breed Tract. The small settlement served as a trading center and gathering point for nearby farmers; it was essentially a rural neighborhood (Fig. 20). By 1890, Barada had a post office and nine services, including two blacksmiths, three general stores, a physician, and a population of seventy. Ten years later, Barada reached its maximum population of 147, before beginning a long decline as the number of farmers in its hinterland dwindled, and there was no longer a compelling reason for its existence.[21]

The railroads continued to make and break Richardson County towns well into the twentieth century, and no place was a bigger beneficiary than Falls City, which after 1910 became the leading transportation and manufacturing center in the southeastern corner of Nebraska.

Falls City's ongoing population growth had faltered from 1900 to 1910, with only 233 residents added over the decade. It seemed likely that it would follow neighboring county seats, Pawnee City, Tecumseh, and Auburn, into a decline. But this trajectory was reversed from 1910 to 1920 with a spurt of growth that added 1,675 to the total, an increase of 51.5 percent. A single decision by the Missouri Pacific in 1909 was responsible for this recovery.[22]

20. First Sawmill in the Barada Area. 1879.
Courtesy Nebraska State Historical Society. Folder RG2457.

As early as 1904, Falls City's business community began pressuring the Missouri Pacific to move its crew-changing division headquarters from Atchison. The argument was that Falls City was midway between the railroad's major hubs at Omaha and Kansas City. The deal was finally made in 1909 when Falls City donated fifteen acres at the south edge of town for the railroad's twenty-four stall roundhouse and extensive marshalling yards. The *Falls City Tribune* was jubilant, declaring "the division is here" and Atchison "has lost out." [23]

In 1910-11, between 500 and 1,000 workers moved from Atchison to Falls City. Most had been reluctant to make the move from their homes to a more isolated place, but they did so to keep their jobs. There were immediate growing pains. Towle Lumber Company had promised to build 200 houses for the workers, but these materialized slowly. In early 1910, the *Tribune* reported that there was "not an available room anywhere" in town, and prices of hotels and boarding houses were "through the roof." Scarce beds were shared sequentially by day shift and night shift workers.[24]

The promised working men's houses were still unbuilt in 1911. Instead, shacks and stables were moved in as "semblances of houses," leaving the *Tribune* to worry that this shanty town would attract the "loose and vagrant element." By about 1917 the "cottages" had been built, the housing problem was solved, and Falls City was benefiting in multiple ways.[25]

There was an immediate injection of more than $20,000 a month in payroll into the Falls City economy, a shot in the arm of purchasing power. By 1915, Falls City offered 221 services of all kinds, including those not available elsewhere in the county, such as a Studebaker automobile dealer, and places to get piano and art lessons. There were also five hotels, two opera houses, three grain elevators, an electric light plant, a flour mill, a waterworks, and two newspapers in town.[26]

The convenient rail transportation attracted industries. The National Poultry and Egg Company operated a processing plant near the Missouri Pacific depot that employed sixty-five men and women, and did an annual business of more than one million dollars' worth of the "purest apple-vinegar cider" from the windfalls and culls of the local orchards. Another large enterprise, the Monarch Engineering Company, erected bridges, irrigation dams, and public works throughout the Great Plains, and employed more than fifty men at its steel fabrication plant and associated workshops. Many other industrial concerns, including the Falls City Bottling Works, the Putnam Glove Factory, the Hermes Creamery, the Southeast Nebraska Telephone Company, and the Western Cereal Company, attracted workers from the countryside and kept Falls City growing.[27]

21. Business Section, Falls City, Nebr. 1913.
Courtesy Nebraska State Historical Society. Folder RG2457.

As its economy boomed, all kinds of civic improvements were made: sewers, water mains, and electric lines were laid throughout the city, a new high school opened, three new churches and two new railroad depots were built, and a fine post office, so grand that even the lavatories had "marble wainscot and terrazzo floors," was completed in the courthouse square. Beginning in 1904, sidewalks were paved, though in piecemeal fashion, alternating brick pavements with mud holes, and after 1911 some streets were laid with bricks, much of that work being done by the Monarch Engineering Company. Stone Street, the main business thoroughfare, was lined by scores of banks and businesses housed in impressive two- and three-story brick buildings. The brick sidewalks were adorned with stately electric lampposts and shaded by awnings that reached out to the street. On the street itself, horse-drawn carriages and wagons shared the space with the first automobiles, an uneasy juxtaposition that resulted in frequent accidents as startled horses bolted. An observer in 1917, seeing all this energy and growth, marveled at how the "little city on the Nemaha had taken on the airs of a metropolis" [28] (Fig. 21).

RURAL SCENES

Despite the rapid growth of Falls City, Richardson County was still a rural place in 1930, with 71 percent of the population living on farms or in the small towns that served them. The county was filled to the brim with agriculture: more than 90 percent of its area was in farms and almost 90 percent of that farmland was "improved" (meaning cultivated in some manner, pastured, or held in fallow). The number of farms was slowly declining, and their average size was slowly increasing as mechanization, first of plowing, then of harvesting, allowed operators to bring more land into production. The total value of farm implements and machinery in the county increased gradually from $246,879 in 1880 to $433,460 in 1900, and $686,050 in 1910. By that last date, an established farmer might own a gang or sulky plow, a disc harrow, a corn planter, a lister, a mowing machine, a hay loader, a binder, wagons, and maybe a steam-powered threshing machine. There were very few gasoline tractors in the county at that time.[29]

That situation was changing, however. By 1920, the total value of farm implements and machinery had soared to $2,591,711. The high crop prices of the war years (the "parity years," when farmers' standards of living were on a par with those of urban Americans) allowed the purchase of tractors. The number of horses correspondingly fell, from a high of 13,202 in 1910, to 9,933 in 1925, and 7,345 in 1935. The era of horse power was passing, but it gave way slowly. Gasoline powered tractors had the advantage of allowing farmers to work more land in a given time, and unlike horses, they did not flag in the heat of the summer. Also, when horses were replaced by tractors this freed up acreages that had been put aside for feed crops and now could be put into corn, the main money-maker. But the initial cost of tractors was high, as were the operating expenses, and their value quickly depreciated. So when agricultural prices fell in the 1920s, wary farmers were reluctant to invest in expensive new machines and continued with tried-and-true horse power. A Richardson County farmer with a new tractor might also keep six or eight horses to hedge his bets.[30]

The average size of the 2,097 farms in Richardson County in 1910 was 158 acres, although a few farmers owned more than 1,000 acres, while others had to get by on less than eighty. Arthur J. Weaver, for example, vice president of the First National Bank in Falls City, owned 3,000 acres of farmland in the county, raised 2,000 hogs and 500 cattle annually, and nurtured the largest apple orchard in the state. His payroll for hired help ran to $40,000 a year. It was not uncommon for Falls City luminaries, like Weaver, to have substantial investments in land across the county.[31]

In 1910, 52 percent of Richardson County farms were operated by owners, and the remainder by tenants. Tenancy had been increasing (in 1880, 67 percent of the farms were run by owners) because already by this time it was becoming too expensive for young people to buy into farming, with its escalating land prices and increasingly expensive machines. Tenants rented the land they worked by paying cash (three to six dollars an acre, depending on the quality of the soil), or by means of a share system, whereby the owner received perhaps one-half of the products of the farm, or through a combination of the two.[32]

Corn was by far the most important crop in 1910, in acreage, production, and revenue. More than half the improved area of the county was in corn. It was grown on practically all kinds of soils, except poorly drained wetlands along the lower Big Nemaha and the stony, thin soils of the steep wooded bluffs. But corn did best on the silty loams of the rolling uplands, yielding about thirty bushels an acre. Most of the corn was sold locally for animal feed, though a good amount was just fed to hogs and cattle on the farms where it was grown.[33]

Oats ranked second to corn in 1910. Acreage and production of the crop had increased steadily over the course of the second half of the nineteenth century, in tandem with the growing number of horses and mules. Most of the oats were consumed on the farms that produced them, though some were shipped to Kansas City, where horses were still a major means of movement and haulage, despite the appearance of automobiles and electric-powered streetcars. The market for oats, of course, contracted as horses were replaced by machinery in farming and transportation in the 1920s and 1930s, until very little was grown at all.[34]

Wheat was the third crop of importance in Richardson County in 1910. Initially, in the second half of the nineteenth century, spring wheat, sown in March and harvested in late summer, was universally grown. But by 1910, winter wheat, especially the hardy Turkey Red variety, had taken over. Winter wheat had a number of advantages: it was winter hardy and drought-resistant; it yielded more than spring wheat; it was sown in October, after the summer crops had been harvested and other demands on the farmers' labor were fewer; and it matured in early summer, before the scorching heat. Wheat was entirely a commercial crop, sold directly after harvest to the local elevators, then moved on to the urban markets of St. Joseph and Kansas City.

Various types of hay, including timothy and clover, were widely grown in 1910. Most were fed to local horses and mules. Additional hay was brought in from western Nebraska to fill this need. Alfalfa was a recent innovation and would soon become the main hay crop, yielding three or four cuttings a year. Smaller amounts of other crops, including potatoes, barley, rye, and another innovation, sorghum, were grown in Richardson County in 1910.

At that time, the value of orchard fruits was $284,365, the highest of any county in Nebraska. Most farms had small orchards of apples, and to a lesser extent, pears, peaches, and plums. But they typically were not properly cared for, and they produced little in the way of quality and quantity. Most of the successful production came from large commercial apple orchards, mainly in the vicinity of Falls City and Shubert, which shipped their produce to Kansas, South Dakota, and western Nebraska, and their culls to cider and vinegar plants, such as Falls City's Leo Vinegar factory (Figs. 22, 23).

22. "Loading Apples" in Stella, Nebr. Aug. 1, 1897.
Courtesy Nebraska State Historical Society. Folder RG2457.

One successful "pomologist," James Franklin Shubert, of the town of the same name, shipped out 400 carloads annually from his 300-acre orchard.[35] The sheltered bluffs along the Missouri offered the best microclimate for apples, but the area was too distant from the railroads to be commercially competitive.

Dairying was a growing concern in Richardson County in 1910, with a total of 6,726 dairy cows, mainly Shorthorns, listed in the census.[36] Most farmers kept a few dairy cows, though some in the vicinity of the urban market of Falls City kept more than forty.

23. Leo Vinegar Mfg. Falls City, Nebr. 1913.
Courtesy Nebraska State Historical Society. Folder RG2457.

Milk was produced only in the summer months, when the cows were at their best, because they were not capable of yielding year-round. Cream was separated on the farm and shipped mainly to St. Joseph. Butter was sold locally in Falls City and in nearby villages.

Herds of beef cattle grazed on the dissected, stony grasslands in the southwestern corner of the state. A total of 19,246 cattle were sold or slaughtered in 1910. Some farmers also brought in cattle from elsewhere and fattened them before dispatching them to the stockyards of St. Joseph and Kansas City. Every farmer in the county kept chickens and produced them and their eggs for family use, or for the two poultry plants in Falls City. In 1910, thirty-two carloads of dressed chickens and ninety carloads of eggs were shipped out of Falls City to urban markets in the Missouri Valley, and even as far as Buffalo.

It was an age of diversified farms, each with an array of crops and animals, but early signs of specialization were evident. For example, Lewis W. Billings of Humboldt Precinct had delved into the thoroughbred poultry business and built a modern hatchery with a 10,000-egg capacity. An enterprising man, Billings bred "all popular brands of poultry" (Rose Combs, Brown Leghorns, Rhode Island Reds), as well as Belgian hares and Carneau pigeons.[37]

Just about every farmer also kept hogs, with an average of about thirty on each farm. In another example of incipient specialization, however, Joy Nims fattened 200 Poland China hogs each year on his farm near Humboldt.[38] Some hogs were butchered on their home farms, providing meat for the year, but most were shipped to the Omaha, St. Joseph, and Kansas City stockyards. Hogs were the most important livestock sector in Richardson County: 46,982 were sold or slaughtered in 1910, with a total value in excess of $1.8 million.

Over and above the profits of their products, farmers could do very well just by capitalizing on rising land values. Reuben Harshbarger, for example, a Shorthorn breeder in Porter Precinct in the northwest of the county, built his holdings gradually, their cost reflecting the appreciation of land values: he bought 100 acres in 1889 at $35 an acre, added another 100 acres in the same section a few years later at $60 an acre, then later still bought 80 acres at $80 an acre. By 1917, the farm was worth about $200 an acre. It became a pattern for old farmers to capitalize on this appreciation, sell out, then retire in the nearest small town or Falls City. One farmer, William L. Stephens of Barada Precinct, saw himself as an exception to this rule, stating in 1917 that he had "no desire to quit the farm and spend his declining years in town, as so many farmers are doing these days." [39]

In 1910, all this farming, which dominated the space, economy, and life of Richardson County, was done with very little care for the land. It was purely exploitive, drawing from the richness of the soil that had accumulated over countless years. Barns were cleaned out twice a year, and some manure was applied locally, but most was wasted. In any case, it took a large number of stock to provide sufficient manure to fertilize even a few acres. Commercial fertilizer (mainly bone or blood meal) was hardly used at all: in 1920, the total county expenditure on fertilizer was only $150. The small orchards on most farms were not pruned, or sprayed, or fertilized, giving them an uncared-for look, as if (to use Arthur J. Weaver's words) they had been "struck by an epidemic." No attention was paid to restorative crop rotation. From 1860 on, the common sequence was to keep the land in corn for three or four years, followed by two years in wheat or oats, then back to corn. Green manuring, plowing the residue of harvested hay crops into the soil while green, was not practiced. As a consequence, the stored fertility of the soil was exhausted, crop yields fell, and the topsoil washed away into the rivers. The Big Nemaha, especially, became overloaded with sediment and frequently overflowed its banks, inundating farmers' fields, drowning their stock, and washing out the bridges and floodplain roads; its water was so overburdened with silt that the hydraulic flour and saw mills went out of business when their wheels became flooded and clogged with mud (Fig. 24). By 1915, water-powered mills were only a memory in Richardson County.[40]

Times were changing, however. What were called at the time "twentieth century ideas" were being proposed and to some degree adopted. After 1880, Farmers' Institutes brought local farmers together to hear the latest ideas on agriculture from experts associated with state agricultural colleges. This type of extension work was formalized in 1914 with the creation of the Cooperative Extension Service, a partnership between the United States Department of Agriculture and land grant universities. Again, the purpose was to provide farmers with practical advice on modern farming methods. In Nebraska specifically, the weekly Nebraska Farmer (which began publishing in 1859, and is still published today) featured articles on how best to work the land without depleting it.[41]

24. Flood of June 17, 1883, Humboldt. 1883.
Courtesy Nebraska State Historical Society. Folder RG2457.

The *Nebraska Farmer* was an enthusiastic proponent of green manuring, and the practice became common in the 1920s. Some farmers even wrote to the journal advocating the plowing of the entire alfalfa crop (not just the residues) into the earth, sacrificing useful feed for future soil health. Much advice was given on the best types of shelter for poultry and hogs: without windows for the former, because glass increased temperature extremes and thereby lowered egg productivity; and hinged roof windows for the latter, to maximize sunlight, and provide ventilation when opened. Progressive orchardists like Arthur J. Weaver recommended the spraying of insecticides and fungicides three or four times during the growing season, and applying barnyard manure or nitrate of soda annually. So by the early twentieth century, new ideas were being circulated and, to some extent, being adopted by Richardson County farmers.[42]

The rural landscape of Richardson County at this time was richly variegated, a colorful patchwork of crops and with a farmstead on most quarter sections. Even the large farms were full of variety. The Miles Ranch, for example, near Dawson, sprawled over 6,000 acres, an agricultural panorama with 1,500 acres in corn, 500 acres in wheat, 400 acres in timothy hay, 300 acres in oats, 100 acres in barley, and, in addition, 300 acres of timber, and 1,500 acres of grazing land that each year supported 300 head of cattle and more than 1,000 Poland China and Duroc Jersey hogs. The ranch boasted "one of the best-built frame houses" in the county, made entirely of timber cut from the bottomlands of the Big Nemaha, and a massive Pennsylvania-style bank barn constructed of local stones and timber and mortared and fastened entirely with wooden pins. Twelve buildings housed the workers on the ranch, a private silo held the grain until prices were right to release it, and a 2,000-gallon-capacity cistern discharged water throughout the property. This impressive ranch had been founded by Stephen B. Miles in 1856 and was run by his son, Joseph H. Miles, in 1917. Miles was also president of the State Bank of Rulo, another example of Richardson County royalty capitalizing on town and country investments.[43]

Most farms were far more humble, although according to an observer in 1917, generally "well painted and in good repair." Farms were often sheltered by a windbreak of evergreens, and there might be a grove of walnut trees and an apple orchard nearby. A kitchen garden and a row of beehives added more detail to the rustic scene. Some farmers had substantial frame barns, as large as 65 feet by 70 feet; others made do with "slough grass" barns, where brush and grass were laid over a frame of poles. Horses, cattle, hogs, and poultry enlivened the farmsteads.[44]

Inside the farm house, by 1917, the old wood-burning stove was giving way to steam heat, and some farms, like Henry Schrader's place in Liberty Precinct, had hot and cold running water in all the rooms. Some also had electricity, though not mainly from a grid (in 1930 only 10 percent of the country's rural population was serviced with electricity), but from a Delco Electric System, powered by a small kerosene engine. This innovation, invented in 1912, cost a substantial $250, but it brought the comforts of urban living to the farm, allowing such luxuries as electrically percolated coffee and late-night sewing and reading. An up-to-date farm might also have a congoleum (linoleum) kitchen floor, waterproof, durable, easy to clean, and displaying colorful patterns. Many issues of the *Nebraska Farmer* had an advertisement for Gold Seal Congoleum, "satisfaction guaranteed or your money back." [45]

Beginning in the 1870s, pastures were enclosed with barbed wire, but many farmers lacked the means to buy this innovative fence. So, even in the early twentieth century, the Richardson County rural landscape was still lined by hedges, especially Osage orange hedges. These linear, thorny thickets not only confined cattle and protected farmsteads from scorching summer winds from the south and driving wintery blizzards from the north, but they also "set the landscape of the prairie in frames of living green." [46]

The hedges ran alongside the dirt roads that followed the section lines and connected farmers to their small-town markets. These unimproved roads were impassible during rainy seasons, and as a result farmers' crops sometimes rotted before they got to the elevator. Then when the roads dried, farmers swarmed to the elevators, the market was glutted with grain, and crop prices plummeted. Until the 1920s, the upkeep of the roads was left to the counties and, resisting higher taxes, residents made little in the way of improvements. After 1920, however, as automobiles became more common (Richardson County ranked third in per capita ownership of automobiles in the state at that time), the demand for better roads gathered force, and state and federal money was applied to this end. Roads were graded more often and culverts added to improve drainage; gradually roads were graveled and even paved with concrete. However, in rural Nebraska as a whole in 1926, from a total of 5,330 miles of road, only 127 miles were paved, and 726 miles graveled, while 4,477 miles remained just dirt. The proportions for Richardson County were probably similar; it is likely that the only paved roads there were the streets in Falls City.[47]

There was one major, long-lasting alteration to the rural landscape of Richardson County in the early twentieth century: the course of the Big Nemaha and its North Fork was ditched and straightened, cutting thirty-one miles off its length to the Missouri. Some 29,402 acres of marshland and acidic soils were reclaimed for agriculture and the threat of flooding was curtailed. The old, abandoned corkscrew channel can still be seen on maps and on the ground as sinuous fingers of standing water and wetlands, and also in the twisting northern boundary of the Sac and Fox Reservation, which still adheres to the meanders of the original river.[48]

Before 1903, when the idea for the reclamation was first proposed, there were no effective drainage laws in Nebraska, or indeed in the nation. This was remedied by the Nebraska State Legislature, which, following a national trend, established a process in 1905 (amended in 1907 and 1913) for the formation of drainage districts. Richardson County adhered to this process in creating Drainage District No. 1, with jurisdiction over the Nemaha valley from Dawson to the Missouri. In 1906, the affected landowners who chose to be affiliated with the project petitioned the district court of Richardson County to create a drainage district; the landowners convened at the Richardson County courthouse and elected a Board of Supervisors, with Joseph H. Miles as chair; an engineer was hired to survey, map, and assess the value of the land to be reclaimed; the participants agreed to pay a portion of the cost of the project, according to their assessments and the benefits they would derive; and finally bonds were issued by the Board of Supervisors to allow the costs to be paid back over time. A Chicago firm bought most of the bonds, attracted by the 6 percent interest that was payable twice a year.

There was one complication: The Iowa and Sac and Fox had lands (379 acres and 2,393 acres respectively) in Drainage District No. 1 and had to pay their share of the cost of the project. But they were under federal supervision and could not be taxed. So they were dealt with separately. On June 14, 1906, the U. S. Congress passed a law authorizing $57,000 to be taken out of their Treasury funds to pay their share of the cost. These were funds that had accrued from sales of land through treaties in 1837 and 1854, and which were held in trust for them and spent "on their behalf" for annual annuities (cash payments and "useful goods") and single issues like Drainage District No. 1.

Dredging the new channel commenced in 1907 and was completed in 1913. The total cost of the reclamation was $297,564. Surrounding farmers dug their own additional ditches and ran subterranean tile channels into them, all draining excess water into the new course of the Big Nemaha and away. Joseph Miles alone was responsible for adding three miles of open ditch at the western end of the drainage district. In subsequent years, additional drainage districts were created and the reclamation was extended west along the North Fork of the Big Nemaha to beyond Humboldt. By 1920, Richardson County had 35,803 acres in drainage enterprises (one-tenth of the area of the county), of which 27,581 acres were improved and mainly in corn. The Big Nemaha valley stands out on the national map of drainage enterprises published in the first ever census of drainage that year.[49]

By 1900, it would have been difficult to distinguish the rural scenes of the reservations from those of the county as a whole. They both were characterized by dispersed settlement, families living on the lands they farmed. The Iowa and Sac and Fox had gradually moved out from their villages (starting in the 1860s) to live first in bark lodges, then in log and frame houses, in the woodlands along the streams. Often they would build in the bend of a river, leaving only the open side of the property to fence.

They each cultivated ten to fifty acres of what was considered communal land, but was recognized as individually owned as long as it was inhabited and worked.[50]

This fragmentation of the communal land was officially recognized with the issuance of allotments in 1891-2. The entire Iowa Reservation, 11,400 acres, was divided into eighty-acre allotments, essentially confirming the ownership of properties that the Indians already occupied. Similarly, the 8,013 acres of the Sac and Fox Reservation were allotted in eighty-acre parcels to the 76 members of the tribe living there, leaving 2,000 acres of "surplus lands." These were not sold to Americans (the usual practice with surplus lands), but allocated to Indian children born after 1890. In accordance with the terms of the General Allotment Act (the Dawes Act) of February 8, 1887, the titles of the allotments were to be held in trust for the Indians by the United States for twenty-five years to prevent their immediate sale to Americans.[51]

This was a necessary precaution in the case of the Iowa and Sac and Fox because, as their agent wrote in 1889, their fertile reservations had long been "a glittering temptation to whites." [52] In fact, for decades there had been concerted pressure on the Indians to sell their lands and move south to Indian Territory. Some of the more traditional members of the tribes, hoping to continue living in old ways, made the move south, but most Indians stayed and took out allotments. The acceptance of allotments in the early 1890s was not only the fulfillment of long-standing federal policy to individualize and assimilate the Indians, but also a preemptive move by the Iowa and Sac and Fox to secure at least some of their lands.

At eighty acres, the Indians' farms were smaller than the average for Richardson County, but most aspects of their rural landscapes were similar. Both reservations – some of the best land in the area – were fully cultivated or grazed, as well as substantially fenced, including with barbed wire. The crops grown were the same as elsewhere in the county, mostly corn but also wheat, oats, and various types of hay, including the newly introduced alfalfa. Crop yields were on a par with the rest of the county.

The Indians' farmhouses (there were 53 on the Iowa Reservation and 38 on the Sac and Fox Reservation in 1897) were described by the agents as small but comfortable. By 1901, they all had a cook stove, functional furniture, a sewing machine, and carpets on the floor. Sometimes their windows were adorned with lace curtains, and on occasion, one agent noted, the melodic sound of a piano or an organ could be heard drifting out from within. The farmhouses were surrounded by orchards of apples and pears, as well as thickets of grapevines, and wagons, teams of horses, and farming implements (all provided via the annuities) added to the familiar Richardson County rural scene.[53]

The reservation landscapes and ways of life had become more similar to the surrounding areas in other ways too. By the 1890s, according to the agents, the Indians were all wearing "citizens' clothes," and skins, furs, and blankets had become apparel of the past. Some of the Indians had adopted Christianity, or at least grafted some of its teachings onto their existing religious beliefs. By 1902, a Catholic church and a Presbyterian church had been erected on the Iowa Reservation. Also by 1902, there was a day school on each reservation, replacing the old, dilapidated Industrial Boarding School near White Cloud, where Indian children had been subjected to draconian methods to turn them into Americans, the boys as farmers and blacksmiths, the girls as housewives. The parents' annuities had been withheld if their children did not attend the boarding school. As a form of resistance, parents began to place their children in public schools in the surrounding communities. This persuaded the Indian Office to close the boarding school (in 1901) and build a day school on each of the reservations.[54]

The distinction between reservation life and life in the rest of Richardson County had become increasingly blurred. Indians and Americans traded with each other, just as Americans traded amongst themselves. This blurring went even deeper on the Iowa Reservation, where, as a result of frequent intermarriage, there was, as the agents reported, a "preponderance of white blood in the tribe.[55]

There remained differences, however, from one side of the reservation boundaries to the other, and between the reservations too. The Indians, particularly the Sac and Fox, who were mainly full-blood and more traditional, persisted in what the agents described as "dancing," which was a dismissive term for practicing ceremonies. Most agents tried to prevent these sacred celebrations, but one of them, C. H. Grover, refused to intervene, because he understood them to be expressions of a genuine "religious urge." Both the Iowa and the Sac and Fox continued the practice of "visiting," leaving their reservations in large numbers for long periods of time to worship and celebrate with relatives in Wisconsin and Indian Territory. The agents tried hard to stop the Indians' visiting, because it diverted them from their agriculture, but it was to no avail, because to the Indians it was a liberation from a world that had become circumscribed, and it reminded them of freer times.[56]

Americans, whether married into the tribes or not, proliferated on the reservations after 1891, the year that the Dawes Act was amended to allow Indian allottees to lease their allotments to others to cultivate and graze. Many took advantage of this opportunity, leasing out their allotments for $2.50 to $3.50 an acre. Some of the Indians became quite well off, a "class of land lords" in their agents' words, disassociated from their lands, and spending much of their time away from the reservations visiting. When agent K. Nadau took over in 1901, he found that all the allotted lands were leased and had been for a number of years. White lessees and their families settled on the vacated allotments, but given that they could not buy them, but only lease them, they were loath to make long-term improvements, and the reservation landscapes took on a run-down appearance.[57]

The influx of Americans onto the reservations was given added momentum with the passage of the Burke Act in 1906, which allowed "competent" Indians who had "adopted the habits of civilized life" to own the titles of their allotments. This started the process of Americans buying up Indian allotments and becoming the majority of landowners on many reservations. By 1945, on the Iowa Reservation, only 1,019 acres remained in individual trust allotments, and 635 acres were held in trust by the tribe. Similarly, on the Sac and Fox Reservation, allotments were quickly sold, leaving only 865 acres in trust for the tribe.[58] The boundaries of the two reservations remained as they had been defined in the treaty of 1861, and as they are now, but within them the bulk of the land had passed into American hands.

ENJOYING LIFE

Americans had increasing amounts of leisure time at their disposal at the beginning of the twentieth century. The six-day work week and eight-hour work day were being introduced in manufacturing, and the hours that farmers spent in the fields were being reduced by mechanization. The average work week declined from fifty-four hours in 1890 to forty-four hours in 1940. Locally, in Richardson County, many farmers, having profited from high yields and crop prices, as well as rising land values, sold out and retired early in Falls City or the newest small town, where they had time to kill, money to spend, and life to enjoy.[59]

At the same time the modes of leisure were changing quickly, from individual and informal activities, such as the ubiquitous "visiting," to structured group activities sponsored by churches, schools, sports teams, women's clubs, and fraternal organizations, or hosted by civic-minded and sociable individuals. Entertainment was becoming more commercial, with touring vaudeville shows, concerts and plays, circuses of all shapes and sizes, and in 1908 in Falls City, the first flickering one-reel movies. The geographic scope of leisure was expanding too, as railroads brought places once distant to within easy reach, permitting the beginnings of a tourist trade. Meanwhile, automobiles made local traveling easier and faster, thereby freeing up even more time for leisure.

The opportunities for enjoying life in Richardson County were on display in the pages of the *Falls City Tribune*, a weekly newspaper published from 1904 to 1911. This resolutely Republican paper gave admirable attention to national and international affairs (for some reason, the Russian-Japanese War of 1904-05 was of particular interest), but its real focus was on Richardson County. The newspaper even hired "correspondents" to report all the happenings in the small towns and rural precincts, asking only that they be "discriminating… timely… and accurate." The *Tribune* advertised the plays showing at the Gehling Theater, the musicals staged at the Jenne Opera House, and the movies spinning at the Electric Theater; it trumpeted the circuses coming to town and covered the sporting events put on by schools or communities; it announced the picnics and parades, the grand lectures, and the genteel Kensington parties; and in regular sections called "Comings and Goings" and "Happenings of the Week in the Circles of Society," it painted a picture of how people were enjoying life in the early years of the twentieth century.[60]

Each issue of the *Tribune* had scores of announcements of visiting, either planned ahead, or recalled after the fact as "timely" news. For example, the January 3, 1908 issue reported from Barada that Lester Miller had come down from Brock to "shake hands with old acquaintances," that D. E. and Otis Spickler had gone to Rosalie for a short visit, and that C. H. Martin and his wife were Falls City visitors in town. And so on, many more, a small world in motion.[61]

This was different from the Indian practice of visiting, which was more sacred and ceremonial, more communal, and often involved long-distance and long-lasting migrations.[62] Americans typically visited on Sundays, after church, when they already were wearing their best clothes. Generally, they would stay just a short time. Visitors from farther afield and those visiting relatives might stay a few days. Sometimes they didn't even visit, but just took pleasure in "riding around" in their carriage, taking in the countryside, a practice that smoothly transitioned into the automobile era. Cars and trucks were becoming common in Richardson County by 1910, especially among the farmers, which widened the range of visiting; and telephones – unconnected local networks at first – may have changed the nature of visiting, making it less spontaneous and more arranged.

The Society pages in the *Tribune* also listed the celebratory events taking place in people's homes and at local venues. Dances were common, like the one on Valentine's Day in Rulo in 1906 hosted by the town's Bachelor Girls Club, with music by the White Cloud Orchestra. The *Tribune* commented "the best of order was maintained," as if it might have been expected to be otherwise. Surprise parties were common too: on February 13, 1908, for example, the correspondent from Shubert wrote that Peter Gurgen and his wife were "pleasantly surprised" by 100 of their friends who gathered to recognize their twenty years of marriage (though it does strain credulity that 100 friends could have kept this secret in a town of only 300 people).[63]

Most of the local entertainments were hosted by women, either individuals or as members of small clubs created for the purposes of "study and social amusements." Kensington clubs and parties focused more on the "social amusements" side of things. Strictly speaking, these gatherings emphasized sewing and needlework (the name comes from an English style of needlework), but their scope went beyond this mission to include musical events and games. The Married Ladies Kensington Club of Falls

City even invited their husbands to one meeting in 1909, where together they made up "six whist tables." Card games were the most popular of the in-home entertainments, as when Miss Leah Potter of Falls City invited thirty of her friends to her "spacious home" in 1904 to play whist, somerset, and flinch (the last two being recently invented card games that were very much in vogue). Refreshments were always served at these events, and invariably they were said to be "delicious," "lovely," "sumptuous," "dainty," and even "toothsome." [64]

Organized women's clubs, with elected officials and national networks, concentrated on the "study" side of things. In an astute article in the *Tribune* in 1909, "Falls City Lady" recalled the growth of women's clubs in the county seat and how they had been received. She admitted to being "guilty" of organizing the first club, the "Research Club," in 1893. Its members were almost all school teachers and its focus was "entirely literary." At first, she recalled, the women's clubs were met with "derision," then gradually "tolerated," and finally viewed, begrudgingly, with "something akin to respect." A woman could still be a good wife and a mother, the "Falls City Lady" argued, while being affiliated with a club that was "recreation, an enjoyment, a stimulus, and a diversion." [65] Clubs were an enrichment of life in a world where opportunities for women outside the home were limited; they became known as "women's universities."

In 1909, according to the "Falls City Lady," there were four women's clubs active in town, with a combined membership of about ninety – Sorosis, Shakespeare, Friends in Council, and the Women's Club. Each was part of a national organization, and each was primarily concerned with literary and musical activities. The Sorosis, for example, hosted lectures at the Gehling Theater and Jenne Opera House on such weighty topics as "France From 1776-1804," "Coleridge," and "City Ordinances, Past, Present, and Prospective" (Fig. 25). The latter shows that women's clubs were also civic-minded, supporting schools, protecting children's welfare, and promoting sanitary reforms and "clean towns." But they could also just be about fun, as when Sorosis brought a "company of clever Tyrolean yodellers" to the Jenne.[66]

25. Sorosis Club, Falls City, Nebr. 1903.
Courtesy Nebraska State Historical Society. Folder RG2457.

The Falls City women's clubs were not overtly political, and two of the burning issues of the day, temperance and women's suffrage, were given little attention. In fact, at the District Convention of Women's Clubs, held in Falls City in 1905, the president asserted that the majority of club members were against extending the vote to women. She argued conventionally that it was only the man's role to "put shoulder to the wheel," and quite enough for women to act in a supporting role, "furnishing axel grease of encouragement and help." Richardson County men would certainly have agreed: they voted overwhelmingly three times (1871, 1882, and 1914) to reject state referenda that would have given women the vote and, like Nebraska as a whole, only passed the suffrage referendum in 1920 when it was a done deal, following the Nineteenth Amendment to the Constitution.[67]

Men had their own clubs, fraternal orders that, with their initiation rites and bonding rituals, as well as their insurance plans, served mainly as mutual aid societies. There were at least ten fraternal orders in Falls City in 1910, from national organizations like the Independent Order of Odd Fellows and the Knights of Pythias to local orders like Die Deauche Gelsellschaft, which was limited to Germans and had the dual purpose of supporting anything German, while confirming their patriotism to their adopted country. According to one member, their clubhouse had "ever been scenes of pleasure and profit," which serves as a good encapsulalization of the purposes of the fraternal orders in general.[68]

Like women's clubs, fraternal orders flourished from the 1880s to the 1920s, then went into decline. Unlike women's clubs, however, with their active social role in the community, fraternal clubs looked inward and were indeed more concerned with "pleasure and profit." There were exceptions: the Knights of Pythias brought the "rising Shakespearean actor," Stanford Dodge, to the Gehling in 1904 to star in *Damon and Pythias*; and one of the biggest events of the year was the Fraternal Union Picnic, with its parades, musical events, baseball games, drill contests, and many speeches. This event, and other red-letter days like July 4 and the annual chautauqua, brought the entire Richardson County community together for festivities[69] (Fig. 26).

From 1882 until the early twentieth century, these big events were held in Hinton Park, a thirty-acre resort with a horse racing track, a boating lake, and groves of walnut trees set in a bend of the Big Nemaha, just south of Falls City. Hinton Park was itself a tourist destination, drawing vacationers from southwestern Iowa, northwestern Missouri, and northeastern Kansas, as well as southeastern Nebraska. This popular attraction was destroyed by the marauding Big Nemaha. Thereafter, the Show Grounds, in the eastern part of Falls City, became the venue for the big events.[70]

26. Tents Set Up for Salem Chautauqua nd.
Courtesy Nebraska State Historical Society. Folder RG2457.

Men had their own particular leisure activities that took place outdoors, rather than in the drawing rooms where women hosted their events. Hunting was particularly popular. Parties would go out to the western reaches of the county to hunt prairie chickens, and men would take their hounds out coursing for rabbits. But the main hunting interest was migratory birds like ducks, snipes, and the elusive "Jacks," a variety of snipe, that were taken from October to April. The prime locations were the marshy bottoms of the Big Nemaha and Big Muddy, and the sandbars south of Rulo. The *Tribune* was filled with accounts of the kills, as in early March of 1907, when two sets of hunters brought in a total of seventy-nine ducks in a single day. A Nebraska game law regulated the hunting of migratory birds: the season ended in April as the agricultural season began, because the birds ate insects, which prevented the insects from eating crops. Nebraska was ahead of the nation here, because it was not until the Migratory Bird Act of 1913 that federal legislation sought to restrict the hunting of insectivorous birds, and not until the Migratory Bird Treaty Act of 1918 that such protection was implemented.[71]

Fishing was mainly a man's world too, although one account in the *Tribune* in August 1908 did tell of a fishing party of men, women, and children (complete with chaperones) that went for an extended outing to Big Lake, in Holt County, Missouri. Fish were there for the taking in the Missouri floodplain lakes and the Big Nemaha. In November 1904, for example, the "largest catch of the year" was taken out of Big Lake on the Missouri bottoms – "innumerable crappy," six bass, the largest weighing seven pounds, and an "immense walleye." At about the same time, Hank Snow reported that he had caught 716 fish and a turtle in the Big Nemaha over the course of the season, and was now ready to "hang up his pole." As with hunting, there were some incipient regulations for fishing, as Joe Burns found out at his own expense in 1904: Burns was arrested by the State Game Department for using traps in the Big Nemaha to catch sixty-two catfish, and he faced a hefty fine of $5 for each fish he had taken illegally.[72]

It was also mostly men (and boys) who were involved in organized sports, although Falls City High School did have a girls' basketball team that played, with some success, teams from other schools in Richardson County and neighboring counties (Fig. 27). This was not unusual: basketball was the cutting edge of womens' entrance into competitive sports at the turn of the century. But in the early 1900s especially in rural areas, sports were considered unsuitable for women and girls, the argument being that sports were unfeminine and unhealthy. At the annual field day, for example, held at the Falls City Show Grounds in May 1904, all the county's high schools competed in baseball, basketball, and an array of track and field events, but only boys participated. Moreover, whereas superintendents and principals (all men) got to compete in a special half-mile race, women teachers (who were the majority) had to settle for the less strenuous and more demure baseball throw.[73]

27. Shubert Basketball Champions. 1925(?).
Courtesy Nebraska State Historical Society. Folder RG2457.

High school boys had basketball, baseball, and football seasons, though the rules of play were sometimes fluid, and the competitions could get rowdy. The October 21, 1904, basketball game between Dawson and Humboldt, for example, was suspended when the players "got into a controversy" over a "misunderstanding of the rules." The victory was given to Humboldt "by default." Later that year, Tecumseh beat the visiting Falls City High School football team 15-5, but only "on account of interference of spectators." "Our boys were not given a chance," lamented the *Tribune*. In November of the same year, the Nebraska City High School team failed to show up for the Falls City game. High school sports were still in their infancy in the early 1900s, and not yet the talisman of community identity that they would become.[74]

28. Falls City Baseball. 1911. Courtesy Nebraska State Historical Society. Folder RG2457.

Communities fielded baseball and football teams too, if the local business leaders were willing to finance them and give their workers time off to participate (Fig. 28). Most of the time, Falls City was without a football team, much to the dismay of the *Tribune*, which pointed out that rival towns like Pawnee City, Tecumseh, and Hiawatha all had fine teams. A team was organized in November of 1904, but its first practice was marred by "a fight every thirty seconds." Their first game, against Padonia (Brown County, Kansas) ended in a 0-0 tie. Apparently the Falls City team had no coach, and some players were completely inexperienced. Moreover, the *Tribune* added, the team might have done better if they had "cut out the stuff that made Milwaukee famous" before playing. Rivalries often spilled over from the field into the crowd: the final game of the 1904 baseball season, featuring Falls City away at Rulo, ended early in a drunken brawl started by the home fans.[75] Organized sports were certainly a way to enjoy life, for players and speculators alike, but sometimes the circumstances were chaotic.

Alcohol was readily available as a lubricant for having a good time in Richardson County in the early 1900s, though the consequences were sometimes dire. There was an active Anti-Saloon League in the county, but despite its efforts, saloons abounded in the towns: the Sanborn Fire Insurance Map for 1908-09 showed three saloons plus a billiard hall on a single block of Stone Street; and one issue of the *Tribune* listed six new licenses issued to saloon keepers to sell "malt, spiritous and vinous liquors." It was even possible to order a case of Luxus beer from Krug Brewery in Omaha and have it delivered to the door.[76]

This side of Falls City's social life did not feature in the pages of the *Tribune*, except when things went wrong. The July 4 party in Barada in 1905, for example, was dampened when the sheriff confiscated numerous cases of beer and whisky, and things went very wrong in Salem the following year when the "usual crowd" got hold of "diverse kegs of beer" and had a "high old time," which led to violence and incarcerations. Rulo was considered a particularly volatile place, with frequent public drinking and "gun-play." Nims City was even worse, and one "drunken affray" there in 1904 almost resulted in a murder, and did result in the closing of its drinking establishments. Alcohol was also carried illegally to the reservations, especially just when annuities or per-capita payments were dispensed and there was money to spend on revelry.[77]

The first decade of the twentieth century saw an expansion of commercial entertainment in Richardson County, and in the country as a whole. It also witnessed the transition from the old, the live plays and vaudeville at the Gehling Theater and the Jenne Opera House, to the new, the electric theaters showing motion pictures. These entertainments overlapped for a while, before the old gave way to the new.

There was a great deal of variety in the entertainment offered at the Gehling and Jenne, from local performers like Mrs. Wm. Chilton, a monologist presenting readings and impersonations, to touring ensembles like the Kingsley-Russell Company, which billed itself as the "acknowledged monarchs of repertoire" featuring the "latest and best comedies and dramas," as well as a "wide array of vaudeville features." Some companies might have a week-long engagement; others played for just one night. Tickets were affordable: 75 cents for the first two rows in the dress circle, 50 cents for the remainder of the dress circle, and 35 cents for the balcony. According to the *Tribune*, the shows were generally well-attended.[78]

Some of the shows were sheer entertainment, like *Phantom Detective*, a "Melodramatic, Mystifying, Musical Suprize" that played at the Gehling in 1910, with its cast of thirty, a chorus of "Prettily-Costumed Showgirls," a quartet of "Singing Comedians," and a "cage of real lions." But many came with a moral message to mollify critics in communities like Falls City who saw the acting, singing, and dancing as a threat to decency. So, for example, *The Little Homestead*, which showed at the Gehling in 1904, was about the "repentance" and "remorse" of a woman who left her husband for an "unscrupulous scoundrel," only to come to her senses and be forgiven in the end. *Thorns and Orange Blossoms* was likewise a "drama of love lost and gained," aimed specifically at an audience of women, and *The Kansas Sunflower* was advertised as a "sincere heart story, clean, pure, and simple."[79]

The types of shows that played in Richardson County during these years, and the ways the performers were received, expose prevailing attitudes to ethnicity and race. *The Old Clothes Man* was publicized defensively in the *Tribune* as the "best Hebrew play on the American stage today," with, it was claimed, none of the usual "buffoonery and ridicule" associated with the genre.[80] Such damning with faint praise was even more evident in attitudes to Black performers.

There were few African Americans in Richardson County in 1910, only 83 from a total population of 17,448. But performances on the stage often involved Black artists, as well as pretend-Black artists, white minstrels doing their ridiculing mimicry in blackface. The nonsensical farce *Yon Yonson* (an "avalanche of laughter") was performed in this manner, and *The Palace of Aladdin* staged by "Henry's Greatest Minstralls" at the Gehling in 1906, included in its advertising the assurance that the black-face performers in the vaudeville were actually "all-white artists." [81]

The reception of Black actors and singers was sometimes enthusiastic, but often infused with latent and blatant racism. "Slayton's Tennesseans," for example, who played at the Gehling in 1908, were hailed in the *Tribune* as the "greatest colored singers of the time," but this praise was tarnished by the stereotypical and demeaning explanation of their talents: "the negro is a natural in his musical entertainment," having a "childlike enthusiasm," and being "by nature dramatic." [82]

It is not clear where Slayton's Tennesseans stayed while they were in Falls City, but two years before in Stella, the Black performers in a medicine show were not allowed to stay at the hotel and had to bed down in the Opera House where they had just played. The racism was even more blatant in Stella in 1905 when a "company of colored people" called the Alabama Jubilee Singers put on a concert at the Opera House. The local correspondent to the *Tribune*, in reprehensible language, mocked them as "______" from Hiawatha and Falls City, and seemed to take a pleasure in reporting that the audience walked out on them.[83]

The first mention of movie houses in the *Tribune* came in 1908, when the apparently short-lived Lyric Theater began showing "high class moving pictures." Later, in 1911, an Electric Theater opened, presenting the "latest in motion pictures" and promising the audience ample electric fans to keep them cool during the hot summer months. Movies offered more varied entertainment than the live shows at the Gehling and Jenne, changing their programs every Monday, Wednesday, and Friday, and they were cheaper, costing only ten cents for adults and five cents for children. The Gehling could not withstand the competition, and closed its doors as a theater in 1915.[84]

It may have been a new era, but moral opposition to entertainment remained. The *Tribune* was a case in point, lambasting movies as "course and indecent," a "menace to society." In response, the Electric Theater sought to placate its audiences by promising that "no picture will offend even the most refined."[85]

Typically, a program would include three or four short (about twelve minutes each) one-reelers, presented by one of the innumerable small production companies (Selig, Essany, Lubin, Vitagraph and others, all controlled by Edison Studios) that ran the business. The show at the Electric Theater on March 17, 1911, for example, featured *Haunted By Conscience*, a drama with "several intense situations;" *Under the Old Apple Tree*, a picture "better than the best;" and *Hanks and Lanks Joy Riding*, one of a series of comedy shorts that were "bound to please." Moral stories, nostalgic westerns, slapstick comedies, and exotic travelogues such as *A Ramble Through Celon* and *In the Spreewald*, "photo-plays" of Prussia, were popular genres. And if a hit movie didn't make it to Falls City, there was always the possibility of taking a train to St. Joseph and seeing it there: in 1908, a number of enthusiasts did just that to see the blockbuster (fifteen minutes, almost all chariot race) *Ben Hur* at the grand Tootle Opera House.[86]

Movies were all the rage, but the biggest single event in the social calendar was when the circus came to town. The first decades of the twentieth century were in the middle of the golden age of American circuses, made possible by the railroads that facilitated the bulk transportation of people, animals, and equipment. Falls City, an important rail hub, drew all the major circuses during those years: the big two, Ringling Brothers and Barnum and Bailey (they were really one after 1907, when the former bought out the latter, though they continued to tour separately until 1919); John Robinson Shows, a large family circus, that played Falls City as early as 1873, following the first railroad in; the Great Wallace Circus, which claimed to be second only to the Ringling Brothers; and the Campbell Brothers Show, which claimed the same. Add to these more specialized enterprises, like the Kansas-based C.W. Parker Amusement Company, which was renowned for its ornate carousels, and the Miller Brothers' 101 Ranch Wild West Show, which combined circus acts like performing elephants with re-enactments of an imaginary frontier (and which got into movie production after 1911).[87]

The circuses, more than any other form of entertainment, had a seamy side, so they were constantly re-assuring the public of their decency. The Miller Brothers, for example, claimed to be "thoughtful and polite enough for ladies and children," and the Parker Amusement Company promised "a whirlwind of clear attractions… no grafters, fakers, or gamblers," and just to be sure, they hired two detectives to "see that people are cared for." [88]

The circus began with a free parade (Fig. 29) that gave a taste of what was to come in the three rings at the show grounds – exotic animals, elephants, giraffes, camels, sadly out of place, trudging incongruously down Stone Street, "frolicsome clowns," cages of captive animals, acrobats and aerial artists, and hundreds of decorated horses. An extravaganza, and all for a fifty-cent price of admission.[89]

There was the economic benefit too. The rest of Richardson County emptied into their county seat on circus day, bringing their purchasing power with them. The circus itself was a jolt to the economy. In 1910 the *Tribune* calculated that the John Robinson Shows, with a "menagerie not seen since the day of Noah," spent $3,000 during its stay in town, including buying eight tons of hay, seventy-five quarts of milk, and 115 bushels of oats.[90] No wonder towns competed for the circus.

29. Having a Good Time in Falls City, Nebr. 1912.
Courtesy Nebraska State Historical Society. Folder RG2457.

The year 1904 was a particularly rich one for circuses in Falls City. It had not seemed that it would be that way at first. When the Campbell Brothers signed up to come on May 3, the *Tribune* was relieved, but still it lamented that it would be the only one that year. But then the Great Wallace Circus committed to May 31, followed by the Ringling Brothers for July 26. Unfortunately, when the gigantic Ringling Brothers train pulled into the station, with its eighty-five double-length railroad cars, forty elephants, 650 horses, and 1,280 employees, it found that it could not get its heavy wagons through the mud-clogged streets to the show grounds. So it canceled and moved ahead to the next stop. This reversal was overcome with the scheduling of Barnum and Bailey for September 24, and a week after that the Miller Brothers' 101 Ranch rolled in with its Wild West Show.[91] Circuses like these continued to be popular until after World War II, although by 1929 Ringling Brothers had bought out all the major touring companies, and literally ran the show.

Entertainment continued to flow into Richardson County in the form of vaudeville, movies, and circuses, but increasingly residents sought out their own entertainment elsewhere, at tourist destinations easily and reasonably reached by train. A sample from the correspondents' reports in 1906 shows that the well-to-do, at least, traveled widely. On April 7, it was noted that Mrs. W. L. White had just returned from a trip to Niagara Falls; on July 20, Helen Brebeck and Lena Nettleback had just completed an eight-day trip to Sun Springs, Florida; on September 21, Charley Shafer and his wife left for an "extended trip" though the battlefields of the South, where he had served during the Civil War; and on October 26, Dr. and Mrs. Fast, clearly the very well-to-do, departed for a year-long visit to Europe.[92]

The railroads were again the main facilitator of these expanding horizons, serving as tourist agents as well as conveyors. In time, automobiles also opened up tourist destinations, but early on this was constrained by the bad conditions of the roads. Locally, the Burlington and Missouri Pacific offered special rates to the annual chautauquas in Beatrice and Auburn, to the state fair in Lincoln (headlined in 1910 by daily flights of the Wright brothers' plane), and various carnivals and parades at Ak-Sar-Ben in Omaha (a fifty-cent round trip). In 1904, both railroads ran deals to the St. Louis World's Fair: a special train left Falls City at 8:10 pm and arrived in St. Louis at 8:35 am, costing $7.25 round trip.[93]

Both railroads also offered summer vacation rates to the Pacific coast ($45 round trip), "Eastern resorts," and the Rocky Mountains, and winter rates to St. Augustine, New Orleans, and, for those seeking the snow or the reputed health benefits of the mountains, to Colorado Springs. The Missouri Pacific advertised a tour to Hot Springs, Arkansas, and the Burlington organized "Personally Conducted Excursions" to Havana, Cuba. The Burlington even ran a "Visit the Old Folks" special to "many points" in Kentucky, Ohio, and Indiana, a nostalgic return to the homes that had been left behind for a better future in Richardson County.[94]

These day to day turnings, at work and at play, quietly constituted the geography of Richardson County, making it a distinctive place. But it was the big events, mainly the setbacks, that would stand out in the passage of time and become its remembered history.

SETBACKS

Richardson County's impressive growth through 1930 was interrupted by periodic setbacks that temporarily halted the progress. Some of these setbacks were environmental in origin, though by Great Plains standards, Richardson County is a fairly benign place when it comes to environmental hazards. There were droughts, as in 1874, and crops were lost, but lack of rainfall is much less of a problem here than on the western Great Plains, where aridity is a prevailing condition. There were tornadoes too, like the particularly destructive one that targeted the countryside around Stella on April 14, 1911. But in general Richardson County is a rather quiet corner of Nebraska for tornadoes.[95]

Floods were another matter, although floods were caused as much by human agency, by farmers exposing the soil to erosion, as by other forces of nature. Before the reclamation of Drainage District No. 1, completed in 1913, floods were almost an annual occurrence along the lower Big Nemaha. In 1904, for example, twenty-five inches of precipitation fell from April to July, pouring off exposed hillsides into the Big Nemaha and its tributaries, creating a mile-wide lake along its lower reaches. Bridges were washed away, fields inundated, lowland roads destroyed. Making the most of a bad situation, some locals took their boats out on the watery expanse, a new opportunity for recreation. After the reclamation, the flood problem was mitigated, as drainage ditches carried the excess water into the straightened and deepened channel of the Big Nemaha, and away into the Missouri.[96]

One environmental catastrophe that lodged in local memory, even in the early twentieth century, was the grasshopper invasion of 1874-5. More accurately, it was a Rocky Mountain locust invasion, maybe 10 billion of them, riding the westerly winds from the mountain valleys where they lived and reproduced, out onto the Great Plains. The pervasive drought of 1873 may have reduced the capacity of their mountain sanctuaries to support them, and so they found sustenance in the grasslands and in farmers' fields as far east as Minnesota, Iowa, and Missouri. They would reduce a field of corn to stalks in a matter of hours; then they would move on, a cloud rising from the earth, their vibrating wings sounding like rolling thunder. They left behind eggs that would hatch in spring and begin anew the cycle of destruction. Their unworldly appearance, their sheer numbers, the suddenness of their arrival, the completeness of the damage, and the impossibility of preventing it, raised what already was a dramatic event to the level of mythology.[97]

The first mention of the "hateful locust" in the *Nemaha Valley Journal* came on August 6, 1874, when it was reported that they were close at hand, just west of Tecumseh, eating their way across the countryside. They descended on Richardson County soon afterward, filling the furrows between the corn rows to a depth of six inches, and eating everything above ground. They stripped the orchards, leaving only the pits hanging from the bare branches of the peach trees. Then they laid their eggs and moved on to Missouri. Farmers, with no crops to sell, or vegetables to eat, left if they could, and stayed and suffered if they couldn't. A map published in the *Annual Report of the Kansas State Board of Agriculture* in 1874 described Richardson County (and all of eastern Nebraska) as "ravaged." [98]

In May of 1875 the eggs hatched out and a new generation of locusts quickly consumed the young crops, leaving the land "as bare as a desert." The farmers tried multiple ways to get rid of them: heavy rolling to squash the eggs before they hatched, fire and smoke to repel the young grasshoppers as they emerged, pans of kerosene dragged through the fields which seemed to attract and kill them. But it was all in vain. When the locusts did leave, it was of their own accord, and they never returned to Richardson County. There would be other grasshopper invasions, locally experienced, but the Rocky Mountain locust was driven to extinction by 1902, the result of habitat destruction, as farming and ranching transformed the environments of the mountain valleys that had nurtured them.[99]

Rocky Mountain locusts were not the only problem facing Richardson County in 1874. Drought and chinch bugs had already taken a toll on the spring wheat crop by the time the locusts arrived. Then there were serious economic problems, storms brewed in distant places that blew into Richardson County and disrupted life. On September 18, 1873, the banking house of Jay Cooke and Company, overburdened by debt incurred by wild speculating in railroad construction, declared bankruptcy. This triggered the "Panic of 1873" and the resulting failure of other indebted banks and businesses throughout the nation. The New York Stock Exchange was forced to close for ten days. In Richardson County the banks suspended payments for a period of time. By May of 1874, according to the local newspapers, they had recovered and were said to be doing "remarkably well." [100]

Indebtedness was an ongoing problem in Richardson County (and on the frontier in general), but the immediate issue, once the locusts were gone, was overproduction of crops and the consequent loss of agricultural markets. Demand for American wheat in its main foreign market, Europe, declined as it too sank into economic depression. Meanwhile, production at home, but also in Russia and Australia, was at an all time high. Domestic corn production also soared, as new lands were brought under cultivation. Richardson County was "choked with abundance," its corn cribs and elevators brimming with grain that could not be sold anywhere at a profit. From 1874 to 1877, the average selling price of wheat was ninety-four cents a bushel, and of corn forty cents a bushel, not enough to cover the costs of production.

"A glut is as bad as a famine," declared the *Nemaha Valley Journal*, as it described the cascading effects of the crisis: farmers had no cash to pay taxes, mortgages, and store bills; some had invested in reapers and other expensive machinery during better times, and now they couldn't pay them off; to save money they laid off their hired hands, widening the distress; with no markets for their flour, millers discharged their workers too; merchants failed when farmers and millers couldn't pay their bills. The *Nemaha Valley Journal* ended its editorial with the lament, "men break right and left." [101]

The areas hit worst by the combination of drought, locusts, and economic downturn were in central Nebraska and Kansas, which had just been settled, and farmers there had no reserves to fall back on. But even in Richardson County, which had been settled for two decades, a "state of destitution existed universally." The Roman Catholic churches in the county held a mass meeting and sent a member to the eastern United States to "appeal to the charity of all persons." Such charity was the preferred form of relief, because ravaged states like Nebraska were reluctant to draw upon their own reserves, or to seek help from the Federal Government, because this would reflect badly on their ability to fend for themselves. But as the condition of the settlers continued to deteriorate over the winter of 1874-5, the Nebraska Legislature authorized an expenditure of $50,000 for seeds, so that ruined farmers could start again. Congress also took the unprecedented step of providing $30,000 for seeds and $150,000 worth of surplus blankets and clothing to help the destitute.[102] This initial trickle of federal aid to Plains farmers would become a torrent in the 1930s, and the flow has continued ever since.

The seeds paid dividends in Richardson County, and good crops were harvested in the fall of 1875, alleviating the suffering. But crop prices remained low, and the general depression lingered on until 1878-9.

Most of the major reversals in Richardson County, such as the Rocky Mountain locusts, economic panics, and deadly epidemics, came in from the outside. Of those generated locally, fires were the worst. Fires were ubiquitous and repetitive. In the early years of American settlement, grassland fires, started by lightning or human error, were the main hazard. Often the first furrows plowed were not for crops, but to create a firebreak around a home. As the combustible natural prairie was replaced by less flammable crops, and as roads themselves became fire breaks, the incidence of destructive grassland fires declined and the principal threat moved into towns, where densely packed wooden buildings were a tinderbox just waiting for a spark from a machine, or the flame from a toppled candle, to cause a conflagration. Not a single town in the county escaped at least one destructive fire, and most towns had many.[103]

Falls City had its "long looked for fire… the greatest ever witnessed" on April 12, 1877. The fire broke out in a feed store that housed a dwelling on the second floor. The cause was unknown, although two men had been seen smoking cigars nearby earlier in the evening. The entire building was quickly engulfed in flames, and the residents upstairs barely (literally) escaped with their lives. Within forty minutes seven other buildings had been burned to the ground. The streets were filled with "excited people," but there was nothing to be done: the city didn't have a fire wagon, and buckets of water were only a vain gesture. Most of the owners of the destroyed buildings carried no insurance. In the aftermath, Falls City's council passed an ordinance preventing the erection of frame buildings in the business district.[104]

This was a wise move, but it didn't prevent fires. The year 1919 was particularly blighted. On May 7, a fire broke out in the dome of the county courthouse and reduced it to ashes in a matter of minutes. The massive brick walls were left standing on all sides, surrounding a gutted interior. Any efforts to control it were thwarted by lack of water, because the city's system was down. *The Falls City News* estimated that insurance would cover only half of the loss.[105]

This was an opportunity for Humboldt to make a bid for the county seat, arguing that Falls City had lost that right because of its abysmal fire record. Humboldt had not been around for the early courthouse wars, but it clearly had ambitions from the start when it built around a public square, just begging for the county courthouse. In May 1919, while the courthouse was still smoldering, Humboldt businessmen pledged $100,000 to have a new one built in its public square. The competition was fought on in the respective towns' newspapers over the next few months, and only settled on September 9 in a county-wide election that was decisively in Falls City's favor. The Humboldt paper lamented that Falls City's business interests had come out on top again.[106]

Falls City's fire record did not improve. On October 1, 1919, the Leo Vinegar Works caught fire, possibly started by sparks from a passing engine. The fire burned a long time before anyone noticed because the factory's fire alarm was broken. The factory was totally destroyed, an estimated loss of $100,000. By the end of the year, the J. C. Penney store, a bakery, and the YMCA had all burned down.[107]

Stella may have been the hardest hit of all the towns. In short, here is Stella's late nineteenth century fire history: the first house built in town was destroyed by a lightning strike in 1882; five years later the Metzger and Clark mill burned to the ground and was replaced by a new building that in turn burned down in 1896; in 1888, the general store and millenary store were destroyed by fire; the next year, the school burned down; also in 1889, the grain elevator was taken out by fire, rebuilt, and then burned again in 1896, rebuilt once more, only to be burned yet again in the 1930s.[108]

Surprisingly, none of these fires seem to have resulted in deaths (except for the guard dog at the Leo Vinegar Works). And there was always the compensation that a building boom followed a fire, providing jobs for carpenters, masons, and other workers, and new business for hardware stores, lumberyards, and brickworks. Following the Rulo fire of April 27, 1904, for example, which just about destroyed the main street, the *Rulo Register* seemed almost jubilant in declaring that the new brick buildings would be "a big improvement to the town."[109]

There was no bright side to epidemics. The 1870 mortality census, covering those who had died between June 1, 1869 and May 31, 1870, paints a bleak picture of the tenuous nature of life, especially for children. Of the 114 deaths in the county that year, 32, or 28 percent, were of children aged 5 and younger, and 80, or 70 percent, were of children aged 10 and younger. They died of typhoid fever, cholera infantum, whooping cough, and measles. But most of all, they died of scarlet fever: 32, or 40 percent of all children's deaths were caused by this infectious bacterial disease, sometimes within only 48 hours of contracting it.

Scarlet fever was a simmering pandemic from about 1820 to 1880 that periodically boiled over in ferocious epidemics, such as the one that ran its course through the United States in 1870-72. An entire generation of children in Richardson County was lost to this disease during these years: the Pribbens family lost Sophia (2) and Emma (1); The John family lost Barbara (9) and Matilda (7); and the Geloe family lost Dora (9), Charles (6), and John (2), to name only a few of these mortalities. There was no effective treatment for the disease. When the epidemic finally waned it was because of preventative measures, such as better nutrition, improved sanitation, and quarantining.[110]

Despite such improvements, the epidemics kept coming, even in the early twentieth century. There was a smallpox epidemic on the reservations in 1901, a dreadful echo from the past, and in the spring of 1904, the schools were forced to close because of a raging measles epidemic that also targeted the aged. But the sickness that set back life most seriously, and which lodged in the collective memory longest, was the influenza epidemic of 1918, the so-called "Spanish flu." [111]

It wasn't really the Spanish flu. The first cases of what later was identified as the H1N1 influenza virus likely occurred in Haskell County, southwestern Kansas, in January of 1918. From there the virus was carried to Camp Funston, an overcrowded army camp in northern Kansas, just 120 miles to the west of Richardson County. By March 1,100 soldiers were hospitalized, and forty-six were dead from bacterial pneumonia and other secondary infections that developed from the flu. The virus then disseminated widely with deployed troops in camps throughout the United States and in the arena of war in Europe, where they died more often from its dreadful effects than from the conflict. By July the tide of infection had washed around the world.[112]

The virus came back to the United States with returning troops in early October, having mutated into a more virulent form. It surged in East Coast cities like Philadelphia, which was brought to its knees, then it quickly diffused inland, arriving in Richardson County in mid-October.

Altogether, at least 675,000 Americans would die, many of them otherwise healthy young men and women.

The first deaths of Richardson County residents actually occurred in distant army camps, and they kept occurring there throughout the morbid fall of 1918. Their obituaries were printed in the local newspaper alongside those of the young men who were dying in the trenches of World War I.[113]

Then the sickness came home. On October 10, *The Humboldt Leader* ran the headline, "The Influenza Scare Has Reached Humboldt." By November 2, there were 100 cases in Humboldt and the surrounding countryside; by November 23 there were 403 cases in Falls City and seventeen of them had died. Entire families died, so many that the monument makers could not keep up, and the deceased were buried together, with only a pile of stones to mark the tragic place. *The Falls City News* lamented that there was "a general sadness among our people." [114]

The disease seemed to relent in December, but there were still at least 157 infected people in the county on December 13: 45 in Falls City, 3 in Salem, 12 in Barada, 11 in Humboldt, 7 in Stella, 13 in Shubert, 10 in Rulo, and 3 in Preston. The rural areas outside the towns had even higher numbers proportionate to their populations. The epidemic finally waned in the spring of 1919, because so many people had been infected, and were thereby protected, that the virus could not readily spread. As elsewhere in the United States, the worst of the epidemic was over in Richardson County in about eight weeks.[115]

There was nothing known about viruses in 1918. It was understood that influenza was a "crowd disease" that spread through "droplets" in the air, so efforts to contain it consisted of restricting public assemblies and quarantining those who were sick. Fresh air was thought to be beneficial, and Vicks VapoRub was widely advertised as a means of allaying symptoms.

On October 7, as the first cases hit home, the Nebraska State Board of Health ordered the closing of "schools, churches, places of entertainment or public congregation, pool halls, and other places of amusement." Implementation of this ban was left to local authorities. Humboldt and Falls City complied, although businessmen complained loudly of the financial loss. Stella and Rulo refused to recognize the epidemic at all. Humboldt also put strict quarantine measures in place: all cases of flu had to be reported to the city's Board of Health, and failure to do so would result in a fine; patients had to be isolated, with only attending physicians and nurses allowed in the room; houses with sick people were placarded in town and up to a radius of five miles around town; and sick people would be arrested if they didn't stay home. Falls City's quarantine laws were less strict, allowing healthy members of afflicted families to be "permitted their liberty." Quarantine laws were not strictly imposed or observed in the countryside, which explains the higher incidence of disease there.[116]

On November 14, anxious for an ending, the mayor of Humboldt lifted the ban and re-opened the schools and churches. Quarantine restrictions were relaxed, allowing people to "resume their normal pursuits." The result was a proliferation of new cases: nearly all the high school students became ill, as did many of their teachers. So the "lid" was clamped on tightly again in late November, and stricter quarantine rules were put in place (Fig. 30), and people were urged to wear masks. The ban was finally lifted in Humboldt on December 19, and schools re-opened, although children from homes where there was influenza could not attend. *The Humboldt Leader* was able to claim that "the situation is very favorable here." [117]

That was certainly an exaggeration. Throughout the epidemic communities like Falls City and Humboldt downplayed the seriousness in order to protect their images and their businesses. Humboldt, for example, admitted to only one death (from more than 400 cases) and claimed that it was actually caused by Bright's disease, not influenza. As late as October 31, *The Humboldt Leader* was still maintaining that it was not a serious matter, no worse than the "French Grip," a previous influenza epidemic that had run through Richardson County in the winter of 1889-90. Similarly, an editorial in the *Falls City News* on December 11, at the height of the epidemic, claimed that there was no need to fear visiting Falls City – that it was "quite safe for country folk to come in and do their business.[118]

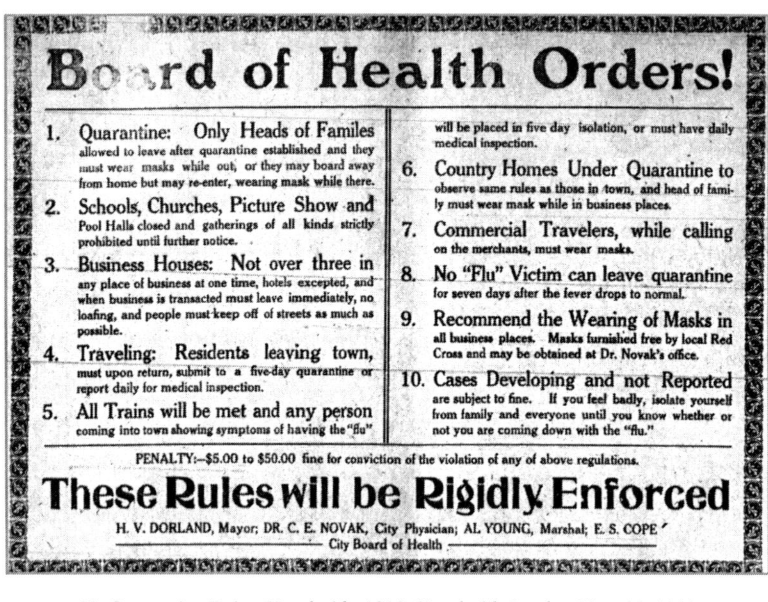

Board of Health Orders!

1. **Quarantine: Only Heads of Familes** allowed to leave after quarantine established and they must wear masks while out, or they may board away from home but may re-enter, wearing mask while there.
2. **Schools, Churches, Picture Show and** Pool Halls closed and gatherings of all kinds strictly prohibited until further notice.
3. **Business Houses: Not over three in** any place of business at one time, hotels excepted, and when business is transacted must leave immediately, no loafing, and people must keep off of streets as much as possible.
4. **Traveling: Residents leaving town,** must upon return, submit to a five-day quarantine or report daily for medical inspection.
5. **All Trains will be met and any person** coming into town showing symptoms of having the "flu" will be placed in five day isolation, or must have daily medical inspection.
6. **Country Homes Under Quarantine to** observe same rules as those in town, and head of family must wear mask while in business places.
7. **Commercial Travelers, while calling** on the merchants, must wear masks.
8. **No "Flu" Victim can leave quarantine** for seven days after the fever drops to normal.
9. **Recommend the Wearing of Masks in** all business places. Masks furnished free by local Red Cross and may be obtained at Dr. Novak's office.
10. **Cases Developing and not Reported** are subject to fine. If you feel badly, isolate yourself from family and everyone until you know whether or not you are coming down with the "flu."

PENALTY:—$5.00 to $50.00 fine for conviction of the violation of any of above regulations.

These Rules will be Rigidly Enforced

H. V. DORLAND, Mayor; DR. C. E. NOVAK, City Physician; AL YOUNG, Marshal; E. S. COPE

City Board of Health

30. Quarantine Rules, Humboldt, 1918. Humboldt Leader, Nov. 28, 1918.

The epidemic was also downplayed because to admit its severity would undermine the war effort. And indeed, articles on the war took up far more space in the Richardson County newspapers than did news about the epidemic. Of course, the obituaries in the newspapers, and the fresh burials in the graveyards, belied all the protestations.

The stress of the epidemic brought to the surface the deep-rooted tensions among Richardson County towns, and between these towns and the countryside. Falls City's newspapers mocked Humboldt's claim that it had only suffered one death. In a retort, the mayor of Humboldt complained that Falls City was purposefully spreading rumors in an attempt to hurt businesses in his town. Meanwhile, the "country people" suspected that the ban and quarantine rules were specifically aimed at them, and they refused to comply. There was also a tendency to blame other places for the predicament: on December 5, for example, *The Humboldt Leader* expressed that many of their cases of influenza were caused by visitors from neighboring towns where there were no restrictions in place, and on December 23, the *Falls City News* put the blame for their winter upsurge on Kansas, where there were no quarantine laws in effect.[119]

As the epidemic retreated in late winter and spring 1919, the presence of the influenza virus became just another facet of life, along with other trials and tribulations. It moved to the back of peoples' minds, unless it came too close, as it did for Humboldt's Mr. and Mrs. Philpot and their newborn child, who all perished from the "dread disease" in late February.[120] It would be a century before another pandemic of equal virulency found its way into Richardson County, sowing sickness and death anew.

Chapter 4

Contraction, 1931-2023

After a few decades of meteoric growth, Richardson County's population began its long decline to the present. Rural areas, farms, and small towns repeatedly lost population, census by census, after 1930, and they continue to lose population today. There were variations from town to town, because each was a particular story, but these were only variations on a common theme of decline. Even the short-lived oil boom from 1938 to 1941, drawing from oil fields near Falls City, Dawson, and Shubert (Fig. 31), did nothing to halt the downward plunge.[1]

31. Oil Fields Richardson County, Eickhoff no. 1. Circa 1940. Courtesy Nebraska State Historical Society. Folder RG 2457.

The draining of the population from farms, due in considerable part to the mechanization of farming, displacing labor, carried the small towns down with it: fewer customers at the elevator, fewer men at the barbers and the bars, fewer faces in the desks and pews. And this was all the result not of failure, but of resounding success, increased production of crops and livestock from the same, or even less, acreage, and with reduced need for workers. This success, however, came at the cost of the unraveling of the dense patchwork quilt of farms and towns that had been woven in the late nineteenth and early twentieth centuries.

As the population of the countryside thinned, Falls City benefited from the drift into town, and the county seat continued to grow until 1950, after which it joined the contraction. But Falls City declined more slowly than the surrounding areas, so that as each decade went by it contained a greater and greater share of the county's population. By 2020, Falls City accounted for 52 percent of the total, an incongruous situation whereby a rural county with more than 90 percent of its area in farms, is actually (by census definition) an urban county, where the majority of its population is concentrated in a single town.

CONSOLIDATION

Against this backdrop of steady population decline, Richardson County's geography was transformed by the consolidation of its parts. The railroads, for example, began to tear up unprofitable branch lines, leaving towns stranded. This happened to Rulo, which lost its rail connection to Atchison in 1933. And it happened to Shubert in 1942, when the Burlington pulled up the track from Salem to provide steel for the war effort. Shubert retained the track to Nemaha City until 1982, when it too was abandoned. And so Shubert became an "inland town," five miles from the nearest rails.[2] There's still a functioning elevator, serviced by trucks, but there's no sign of the old railroad, except for the elevator's rusted grain chute, dangling over where the railcars once rolled.

Consolidation of railroads also had a damaging impact on Falls City. This was explained by Bill Schock, a forty-three-year veteran of the Missouri Pacific, in a nostalgic lecture to the Richardson County Historical Society in 2013. Schock explained that the arrival of low-maintenance diesel engines in Richardson County in 1952 resulted in large numbers of roundhouse repair crews losing their jobs and having to move elsewhere. Then in 1962 the Missouri Pacific moved its division headquarters, with all its officers and staff, to Kansas City and Atchison. Continuing the downsizing, all telegraphers' positions in Falls City were abolished in 1982 when train movements became monitored by radio (and later computer) from Omaha. And in 1992, the position of station agent at Falls City was terminated.[3] The acquisition of division headquarters from Atchison in 1910 had kept Falls City growing in the early twentieth century, and just as surely the loss of this function in the second half of that century kept the town's population declining.

The most evident consolidation in Richardson County after 1930 took place in farming and the rural landscape. The number of farms steadily decreased from census to census, while their size steadily increased. In 1930, there were 1,964 farms in the county, with an average size of 166 acres – most quarter-sections had a farm; by 1959, the number of farms was down to 1,384 and their average size had increased to 239 acres. By 2017 only 708 farms remained, with an average size of 483 acres. Of those farms, 111, or 16 percent of the total, had more than 1,000 acres.[4]

Fewer farmers were able to manage more acres more intensely after World War II because of the adoption of increasingly sophisticated machinery to prepare the soil, and to plant, spray, and harvest the crops. The introduction of hybrid seeds, synthetic fertilizers, and insecticides was also instrumental to this modernization of farming, which produced greatly increased yields per acre.[5] By 1959, almost all the farms in Richardson County had tractors, and the vast majority also had combines and corn pickers. Horses disappeared from the rural landscape, the end of an era: by 2017, only 266 horses and ponies were on Richardson County farms; the value of their sales was so small that the census withheld reporting the figure "to avoid disclosing data for individual operations." [6] And so horses, as beasts of burden, went the way of oxen into the past.

As the farms became larger, they also became more specialized. A typical Richardson County farm in 1930 would have had a dairy, a poultry barn, a hog house, and pastures for horses, cattle, and sheep. A variety of crops – corn, oats, sorghum, winter wheat, and various hays were grown in small, colorful fields. Altogether, the typical farm might yield four or five commercial products from the crops and livestock.

A typical Richardson County farm now focuses on one or two products, mainly corn and soybeans (the latter first appeared in the 1950 census, and now almost matches corn in acreage). Together corn and soybeans account for 95 percent of the acres in crops in the county.[7] Oats disappeared with the horses, sorghum moved to drier places, and wheat gave way almost completely to more profitable corn and soybeans. And so was lost the first fresh green of spring. Animals vanished from the farmyards and pastures, the dairy cow unnecessary after refrigerated milk, and the hogs and poultry crammed into massive confinement-feeding operations that seem more like manufacturing than farming. Only beef cow-calf operations on Richardson County pastures (12 percent of the area in farms in 2017) have resisted consolidation, a situation that pertains across the nation as a whole.[8]

Consolidation, in the sense of things being brought together, was implicit in the modernization of rural life in Richardson County during the decades following World War II. By 1959, for example, 1,250 of the county's farms had telephones and 1,348 had automobiles (873 farms also had "motortrucks"). Roads were improved, bringing everything closer: in 1950, 543 farms fronted on a gravel road and 883 on a dirt road; by 1959, the numbers were 920 and 203 respectively. It was an increasingly mobile and connected world: as reported in the 1950 Census of Agriculture, the average distance that Richardson County farmers traveled to their "most visited trade center" was six miles.[9]

The most dramatic change came with rural electrification in the 1930s and 1940s, replacing locally generated electricity with service from a single power line. In 1940, only 634 of Richardson County's farms had electricity, and only 329 of those received their current from a power line; ten years later 1,396 farms had electricity, of which 1,371 were supplied by a power line. There was some resistance to rural electrification on the basis of expense – it could cost a hefty $600 to get hooked up, and in 1950 the average monthly electricity bill was $8.46. But the attractions were too great and resistance was quickly overcome. Farm families readily adopted electric water pumps, electric water heaters, home freezers, electric washing machines, in addition to electric coffee pots and radios. Electric ranges were accepted more slowly: the old coal or wood stove cost less and provided more because in addition to cooking and baking it was also used to heat the kitchen in winter.[10]

Consolidation, in another sense of solidifying, or making more firm, was also evident in the increasing amount of the farmers' incomes that came from the federal government.

Federal aid to Richardson County farmers first came in the drought and depression of the 1930s. Before that, in a similar drought and depression in the mid-1890s, Great Plains farmers were mainly left to sink or swim by themselves. The first infusion of federal money came through the Agricultural Adjustment Acts of 1933, which paid farmers to limit crop acreages in order to reduce the supply and thereby raise flagging crop prices. A map of federal aid per capita from 1933 to 1936, compiled at the latter date, puts Richardson County in the second highest category, $119 to $175, not as high as the Dust Bowl area of the southern Plains, but higher than most of the surrounding counties.[11]

The Agricultural Adjustment Acts and other federal aid, such as emergency purchases of starving cattle, set the pattern for government involvement in farming. In 1956, the Soil Bank program provided cash payments to farmers to take cropland out of production in order to reduce surpluses and raise prices. This was also a boon to conservation and wildlife habitat, because the retired acres were to be left idle, or put under perennial grasses. It was risk-free income with little or no work; some farmers retired all their lands and lived on the proceeds.[12]

This river of federal support flows right through to the present in the form of the Conservation Reserve Program. The CRP was created in 1985, permitting farmers to enter into contracts with the government that pay them to retire cropland and put it instead under vegetative cover. Again, this benefited wildlife in places like Richardson County where the monocultural duopoly of corn and soybeans had left the land exceedingly productive for those crops, but for very little else. Specifically, Richardson County farmers received more than $2 million each year from 2001 to 2015 through the CRP. In 2014, for example, a total of 20,155 acres were retired under this program in the following categories: 2,588 acres in already established grass, 2,205 acres in filter strips, 1,148 acres in introduced grasses and legumes, 2,588 acres designated as "rare and declining habitat," 8,284 acres in introduced grasses, and 3,170 acres categorized as "other." The amount of acreage sheltered under the CRP in Richardson County's maximum participation came in the period from 2003 to 2009, with more than 30,000 acres put aside each year.[13]

In recent years, federal programs to support farmers have diversified beyond conservation measures to subsidies that protect them from variations in agricultural production, profitability, weather extremes, and market loss. Richardson County farmers received a total of $300 million in such subsidies from 1995 to 2020. The breakdown in payments over these years is as follows: $67.4 million in crop insurance subsidies (payments for crop yield losses and revenue below a target level), $9.98 million in disaster payments, $63.3 in conservation programs, including the CRP, and $159 million in commodity subsidies. Corn accounts for most of the various subsidies in Richardson County, with $123,489,843 paid out to 2,268 recipients. Soybeans brought in $58,833,299 over that same period, shared by 1,888 recipients. However, the emphasis shifted to soybean subsidies in 2018-19, to make up for the loss of the Chinese market brought about by the Trump administration's trade war. Nebraska farmers received $694 million from the U.S. Department of Agriculture from September 2018 to August 2019; a state map showing payments by county put Richardson County in the middle category of payments, receiving $9 to $14 million in support that year.[14]

It should be said that the majority of this federal aid has gone to large farms that make more than $250,000 a year, and small farmers don't benefit nearly as much. The three top beneficiaries in Richardson County in 2020, for example, each reaped about $200,000 from these programs. The average amount paid to Richardson County farmers was much smaller – $16,726 in 2017, up from $8,047 in 2007. In 2020, for the country as a whole, 38 percent of farmers' net incomes came from federal aid, and Richardson County farmers were surely no exception.[15]

The consolidation that is most personal, however, that cuts to the heart of a Richardson County community, is the loss of a school.

The one-room, one-teacher schools were the first to go. These mainly wooden, but sometimes brick, schoolhouses were ubiquitous in Richardson County, and throughout the Great Plains, in the early twentieth century. In 1918, Daniel Weber, Superintendent of Public Instruction for the County, reported that there was a school for every four or five sections of land, meaning that students rarely had to walk (or ride) more than two miles to get an education. It was all very local: parents were involved in the classroom and in the construction and upkeep of the schools; multiple generations had experienced the basics of learning and life at the same school, fostering a sense of belonging to a place and a community.[16]

But after 1930, as the rural population thinned, and as automobiles and improved roads allowed wider circulation, there were too many schools. So they were combined with each other, or folded into larger K-12 school districts. The educational argument, more assertion than fact, was that the larger schools could offer better instruction and a fuller curriculum. The economic argument, that the tax base could not support so many dispersed schools, and that expenses were saved by economies of scale, was even more imperative. The county's Comprehensive Plan (1977), which set minimum enrollments for levels from kindergarten to high school, put this bluntly: "the small school district is economically unfeasible to operate and provides only limited educational opportunities." The Nebraska State Legislature made consolidation official in 2005 when it passed a statute mandating the merger of school districts with only elementary schools and those with only high schools into K-12 districts. But by that time, the small schools were just about gone. Some of the abandoned buildings still stand on the Richardson County landscape, humble monuments to a bygone age.[17]

In the early twenty-first century, only a solitary one-room schoolhouse, Maple Grove, remained open in Richardson County. Located at the county corner six miles northwest of Falls City, Maple Grove had been founded in 1859 by parents who donated the logs. Almost inevitably, the building burned down (in 1880), and was replaced by a new schoolhouse that sufficed for education for more than a century. Its last class, in 2009, had an enrollment of seven, six boys and one girl, three second graders, two third graders, and two fourth graders, altogether three sets of siblings. The students (and their desks) were dispatched to the Falls City public schools. This may well have broadened their educational and social opportunities, but much that is unquantifiable was lost: as one of the dislocated pupils wistfully remarked, "in town we couldn't see any tractors or vultures eating possums out the window." [18]

The loss to a community is magnified when it is the high school that closes. Towns lose their most treasured icon. Friday nights, once bustling with football crowds, become eerily silent, and restaurants and bars are deprived of customers. Students are obliged to travel farther to school, leaving them already halfway gone from home. Residents become disaffected, their lives turned upside down by decisions made elsewhere.[19]

There are many examples of such loss in Richardson County. In 1950, the county supported ten public high schools (Bratton Union, Dawson, Falls City, Honey Creek Union Consolidated, Humboldt, Rulo, Salem, Shubert, Stella, and Verdon); by 2009, only two (Falls City and Humboldt-Table Rock-Steinauer) remained.

It was a familiar story of falling enrollments, increased expenses, and declining state aid. Dawson and Verdon, which had supported high schools since 1887, merged in 1959 in an attempt to cut costs. The last graduating senior class at Verdon amounted to twelve students. The red and white colors of the Dawson Lions were combined with the blue and white colors of the Verdon Bulldogs to become the patriotic red, white, and blue of the Dawson-Verdon Jets – a confusion of identities and allegiances, as former rivals instantly became cohorts. High schools at Salem, Rulo, and Honey Creek also closed from 1951 to 1962. Honey Creek's last graduating senior class had only four students.[20]

The next major consolidation came in 1966, when the high schools at Bratton Union, Shubert, and Stella joined forces to become Southeast Nebraska Consolidated High School, located in a "state of the art" building at Stella. Students from Nemaha High School (in Nemaha County) and from the small school in Barada also became commuters to Southeast Nebraska Consolidated for their K-12 education. The enlarged school became the hub of the community: long-time faculty member Wayne Shafer later recalled that "the kids were number one… faculty and staff were like family… We could count on anyone for anything." [21]

Consolidation continued in 2004 when Dawson-Verdon closed. Half the students were relocated to a new, enlarged consolidated school in Humboldt; the others chose to attend the Falls City Public Schools. It was an inevitable outcome, Dawson-Verdon Superintendent John James explained: another year would have been "impossible financially." The consolidated school in Humboldt also absorbed the previously merged schools of Table Rock and Steinhauer, Pawnee County, in 2004. The new school, a major boon for a fading town, became Humboldt-Table Rock-Steinhauer.[22]

The largest combination of school districts came in 2009, when Southeast Nebraska Consolidated Schools closed its doors in Stella. Student numbers had been falling for years, not just because of general population loss, but also because of freeholding petitions, which permitted a landowner, under some conditions, to transfer his or her land to a contiguous school district. By one estimate, Southeast Nebraska Consolidated had lost 40 percent of its student body by such voluntary defections, mainly to Humboldt-Table Rock-Steinhauer. After the closure, most of the remaining elementary and high school students had to travel the extra fourteen miles to Humboldt-Table Rock-Steinhauer, which became (at 384 square miles) one of the largest school districts in Nebraska. Five bus routes bring the students into Humboldt each day. Stella's loss was profound: "I've been in this building since kindergarten" lamented fifth grader Taylor O'Brian, "It's been my home." Superintendent Michael Montgomery called the closing "heart breaking." [23] The old school is now just a shell of a building, its dusty corridors silent, vegetation closing in all around (Fig. 32).

32. The Abandoned Southeast Consolidated School at Stella, Sept.25, 2021. Courtesy of Sarah Disbrow.

Stella's loss was Humboldt's gain. As Humboldt-Table Rock-Steinhauer's Board of Education President Neal Kanel explained: "It no doubt makes us a stronger district. With a larger land base and more students it makes us have a pretty good position." But for how long? Reflecting the shrinking of Richardson County's population in general, Humboldt-Table Rock-Steinhauer's total enrollment fell from 427 in 2011-12 to 353 in

2019-20. The number of high school students there declined from 131 to 98 over the same period.[24] The small town of Humboldt was the beneficiary of school consolidation in 2009, but it could just as easily become its victim in a depopulating county that eventually may be able to support only one K-12 public school.

The most recent consolidation effort in Richardson County involves the planned absorption of its 911 emergency dispatch services by the Southeast Communications 911 Center in Beatrice. Such consolidations have become increasingly common in rural Nebraska, because small dispatch services (like small schools) cannot afford the costs of updating equipment and providing services to a diminishing population. Southeast Communications was already a consolidated unit, having previously incorporated small dispatch centers elsewhere in Gage County and also at nearby towns of Wymore and Crete. Beatrice Police Chief Bruce Lang explained the logic of consolidation: "we're going to save them [Richardson County] money in almost every scenario… having a stand-alone dispatch center for a county that has five thousand people… doesn't make any economic sense." Lang said that centralized dispatch centers could readily serve an area with a radius of seventy miles. He looked forward to a time when all southeastern Nebraska would be served by a single dispatch center, the epitome of consolidation.[25]

Richardson County Board of Commissioners agreed, and on June 22, 2021, they contracted to join the Southeast Communications 911 Center in Beatrice. The Beatrice City Council approved the agreement on July 22. Richardson County agreed to pay a fee of $180,000 for the first year of a three-year contract to use the enhanced services.[26]

The planned consolidation did not get a chance to work. Falls City officials had been skeptical of the arrangement from the start, maintaining that the County Board of Commissioners had overstepped its authority in making the contract. After a year of disagreement, Richardson County asked to terminate the agreement with the Southeast Communications 911 Center. The city of Beatrice responded by requesting $300,000 to cover the first year's fee, plus additional expenses incurred in preparing the consolidation. The consolidation had still not been effected at the beginning of 2024.[27] It seems that consolidation, successful or not, always comes at a cost.

ON THE RESERVATIONS

The decade of the 1930s also marked a break from the past in federal Indian policy, and the impact was felt on reservations across the country, including those in Richardson County. The relentless, abiding policy of assimilation was overturned in favor of self-determination under the more enlightened supervision of the John Collier administration. The Indian Reorganization Act of 1934 was particularly significant because it abolished the practice of allotment and facilitated the return of reservation lands to tribal ownership. Tribes were encouraged to adopt constitutions and bylaws, as well as a charter of incorporation, so that they could effectively manage their assets. Indian cultures and traditions were to be celebrated and promoted, not denigrated and suppressed, as had been the rule in the past. A sizable fund was set aside for the tribes to finance economic development; it truly was an "Indian New Deal."

Across the nation, 181 tribes (a majority) voted to accept the conditions of the Indian Reorganization Act. Of these ninety-three tribes and bands eventually agreed to constitutions, and seventy-three were granted charters.[28] Among them were the Iowa and Sac and Fox of Kansas and Nebraska.

The constitutions of the Iowa and Sac and Fox were quite similar, which is not surprising because the Collier administration had provided templates and sent out superintendents to oversee the completion of the documents. The constitutions both included articles on tribal membership, territory, election of the Tribal Council, and powers of the Tribal Council. But there were differences too, indicating that each tribe shaped the agreement to suit its own situation. For example, the Iowa restricted future membership to children born to any member of the tribe living on the reservation at the time of birth, whereas the Sac and Fox threw a wider net, admitting children born of a member on their own reservation, but also on the nearby Iowa, Kickapoo, and the Prairie Band of Potawatomi reservations (which all fell under the administration of the Bureau of Indian Affairs' Potawatomi Field Office located at Horton, Kansas).[29] Perhaps this indicated a greater degree of intermarriage with the other tribes on the part of the Sac and Fox.

The two tribes ratified their constitutions and bylaws on January 23, 1937. The Sac and Fox vote was twenty-two in favor and two against; the Iowa vote was eighty-eight in favor and one against. The turnout in both cases was only 30 percent of those eligible to vote. The constitutions, and the Indian Reorganization Act in general, did not alter Indian sovereignty in relation to the United States, but they did set up what were called at the time "organized governments," which made it easier to access federal programs and funds. In subsequent years, the constitutions were amended to keep up with changing times and, to quote from an Iowa amendment in 2013, "to form a more functional government, develop our tribal resources, and promote the economic and social welfare of ourselves and our descendents." [30]

The Indian Reorganization Act did indeed stimulate tribal identity and pride, and federal loans provided needed support. But by mid-century the Iowa and Sac and Fox (and the other two associated tribes) were mired in poverty. The allotment process and other efforts to break down traditional ways had done their damage. Many young Indians had left the reservations to find jobs at the foundry in Atkinson, the Goodyear Tire and Rubber Company at Topeka, and "pick and shovel work" elsewhere. The reservations were left to the elderly. Tribal membership for the Sac and Fox stood at 190, but only forty remained on the reservation; the Iowa situation was similar, with 524 enrolled members, but only sixty of them living on the reservation.

The vast majority of the land on the reservations was owned by whites, who bought the Indians' allotments as soon as the trust period of twenty-five years expired or even earlier when "competent Indians" received their titles. The Indians could not pay the taxes on their newly privatized property, and they sold out. When the Iowa reservation was allotted following the act of January 28, 1887, there had been 11,771 acres held in trust; by 1954 all but 916 acres had been transferred to whites. Seven of the remaining allotments held in trust were shared among multiple owners as a result of heirship division. It was a similar picture on the Sac and Fox reservation, where the original allotted acreage of 7,924 acres had been whittled away through sales to 619 acres by 1954. Of the nineteen tracts still held in trust by the Indians, seven were fractionated by partible inheritance. These tracts were located in the bend of the Nemaha River and averaged twenty-five acres. Ninety percent of the Iowa and Sac and Fox who still had allotments leased them to whites for payments of $1 to $2 an acre. This was their main source of income.[31] At a time when farms elsewhere in Richardson County were increasing in size in order to be competitive, Indian holdings were getting smaller, too small to support a family.

The Indians' diminished presence on their own reservations, the relatively few federal services that remained as treaty obligations expired, the reality that there were few full-blooded Indians left, and the fact that most of the Indians could speak English, and therefore, it was claimed, were capable of getting by in the larger society, all put the four tribes in a vulnerable position when, following World War II, federal policy lurched back to assimilation, mandatory assimilation, in the form of termination.

Termination aimed at the prompt withdrawal of federal supervision over reservations and the immediate absorption of the Indians into the general population as individual tax-paying citizens. It was offered as a beneficence, something for the Indians' own good, freeing them from stifling government oversight, giving them a "chance to succeed." The policy was promoted rigorously by the Bureau of Indian Affairs and by congressmen, especially those from the western states, where most reservations were located. As usual, however, the motivations were more avaricious than the rhetoric: it was just the latest, and most concerted, effort to acquire the remaining Indian lands.[32]

The termination policy was enacted through House Resolution No. 8, passed on August 1, 1953. To begin the process, the Bureau of Indian Affairs identified a group of tribes that it deemed to be particularly prepared for elimination. Among them were the four tribes of the Potawatomi Field Office.

A proposed bill for the withdrawal of federal responsibility for the four tribes was drafted in early January 1954. Federal oversight would be canceled; tribal property would be assessed and the proceeds divided among enrolled members; allotments would be privatized and their owners would become subject to the same federal and state taxes as non-Indians; tribal constitutions and charters established under the Indian Reorganization Act would be revoked. In a letter conveying the proposed bill to the Senate on January 4, 1954, Assistant Secretary of the Interior Orme Lewis blithely asserted that the terminations could proceed with "no hardship on the Indians and little administrative difficulty." [33]

The Indians disagreed, or at least those who still lived on the reservations did; those who had migrated away were less likely to care, because any provided federal services (such as the single field nurse, who served all four reservations) were out of reach. The main fear was that old and poor Indians who received titles to their allotments would not have the means to pay their taxes, and their homes would be lost. Three of the four tribes (the Sac and Fox were strangely silent) strongly opposed the bill. The Iowa sent a written protest to their senator, Hugh Butler, explaining that termination would "force them off their homes." The Prairie Band of Potawatomi and Kickapoo took the protest even further and sent delegates to hearings on the bill that were held in Washington D.C. from February 18-23, 1954.

The Indians had argued that the congressmen should travel to the reservations for the hearings and see the situation there for themselves. This proposal was rejected, on the grounds that it would cost too much, and also that they didn't have the time. The Indians then proposed that the committees conducting the hearings should pay their expenses for the trip, but this too was rejected because of the precedent it would set. In the end, after much argumentation, the delegations were subsidized from the Indians' own trust funds.[34]

The delegates, three Potawatomis (accompanied by their able lawyer, O.R. McGuire) and two Kickapoos, each had their say before the committees. Mrs. Minnie Evans, chair of the Tribal Council of the Prairie Band of Potawatomi, was a particularly effective spokesperson. She arrived at the hearings with a briefcase filled with documents and an unyielding attitude. In response to the committee's questions, aimed at proving that the Indians were ready to assimilate (How many full bloods were left? Does anyone still speak the old language? How many Indians had already left the reservations? How many federal services were still active?), Mrs. Evans repeatedly referred back to the treaties that had promised her people a reservation in perpetuity. Furthermore, she argued that the Indians were not ready to make it in white society on their own, and that it was not just a matter of taxes, but that the reservation was "a home for our parents, ourselves, and our children." Her people, she said, did not want to be let loose from federal oversight, but wanted that supervision to continue, in accordance with their treaties. When Mrs. Evans returned to Kansas, she gathered her people together, and she and seventy-nine others sent a petition to the Senate and House of Representatives stating that they were "unalterably opposed" to the legislation.[35]

This staunch opposition by the Kansas/Nebraska Indians to proposed termination was decisive in assuring that they would keep their reservations. Elsewhere, other tribes were not so successful. The Klamath of Oregon and the Menominee of Wisconsin both lost their reservation and tribal status in 1961, with disastrous results, as unprepared Indians were left to compete alone in American society. And in 1968, a decade after the termination policy had begun to wane, the Poncas, another Nebraska tribe, were officially "liquidated" as an entity, and they lost their reservation on the Niobrara forever.[36]

The Indian Claims Commission, which was set up in 1948, can be seen as another arm of termination. The Commission's purpose was to consider outstanding Indian claims against the United States, often for lands that had been taken illegally, or for too low a price, in the past. Previously Indians had been barred from suing the United States, unless they could first obtain an enabling act from Congress, an unwieldy and time-consuming process that had resulted in a backed-up catalog of claims. The Commission, which functioned as a "highly specialized court," would hear arguments from the Indians, as plaintiffs, and the Government, as defendant, before deciding if a second compensation was due. There was no option of a return of land, and once a decision was accepted that claim was settled for good. Supporters of Indian rights saw it as an opportunity for them to have "their day in court;" termination supporters saw it as a chance to "clean the slate" of outstanding claims before canceling out the tribes. As Harvey D. Rosenthal, a contemporary authority, put it, "[t]he problem of giving the Indian his due had to be balanced somehow with giving him his walking papers…." Almost all the nations, 176 tribes and bands, filed claims.[37] These included the Iowa and Sac and Fox of Richardson County.

The two tribes won multiple awards in their claims before the Indian Claims Commission for lands surrendered through nineteenth-century treaties in Iowa and Missouri. Most often the awards were the difference between what they originally had been paid for their territories and the fair market value, or what an "informed purchaser" would have paid at the time of taking. Gratuitous offsets, or payments made to the Indians without obligation (rations to forestall famine, for example) were deducted from the awards in some cases, and the Indians' lawyers were permitted to charge up to 10 percent of the awards for their services. In 1965, for example, the Indian Claims Commission awarded the Sac and Fox $965,560.37 and the Iowa $633,193.77 for a large swath of northern Missouri that they had ceded through a treaty in 1824 for an "unconscionably low" payment.[38]

The Iowa reservation in Kansas and Nebraska was the setting of another claim, one that resulted in a settlement of $1,377,207.27 in 1969. The treaty of May 17, 1854, had reduced the Iowa's original 1836 reservation to fifty square miles. The remaining lands, 94,451 acres of trust lands in Doniphan and Brown counties in Kansas and Richardson County in Nebraska, were to be sold at public auction and the proceeds invested by the government on the Iowa's behalf. The principal would remain untouched, and the 5 percent annual interest would be used to promote the Iowa's "civilization." But the trust lands were quickly overrun by squatters in what the Commission called a time of "confusion and turmoil" following the Kansas-Nebraska Act. The squatters were subsequently allowed to preempt their holdings and legitimize the possession. At the time, the

Iowa were compensated for their loss at an appraised value of $1.95 an acre, altogether $184,466.85. In 1952, the Iowa lodged a claim before the Commission, arguing that the United States had contravened the 1854 treaty by not allowing the promised competitive bidding that a public auction would have produced. An associated claim maintained that there had been a shortage of 4,798 acres in the area of trust lands in southwestern Richardson County, and for this they deserved compensation too.

In 1969, after eighteen years of intermittent litigation, the Indian Claims Commission ruled in favor of the Iowa plaintiffs. The United States had indeed breached the terms of the 1854 treaty by failing to sell the land at public auction. Taking into account the fertile farming land, the valuable stands of timber, and the easy access to transportation lines, the Commission ruled that the hypothetical informed purchaser would have paid $4 an acre for the ceded 94,451 acres, or a total fair market value of $377,805.10. This was $193,358.15 more than they had been paid. To this was added $207,752, that being the fair market value of the 4,798-acre shortfall (the rugged land of southwestern Richardson County was assessed at $3 an acre, because it was less fertile than the trust lands as a whole). The amount due to the Iowa in 1969, therefore, stood at $401,110.15.

The Commission did not stop there, however. Because the Indians did not initially receive the fair amount, those extra funds were not there to be invested for them over time, as the 1854 treaty had promised. So the Commission awarded an interest on the award of $1,377,207 in 1970. No gratuitous offsets were recognized, but the Iowa's lawyers did indeed take the maximum 10 percent of the award, $138,860.[39]

The experiences of the Iowa and Sac and Fox before the Indian Claims Commission were similar to those of tribes and bands across the country. There is much to be said in support of the Commission, despite the mercenary motives of those who saw it as a step to termination. The

United States was ahead of other colonial nations, such as Canada, New Zealand, and Australia, in recognizing claims and issuing second payments to the Indians. But the impressively large awards actually resulted in relatively small per capita payments when divided among large numbers of Indians, and Indian lands were recognized only as real estate, not as the cherished homelands that they actually were. And once the claims were heard, and the awards accepted, then those claims were dead. The Indian Claims Commission was a reconciliation of sorts, but the injustices of dispossession remain unatoned.

The years spanned by the Indian Claims Commission (1948-78) saw another turnaround in federal Indian policy, from termination back to self-determination and economic development, a direction that continues today. American Indians made gains in civil rights, such as the repatriation of skeletal remains and cultural treasures from museum shelves that came with the Native American Graves Protection and Repatriation Act (NAGPRA) in 1990. But probably nothing had as big an impact, especially on economic development, as the Indian Gaming Regulatory Act (IGRA) of 1989, which authorized casino gambling (including Las Vegas-style gambling) on Indian trust lands in states where such gambling was already in place.[40] The Iowa and Sac and Fox were among the many tribes that took advantage of this new economic opportunity.

In 1995, the Iowa and Sac and Fox entered into compacts with the state of Kansas to permit the establishment of casinos on their reservations. The casinos would be located on the Kansas portions of their reservations because, unlike Nebraska, Kansas already allowed what IGRA termed Class III gaming, including blackjack, poker, roulette, baccarat, and slots. Each tribe would appoint a Tribal Gaming Commission to regulate its gaming operations, subject to approval and oversight of the Kansas State Gaming Agency. These exhaustively detailed compacts sought to ensure that the casinos operated legally and safely. Net revenues were to be specifically used for tribal operations and programs, to provide for the general welfare of the tribe, to promote economic development, and for charitable causes. The State of Kansas would not be able to tax the revenues, although it would be permitted to regain "reasonable and necessary costs" associated with its regulation of the tribes' Class III gaming. Local governments could also draw from the casinos' revenues for associated costs, such as road improvements and increased police supervision.[41]

The Sac and Fox chose to locate its casino on a purchased piece of land on the Kickapoo Reservation, because it was more accessible to the major highways, routes 75 and 36, than the isolated uplands of their own reservation. The casino opened on February 28, 1997. The Iowa built their casino in the heart of their country, in the hills west of White Cloud, on Jackpot Drive, just south of the Nebraska state line, and just up the slope from where William Clark had chanced upon the remains of the Oneota agricultural village in 1804. Casino White Cloud opened in May of 1998.

The Sac and Fox Casino, more convenient for busloads of customers converging from large cities like Topeka and Wichita, is the larger of the two, with more than 700 gaming machines and various table games, an adjacent RV park and twenty-four-hour truck stop, two dining facilities, a golf driving range, and the Silver Fox Showroom, featuring live concerts. The smaller Casino White Cloud has 380 slot machines and virtual table games, the Mahasha Restaurant, a bingo hall, and four rustic cabins for accommodation. The rhythms of the two casinos are similar, however, rising each day from quiet mornings and early afternoons to highest attendance in the evening, and over the course of the week from slow Sundays to absolute peaks on Friday and Saturday nights. The atmospheres of the two casinos are similar too: the friendly greeting, the jangling and chiming of the slot machines, the smell of fried food, the smoke-saturated air, all going on under the watchful eye of the closed-circuit television system. But Casino White Cloud is different in one exceptional way: a magnificent bear-claw necklace, made of otter pelt and grizzly claws, perhaps a hundred years old, sits in all its splendor in a display case on the wall, an island of quiet dignity amidst the pandemonium of the casino.[42]

The casinos' revenues are not public information, and online estimates are so disparate as to be unreliable. But it is safe to say that they have earned the tribes millions of dollars for reservation improvements that they would not otherwise have had. By 2005, all four reservations in northeastern Kansas (and overlapping into Richardson County) were benefiting from casino revenues. Kickapoo Tribal Chairman Steve Cadue was able to say, "We have spent our money wisely" on roads, schools, a community center, senior center, and health clinic. The impact was greater than just the money, Cadue explained: "We can take care of ourselves now.... The casino has given us self-esteem." The revenues allowed the tribes to plan for the future; by 2005 the Sac and Fox were funding twenty-five of their members through college.[43]

The casinos themselves became economic growth poles, employing large numbers of people and fueling local economies. Even the small Casino White Cloud employs more than 100 workers, about one-quarter of them Iowa tribal members and their spouses. The comprehensive healthcare coverage offered to employees is a major attraction, although the $1,000 sign-on bonus in 2022 suggests that there are always openings to fill. The casinos have become cultural centers too: the Sac and Fox annual powwow, for example, is held on the last weekend of August at their casino, and Casino White Cloud is just one part of their larger tribal complex.[44]

The Iowa Tribe now has an enrollment of 2,258 members, with about half living on, or in the vicinity of, their reservation. Their population numbers have come a long way since the late nineteenth century, when they were down to about 150. Sac and Fox numbers are much lower, with about 450 enrolled members, again with about one-half of them living on the reservation, or within twenty miles of it. The reservations have the same dimensions as when they were created in 1861, but internally relatively little land remains in Indian hands, because of the sale of allotments. In 2013, the Sac and Fox had 1,446 acres held in tribal trust, while the Iowa now hold about one-third of their 12,038-acre reservation in this manner. The Iowa have been actively buying back their lost lands, one piece at a time, using casino revenues.[45]

There is little to distinguish the landscapes of the Indian lands from those of the surrounding countryside of Richardson and Brown counties. Most is in corn and soybeans, although some alfalfa, millet, and brome are also grown for cattle feeding. The Sac and Fox have a bison herd on land down by Noharts Creek, and the Iowa just recently received approval to develop an industrial hemp enterprise, one of only seven tribes in the country authorized to do so. Like farmers everywhere in Richardson and Brown counties, the tribes take advantage of federal subsidies. In fact, the Iowa Tribe was paid $880,125 from 1995 to 2020 in commodity program subsidies, conservation programs, disaster programs, and crop insurance subsidies, making it one of the largest recipients of federal agricultural aid in Richardson County.[46]

The Sac and Fox and Iowa, like all the other farmers, face the challenge of adapting to rapid climate change. The growing season and harvest time have shifted by two to three weeks over the last twenty years. Rainfall events are more extreme, inundating roads and making it difficult to get the crops in the fields. The Missouri River overflows its banks and backs up the Big Nemaha and its tributary creeks. On May 28, 2019, for example, six inches of rain fell on the Sac and Fox Reservation in forty-eight hours and Noharts Creek overflowed its banks, turning the bison pasture into mud. The herd could not be reached with supplemental feed for several days. Tribal office buildings at Reserve, Kansas, were flooded with the overflow of nearby septic leach fields. Brown County had to step in to help with the recovery.[47]

The Bureau of Indian Affairs has provided the Sac and Fox and Iowa (and also the Kickapoo and Prairie Band of Potawatomi) with a grant to help them adjust to the increasingly temperamental climate and protect threatened environments. In 2021, for example, the Iowa Tribal Fish and Wildlife Department used this money to release 1,000 quail, 1,000 pheasants, and 400 Hungarian partridges at various points on their reservation in an attempt to reverse the longtime decline in wildlife caused by the removal of cover and feeding opportunities in the fertile, yet sterile, spaces of modern one-crop farming.[48]

Having lost most of their country through treaties and the sale of allotments, and having repeatedly fought off removal to Indian Territory and termination, the two Richardson County tribes are now determined to preserve the vitality of the lands they still possess. To this end, in 2020, the Iowa were bequeathed 284 acres in the bluffs south of Rulo by the Nature Conservancy, adding to the 160-acre tract the Conservancy had previously given to the tribe in 2018. This 444-acre gift, described by Iowa Vice-Chair and Historical Preservation Officer Lance Foster as "an act of kindness, justice, and reconciliation," will be protected as a "tribal national park," only the second such park in the country.[49]

The bluffs and their environs are a special place, both physically and culturally. They are covered with old hardwood forests of pin oaks, hickory, pawpaws, and basswood that are home to species of plants and animals not found elsewhere in Nebraska. They tower over the flood plains of the Big Nemaha and Missouri rivers, overlooking the ancient Leary site and the routeway of Lewis and Clark. The park, scheduled to open in 2025, could be developed for agritourism, heritage tourism, and ecotourism, but above all it will be a regenerative place for the tribe. There are plans to preserve the prairie, bring back the buffalo, and create an eagle sanctuary, "so that the land is healed." As Forster explained, "unlike other people, who can buy and sell land and move away, we can never move away. This is our land forever."

Richardson County should hope that Lance Foster is right. In addition to running a casino that provides good jobs and lifts the local economy, and creating a natural preserve for posterity, the Iowa are now playing an active role in the revitalization of Rulo. In August 2022 the tribe received a Rural Business Development Grant worth $855,555 to open the Great Nemaha Trading Post on Rulo's moribund mainstreet. This will not only be a store, but also a cultural center featuring the Indian and French heritage of the area.[50]

DISASTERS

Throughout the century or so of contraction, disastrous events punctuated the passage of time. Some were environmental, changes in the physical geography that had periodically occurred since time immemorial, but now are intensified by the repercussions of human-induced climate change. Some were idiosyncratic, catastrophes that just happened to take place in this part of the world. Still others were outbreaks of violence that were products of place and society, and which indelibly stained the image and reputation of Richardson County.

In 1930 the orchard business of Richardson County was thriving. The agricultural census of that year reported 1,142 farms having land in "orchards, vineyards, and planted nut trees." Most of these were small acreages, just another dimension of the diversified farm of the time. But some, especially around Shubert, were large commercial orchards of apple, pear, peach, and cherry trees. The apples were sent to three "apple houses" in Shubert by truck and cart. There they were washed, sorted, and transferred to rail cars. It was claimed that 300 cars of apples (Winesaps, Jonathans, Delicious) were shipped from Shubert each year from August to October, destined for distant markets in Omaha and Chicago. With some reason, in the 1930s Shubert boasted that it was the "apple metropolis" of Nebraska.[51] Then a series of environmental disasters virtually put an end to Richardson County's orchards.

Southeastern Nebraska, like all the Great Plains, experienced excessive heat and deficient precipitation over much of the 1930s. The years 1934 and 1936 were particularly severe on both counts. Annual precipitation barely reached 22 inches, compared to the 34 inches average; crucially, little precipitation fell in the growing season. Meanwhile, temperatures soared, reaching 114°F in Falls City in August of 1934 and 1936; many days saw temperatures above 100°F. The leaves of the fruit trees yellowed and died. Young trees particularly, with their shallow roots, were stranded above the available soil moisture, which in some parts of the county lay at a depth of 35 feet. Many fruit trees failed to green up in the spring.[52]

Still, according to the 1940 agricultural census, 914 Richardson County farms reported orchard fruits and nuts, and prospects seemed good, with the desiccated decade of the 1930s done. Then, beginning on the night of November 10, 1940, and continuing for five frozen days, the Armistice Day blizzard finished off the fruit trees that had weathered the 1930s.[53]

The storm had moved into the Pacific Northwest on November 7, bringing forty-five-mile-per-hour winds that took down the Tacoma Narrows bridge. By November 10, the storm had crossed the Rockies, and over the next twenty-four hours cut a destructive path across the Great Plains and Midwest to Michigan, killing fruit trees and duck hunters alike.

The onset of the storm was rapid. In Richardson County, temperatures had reached a balmy 60°F on the day of the 10th. The rain, snow, and winds moved in overnight, with the mercury plunging to 10°F by dawn.

The high on the 11th was only 16°F. The temperature dropped to record lows of 4°F on the 13th and −2°F on the 15th, before starting to climb back to normalcy. The county came to a standstill; not expecting such an abrupt and severe onset of winter, few had winterized their trucks and tractors. Not that they could have driven anywhere, because the roads were closed by ice and drifting snow.[54]

The county's fruit trees were devastated. Despite blithe reassurance from the state horticulturalist that reports of damage were "exaggerated," the trees died from trauma to their trunks, brought on by the intense freeze. Farmers, with the economically deprived decade of the 1930s just behind, and the austerity of the war years just ahead, lacked the resources to start over. It would take eight or ten years for the new trees to bear fruit. So the farmers cut down the long rows of dead trees for firewood, and plowed them out and put the land in corn.[55]

Even if they had tried to start anew, their efforts would have been in vain, because the 10 miles of tracks between Salem and Shubert were torn up in 1942 and the main connection to markets was lost. The entire rural economy suffered, because farmers and townsfolk alike had relied on seasonal work in the orchards to supplement their incomes, and the more than 100 workers employed in the apple houses of Shubert lost their jobs.[56] The loss went beyond economic: the countryside was deprived of its orchards' white, pink, and purple blossoms of spring, all those sweet fragrances gone.[57]

The most recent environmental disaster in Richardson County was also its most persistent threat, floods. The severity of Missouri River floods has increased over time, as shown by the crests of the swollen river at Rulo. The 1952 flood, cresting at 25.37 feet (flood stage begins at 17 feet), was the flood of record for 58 years, until surpassed by the 2010 crest of 26.3 feet. That record lasted only one year, until the river crested at 27.26

feet in 2011. All these records were left behind on March 20, 2019, when the marauding Missouri crested at 28.13 at Rulo, inundating the low-lying areas of the town, and creating a lake on the Holt County side of the river that covered 90,000 acres of what just recently had been fertile farmland. It would be 272 days before the river at Rulo again fell below flood level.[58]

The flood was caused by a convergence of circumstances. The immediate cause was winter storm Ulmer, a "bomb cyclone" that dropped heavy rainfall over southeastern South Dakota, southwestern Minnesota, northwestern Iowa, and much of eastern Nebraska on March 13-14. The rain fell on a deep snowpack overlying frozen ground, resulting in widespread melting and rapid runoff. Gavins Point Dam on the Missouri, linking northeast Nebraska and southeast South Dakota, was filled to the brim, obliging its operators to open the spillways, which added to the surge that was coursing downstream. Heavy rainfall over the remainder of the spring and into the summer sustained the disaster. More than thirty levees were breached in western Iowa and northwestern Missouri. Three were breached in Richardson County. In Holt County, 30,000 acres were still underwater in October.[59]

At Rulo, the oil-slicked, debris-laden Missouri engulfed the cabins, campgrounds, and the old Rulo River Club that had lined the western bank, but now were more than 100 feet into the racing river. The highway 159 bridge and the railroad bridge, high above Rulo, descended on the Missouri side into the Holt County lake. Highway 159 was closed until October 31. The Rulo water system was compromised. The old water meters were located underground, and the flood drowned them in water and covered them with silt. There was no way to assess residential water use except by driving around town and seeing which houses had condensation on the windows. A major leak in the water system was eventually located, but not before 200,000 gallons had been lost. In November of 2020, a $485,000 Community Development Block Grant from the Nebraska

Department of Economic Development financed the replacement and modernization of the town's water system, a rare benefit stemming from the traumatic flood.[60]

According to climate predictions, the floods will only get worse in the future. For Nebraska as a whole, annual precipitation has already increased by 2 inches over the last 30 years, with most of that excess coming in spring. The forecast is for this trend to continue, with a 15-35 percent increase in multi-day, extreme precipitation events by mid-century. The climate models only confirm what the farmers know on the ground: weather is becoming more extreme and more difficult to plan for. It is likely that the 2019 disaster will be the flood of record in Richardson County for only a short time.[61]

Floods and droughts and freezes are expected disasters, bound to occur at some time or another. But the plunge of Braniff Airways Flight 250 into Antone Schwang's soybean field eight miles northeast of Falls City at 11:12 p.m. on August 6, 1966, was a singular event. All forty-two people on board died. It remains Nebraska's worst commercial air disaster.

The airliner was on its way from New Orleans to Minneapolis, scheduled to make stops at Shreveport, Fort Smith, Tulsa, Kansas City, and Omaha, dropping off and picking up passengers like a bus. The experienced crew was based in Minneapolis. Many of the thirty-eight passengers were United States military, some returning home from a tour of duty in Vietnam. There were also two sets of teenage sisters on board, and a five-year-old boy returning with his mother from a visit to the Kansas City zoo.[62]

Between Kansas City and Omaha the plane was confronted by a solid wall of thunderstorms. According to eyewitnesses on the ground, the plane did not reach the squall line, but entered the shelf of clouds preceding it, where it fragmented and exploded in a ball of fire. The official accident report later concluded that the plane came down because of "in flight structural failure caused by extreme turbulence," specifically, a large, abrupt "angled wind gust" caused by an outflow of cold air ahead of the approaching thunderstorm. The rear vertical fin and tail and the right wing separated from the body of the plane, which fell in a spin perpendicularly into the field. The pieces of the plane and the mangled, burning bodies were strewn amongst the waist-high soybeans. The official accident report also concluded that the hazardous weather could have been avoided by delaying or diverting the flight, but the intensity of the thunderstorms had been underestimated.[63]

Antone Schwang and his family were driving home from Shubert when they saw the fireball drop into the field, only 150 feet from their farmhouse. Antone later recalled being "scared to death for a while." Soon a crowd gathered along the fence line, standing in silence as lightning illuminated the horrific scene. It started to rain, and the crash site turned to mud.

By 2 a.m. the National Guard had taken charge, and the roads were closed to all but official traffic. "Disposal pouches" were sent from Topeka, and representatives from the four funeral homes in Falls City and Auburn had begun to remove the bodies to Prichard Auditorium, Falls City's grand community center, which was more used to hosting sporting events and weddings than serving as a morgue. The 4-H event scheduled for that day was quickly forgotten about. By one account, "the smell of death was evident a block away from the auditorium." The bodies were identified by dental records, fingerprints, and any possessions that remained, then sent in metal caskets provided by Braniff to Omaha and Kansas City, to be flown home or else carried overland to grieving families.[64]

Representatives from the Civil Aeronautics Board, the Federal Aviation Agency, and the Federal Bureau of Investigation quickly moved in to comb the site for clues to explain the disaster. Among the items found were two Air Force hats sitting quietly side-by-side, and a silver wristwatch, its hands frozen at 11:11 p.m., the time of the explosion. The investigation teams carefully documented and photographed the deadly scene, and by August 18 all the debris had been removed, leaving only the terrible memories of those who had witnessed the scene.[65]

In 1968, the same year that the accident report was released, Braniff and the British Aircraft Corporation (the maker of the plane) agreed to a $2,475,000 settlement with the estates of fifteen of the deceased passengers, one of the largest ever made in a suit for damages in a federal district court. The highest individual payment was $400,000, and many others were in excess of $100,000. The exception was the small $20,000 payment to the survivors of Mrs. Virginia Tejuda of Guatemala, the only one of the passengers from outside the United States.[66]

As the years passed, efforts were made to officially remember this tragic event. A simple, poignant memorial was placed at the site of the crash in 2006, with a reference to John 14:1-3, beginning "Do not let your hearts be troubled." And on August 6, 2016, the fiftieth anniversary of the catastrophe, more than 100 people, many of them family members of those who died, were hosted by the Richardson County Historical Society. They visited the crash site; the names of all forty-two victims were read out; a bell was chimed after each name.[67]

For a while, Richardson County was a famous place. The story of the crash was covered widely, including in the New York Times and the Times of London. This is what Richardson County was known for from afar. That is, until the Rulo murders of 1984 and the Humboldt murders almost a decade later. These were different types of disasters, outbreaks of violence that exposed the dark underside of Richardson County, and American, life.

Richardson County is not a particularly violent place. A map in the Atlas of Nebraska (2017) showing violent crimes per 1,000 people puts Richardson County in the second to lowest category (0.25 to 0.49), well below the state's metropolitan areas, and also below the rates of most of the rural counties.[68] Yet Richardson County is where the most infamous of Nebraska murders took place, matched only by the Charles Starkweather killing spree of 1957.

The backdrop to the Rulo murders was the farm crisis of the early 1980s, and the willingness of unscrupulous men to take advantage of those affected. The second half of the 1970s had been a prosperous time for American farmers: markets, including in the Soviet Union, were insatiable, grain prices were high, production was increasing, land values were soaring. With prospects good, farmers felt confident enough to go into debt to buy new machinery and add to their lands. Then commodity prices began to fall because of overproduction, markets were curtailed when President Jimmy Carter embargoed grain sales to the Soviet Union in retaliation for the invasion of Afghanistan, and the Federal Reserve restricted money supply to combat inflation, resulting in higher interest rates, which increased the costs of operation. Land values fell from their speculative peak in the late 1970s, and farmers no longer had the collateral to pay their loans. As many as one-third of Nebraska farmers were in danger of losing their lands to foreclosure. They looked for someone to blame, and opportunists moved in to feed on their fears and give them targets for their resentments.[69]

The Posse Comitatus, Latin for "power of the county," was the hate group most associated with disaffected farmers. Closely aligned with the Christian Identity movement, the Posse Comitatus was virulently anti-Semitic, white supremacist, opposed to the federal government and its taxes, and an advocate of violence to achieve its goals. In meetings across the heartland in the early 1980s, hate-filled preachers like James Wickstrom recruited farmers and others to their ranks.[70] These included Michael Ryan, a megalomaniac and sadist who made a living as a cattle truck driver in Whiting, northeastern Kansas.

After meeting Wickstrom, Ryan became convinced that God – Yahweh in his iteration – was speaking through him and urging him to prepare for the coming Armageddon. Beginning in 1983, he gathered followers, men and women down on their luck and in need of some meaning in life. One of their number, Rick Stice, had an eighty-acre hog farm two miles north of Rulo on a rolling dirt road, and this suitably remote location became the compound of the Ryan family.[71]

By the summer of 1984, twenty people, half of them children, were living at the compound in two converted trailers. Ryan, a violent man, kept their obedience through intimidation, and through the constant threat that Yahweh would punish them if they resisted his messenger's orders. Yahweh, through Ryan, even decided what they would have for dinner. Eventually, supposedly following Yahweh's orders, Ryan married (by his definition) four of the women living at the compound. At night, Ryan's men would fan out through the countryside stealing cattle and hogs and agricultural and construction equipment, which were sold to assemble a massive stockpile of weapons and food that would allow them to survive the cataclysm of the coming Armageddon.

By the beginning of 1985, the cult was coming apart from the outside and the inside. The families of those who had disappeared into the compound tried to search them out, a private detective was hired, local and state police belatedly began to investigate reports of gunfire and military maneuvers at the site. Ryan was also running out of money. His growing paranoia translated into violence directed at members of the group. Luke Stice, Rick's five-year-old son, was mercilessly tormented and abused by Ryan, who brought his short, sad life to an end by pushing him against a cabinet. This was followed by the humiliation, torture, and murder of James Timm, who had come to this hell from a caring Mennonite family in Beatrice. It was ascertained at the autopsy that Timm could have died from any one of five injuries inflicted over three days. Stice and Timm were buried in shallow graves at the compound.

On August 17, 1985, aided by a remorseful Rick Stice (who had done little to protect his son), and by two of the cult members who had been caught stealing a sprayer rig, a combined force of law officers from the FBI, the Bureau of Alcohol, Tobacco, and Firearms, the Nebraska State Patrol, and the County Sheriff's Office raided the compound and exhumed the decomposing bodies. Authorities arrested Ryan, his fifteen-year-old son Dennis, and another two of his followers who had assisted in the torture and murder of James Timm.

On September 12, 1985, Ryan was found guilty of first-degree murder in the death of James Timm and second-degree murder in the killing of Luke Stice. He was sentenced to die by electric chair. The cult members who had participated in the killing of Timm were given lengthy prison sentences. Over the coming years, Ryan's execution was postponed because of repeated appeals and controversy over the death penalty in Nebraska. When he did die, on May 24, 2015, it was not by execution but from brain cancer. The headline in the *Falls City Journal*, "In the end State never does kill Ryan," carries a suggestion that it was thought that true justice had been evaded.[72]

The ramshackle trailers are long gone from the compound, but the haunting memories remain, making it a dark place even on the sunniest day. This is a legacy that Richardson County will have to carry until enough generations have passed for the Rulo murders to be mercifully forgotten.

The murders of Brandon Teena, Lisa Lambert, and Phillip DeVine in a run-down farmhouse a mile south of Humboldt on New Years Eve, 1993, are another cross that Richardson County has to bear. This was the culmination of a rapidly unfolding disaster that had taken shape over the previous two months in a Richardson County demiworld of drifting, aimless, hopeless young people, eking out an existence in trailers and cheap rentals, holding menial jobs, if any, caught in abusive relationships, and, in some cases, in and out of prison.[73]

Brandon Teena had grown up as Teena Brandon in Lincoln, Nebraska, in a poor but close family headed by single mother JoAnn Brandon. While in high school he began presenting himself as a man, a courageous effort to be true to himself. He began dating girls, who appreciated his consideration. He also began stealing ATM cards and forging checks. In March of 1992 the law caught up with him and he was sentenced to eighteen months' probation. He repeatedly ignored the conditions of the probation and continued stealing and forging checks until, in the fall of 1993, a warrant was issued for his arrest. With his options foreclosing, Brandon absconded to Richardson County, where no one knew him and he hoped to begin life anew as a man. He took refuge in a farmhouse south of Humboldt rented by Lisa Lambert.

In Richardson County he continued to live as a man, beguiling a succession of young women, including Lisa Lambert, with his charm and generosity. Fatefully, within this fringe circle of friends were two malignant ex-convicts, John L. Lotter and Marvin Thomas Nissen.

On December 15, 1993 Brandon Teena was remanded into custody for forging checks in Richardson County. He was placed in the section of the jail reserved for women, and his arrest was publicized in the *Falls City Journal.* His secret was exposed. Out on bail on Christmas Eve he attended a party at Nissen's house. Lotter and Nissen, offended by what they saw as his deception, took Teena into a bathroom, stripped him, and beat him badly. They then forced him into a car and took him to a remote site near the Hormel plant at the edge of Falls City and raped him. They warned him not to go to the police.

But Teena did go to the police, where, on Christmas Day, he filed a rape charge against Lotter and Nissen. In his interview with Teena, Sheriff Charles Laux showed a prurient interest in the details of the rape, and he interrogated the distraught and battered victim as if he had instigated the violence.[74] Teena filed a complaint against Lotter and Nissen, who incongruously remained free while the police investigated the assault.

Teena, afraid of Lotter and Nissen's vengeance, retreated to Lisa Lambert's rented farmhouse. Also there were Lambert's infant son Tanner and a young African American man, Phillip DeVine, who was only briefly in Richardson County and awaiting a bus back to his home in Iowa. Early in the morning of New Year's Eve, Lotter and Nissen kicked in the door of the farmhouse and shot, execution-style, the three adults. Nissen also stabbed Teena in the stomach. It was over in a matter of minutes. Tanner was the only survivor of the massacre.

Lotter and Nissen were arrested later on in the day. Their savagery was matched only by their ineptitude – they had thrown their protective gloves and weapons into the Nemaha, but the river was frozen and the damning evidence lay on the ice for all to see. At his trial in March 1995, Nissen testified against his accomplice and was given a life sentence, which he is serving in the Nebraska State Penitentiary in Lincoln. In 1996, Lotter was found guilty of murder and sentenced to death. After a series of unsuccessful appeals, the latest in 2022, Lotter remains in the State Penitentiary in Tecumseh, just twenty miles up the road from the farmhouse where he ended three young lives.[75]

The notoriety of the case continued to grow in the aftermath of the murders. A thoroughly researched documentary by Susan Muska and Greta Ólafsdóttir, *The Brandon Teena Story* (1998), kept the details of the dreadful story alive, and Kimberly Peirce's compelling dramatization, *Boys Don't Cry* (1999), which won Hilary Swank an Academy Award for her moving portrayal of Teena, projected a version of events and an image of a place to a wide audience. However, the focus was always on Teena, the victim of a hate crime for being a transgender person. Lambert and DeVine had shorter posthumous existences – neither featured in Boys Don't Cry; they were excised from the script because it was believed that they would have made it too complicated. In such ways, history as it happened becomes displaced by history as created.[76]

The tragic story lived on in the courts. In 1999, JoAnn Brandon brought an action suit against Sheriff Laux for "negligence, wrongful death, and intentional infliction of emotional distress" in connection with the events leading up to Teena's death. The district court did find the county negligent, but it reduced the financial award from more than $80,000 to only $17,360. On appeal, the Nebraska Supreme Court issued a scathing rebuke of the lower court's decision, finding Laux's conduct to be "extreme and outrageous," and his tone in the interview "demeaning, accusatory, intimidating." The Supreme Court remanded the case back to the district court, which was ordered to pay JoAnn the full $80,000 plus additional damages for emotional distress.[77] It was justice of a sorts, but scant justice considering all that had been lost.

A LAYER OF LIFE

The years 2020-23 are the latest layer of life in the story of Richardson County, a transitory present slipping away into the past. They were characterized by a continuation of past trends, including steady population loss, by a major event, the coronavirus epidemic, which no doubt is how they will be remembered as history, and by countless small stories of the comings and goings of life that pass unnoticed or are quickly forgotten.

The trend of contraction that defined Richardson County since 1930 continued unabated. The county's population, which had once stood at a mighty 19,614 was down to 7,871 in 2020, and fell to 7,759 in 2022. The rural parts of the county, farms and small towns, continued to empty out and, in the case of the village of Preston, to die completely: on May 24, 2022, the Richardson County Board of Commissioners voted to abolish the town effective June 1, an act of euthanasia for this mortally ill place, whose population had dwindled to only nineteen.[78]

Unless there is an economic windfall, such as happened in 1909 when the Missouri Pacific moved its division headquarters from Atchison to Falls City , it is hard to see how this trend of depopulation can be reversed, because Richardson County's population is old and not being replaced by natural increase or immigration. The median age of the county's population is 47.3, compared to 38.2 for the country as a whole; 24.3 percent of its people are over the age of 65, much higher than the national average of 16.8 percent. The largest cohort (five-year age grouping) in the county's population is 65 to 70, aging baby boomers, while the smallest (other than the cohorts over 80) is the 20 to 25 age group, young people having left for social and economic opportunities in more urban places, taking their reproductive capacity with them. The three nursing homes in the county are filled with the elderly, many of them on the final stage of a journey that started a lifetime ago on a farm.

Unlike many Great Plains counties, particularly those with large meatpacking plants or those adjacent to major urban areas, Richardson County's excess of deaths over births is not being balanced by immigration from domestic or foreign sources. In 2020 only 1 percent of the county's population was foreign-born, way below the national average of 13.6 percent. The county is overwhelmingly white (92.6 percent), much more so than the country as a whole (75.8 percent). Of minority groups, only American Indians are present in numbers above the national average (3.5 percent compared to 1.3 percent), which is hardly surprising given the enduring presence of two reservations in the county. There are few African Americans, for example, amounting to only 0.6 percent of the population, compared to 13.6 percent at the national level.[79] Phillip DeVine must have felt conspicuously out of place during the last weeks of his life in Richardson County.

The trend of fewer farms and operators continues unabated. Operating costs (for fertilizers and pesticides, for example, or for fuels and oils) are soaring, as are costs of breeding stock and land, making it difficult for all but the biggest operators to compete. In 2019, one large Richardson County operator broke a record when he paid $525,000 for a Black Angus bull; and in November of 2022 a choice piece of land at the eastern edge of Falls City sold at auction for an astonishing $27,400 an acre, a total price of $3.2 million for the 117-acre farm.[80] Faced by such intimidating economics, some farmers are obliged to look for ways to supplement their incomes with off-farm employment; still others face the inevitable and sell in yet another wave of consolidation. For those who still have land to farm, however, the prospects are good for 2023, with soaring commodity prices brought about largely by the interruption of life in war-torn Ukraine, a major grain exporter.[81]

One trend that has been dominant in Richardson County almost from the start is its tight affiliation with the Republican Party. The county has voted for Republican candidates for President in 31 of 39 elections since 1868.[82] The 2020 election was no exception. In the run-up to the vote, Trump-Pence signs lined the roads like corn-seed advertisements; Biden-Harris signs were so rare as to qualify as collectors' items. When the votes were counted, 74 percent were for Trump, 1 percent higher than in 2016, despite the fact that he had deprived farmers of their markets with his trade wars, especially their soybean market in China.[83]

Of course, some Richardson County residents did not vote for President Trump. It is likely that many of the seventy or so protestors who attended a Black Lives Matter rally on the east side of the county courthouse on June 6, 2020 were not among his supporters. The rally was organized by two local women on Facebook. They wanted to show that diversity of opinion was alive and well in small towns like Falls City. The community seems to have embraced what was for them an unusual event, although not without some trepidation: the Falls City Police Department, the Richardson County Sheriff's Office, and the Nebraska State Patrol were out in force; when The *Falls City Journal* ran a short article on the demonstration, the words "peaceful" and "peacefully" appeared nine times, a strained effort to make that point; the mayor of Falls City offered her support.[84]

The *Falls City Journal* has covered the news in Richardson County for 115 years, first as a daily, then twice-weekly, and now once a week. At one time, it was filled with national and international news, but now it is decidedly local. There is little overt politics in its pages: a crusty, independent, AP reporter writes a weekly tell-it-like-it-is column on the proceedings of the Nebraska State Legislature, and until 2021 the governor contributed a weekly editorial promoting his own issues (for example, property tax relief and gun rights). The paper does thoroughly inform its readers on local elections and give a balanced view of the candidates and their issues. There is also some in-depth reporting on matters of importance and interest, past and present. But mainly the *Falls City Journal* is a caring community newspaper, dedicated to presenting useful, accurate information and celebrating local achievements and events. As such, it serves as a window into everyday life in Richardson County.

The actual and symbolic importance of high school sports to the community are evident from the amount of space devoted to them in the pages of the paper. Victories – most recently the Lady Irish of Falls City Sacred Heart winning the back-to-back state Class D2 basketball championships in March 2022 and 2023 – are cherished and become part of the folklore of the community. But simple participation in sports is celebrated too, with everyone honored for their efforts. It is clear how the loss of a high school, or even the loss of a sports team, when schools enter into cooperative agreements to pool their declining numbers, leaves a void at the heart of the community.

The *Falls City Journal* also celebrates and promotes the big events in the annual calendar of Richardson County. Nothing is bigger than the Falls City Hot Air Balloon Festival, held each June at Brenner Field Airport. The festival typically attracts aeronauts from around the Midwest and brings in crowds of thousands – an estimated 5,000 in 2019. Unfortunately, the festival was "blown away" by high winds in 2022, leaving the 2,200 people in attendance to enjoy only the music and food.[85]

Nostalgia is a common theme in the *Falls City Journal*, a hearkening back to better days, perhaps, or a deepening of a sense of place. Famous high school sports achievements are often revisited, and every issue of the paper includes a column "From the Journal Files," listing the stories and events of each week 15, 25, and 50 years before. Not surprisingly, many of the remembrances have to do with sports.

The *Falls City Journal* is not all about celebration. Every issue of the paper draws from the public record to identify the crimes committed in the county. Sometimes photographs of those arrested are included, a sad gallery of men and women who look like they have hit rock-bottom, with no easy way up. A few still look defiant, smirking at the camera; one unrepentant man had his tongue stuck out. Most of those booked into the Richardson County jail are there for misdemeanors – failure to appear warrants, reckless driving, disturbing the peace, small amounts of marijuana, and so on. Sometimes more significant amounts of drugs, especially methamphetamine, are involved, and these arrests make the front page. The Richardson County Sheriff's Department seized three pounds of methamphetamine from the fall of 2019 to the spring of 2022.[86]

The *Falls City Journal* does not seem to seek out divisive issues to cover, but sometimes divisive issues intrude, and when that happens they cover the matter in depth. Few issues are more fraught in Richardson County, and across the country, than the role of public schools in teaching "social and emotional learning," a curriculum designed to foster such skills as empathy for others and conflict resolution. This is seen as especially important at a time when bullying in Richardson County schools is at "an all-time high," not least because of the anonymity and impunity of social media. To deal with this, and to fill out the students' education on difficult topics like discrimination and difference, Falls City Middle School introduced the Second Step Program in its homeroom in August of 2021.[87]

Parental concern with this social and emotional learning program grew over the fall of 2021, fueled, in Principal Jack Bangert's opinion, by "rumors and myths" and "social media conspiracy theories." The differences of opinion came to a head at a contentious school board meeting on May 9, 2022.

At the packed meeting, parents and other concerned members of the public were each given five minutes to speak. Some could not shake the belief that Second Step was a covert sex education program, despite assurances given by the teachers; another worried that "progressive activists" were "involving Satan" in the classroom; yet another, "unabashedly Christian," saw the program as an attack on the family unit. All were determined to reserve the right to educate their children on moral matters at home. The meeting disintegrated when members of the audience began speaking out of turn, and the arguments continued as the crowd spilled outside. Faced with such impervious opposition, the Falls City School board suspended the Second Step curriculum.[88]

This opposition to Falls City public schools teaching social and emotional learning is not likely to wane soon. On November 8, 2022, three new members were elected to the school board for District 56, covering the Falls City public schools. Two of the new members ran on platforms that stressed keeping Critical Race Theory and sex and health education out of the schools; one of them wanted a curriculum that promoted "a positive and accurate" history of the United States, without the distractions of race, gender, and sexual orientation. Such views are not shared by Principal Bangert, who sees his job as getting "kids ready for the real world."[89]

On one notable occasion, reporters from the *Falls City Journal* found themselves not only involved in, but also embroiled in, political turmoil. On October 27, 2020, a week before the election, reporters Nikki and Brian McKim drove to Omaha to cover a "historic event," a rally by President Donald Trump. On the way, they noticed many other vehicles with 19-county license plates heading to the same place. They set their cameras up in an area reserved for the media, as a crowd estimated at 10,000 gathered around. Nikki McKim described being "excited like a child" to see Air Force One arrive and the President disembark. But then, in the course of his speech, Trump directed the attention of the crowd to the media, accusing them of manufacturing "fake news." It seemed to Nikki McKim that all 10,000 people were looking their way, shouting abuse and booing. The journalists were now afraid, and they tried to leave, but the angry crowd would not let them. "Words were exchanged," McKim wrote, and "we didn't know what to do." They finally managed to escape the harrowing situation by following a police officer to the exit. The reporters did manage to cover the speech in detail for the *Journal*, but they also related what had happened to them: as Nikki McKim wrote, "'Fake news' would be me telling you how great an experience it was, not reporting how it really happened." [90]

Already, by the time of the rally, Richardson County was experiencing the beginning of the first surge of the coronavirus pandemic, and everything else was soon overshadowed. Ninety-three cases had been confirmed in the county by late October, up from 78 the week before. It was the largest jump in cases since the beginning of the pandemic. The numbers continued to multiply to a peak in late November and early December, before leveling off, then declining as quickly as they had risen. By mid-February 2021, Richardson County had seen 667 cases and 19 deaths.[91]

The virus had taken its time getting to Richardson County. Urban counties in Nebraska, with their denser populations and more frequent connections to other places, were affected first. The initial, ominous mention of the threat in the *Falls City Journal* came on February 20, 2020, in a brief report noting the origins of the disease in Wuhan, China, and the infection of twelve people in the United States.[92] The risk of infection was low in Nebraska, the paper noted, but it warned that the situation was changing rapidly: it was a distant thunder, rolling ever closer.

By March 18, 2020, there were 3,010 confirmed cases nationally in 49 states, but still none in Richardson County. Still, precautions were being taken: the Community Medical Center and the county's nursing homes began to restrict visitors, which was necessary, but heartrending for patients and families alike; all city properties, including city hall, were closed, and eventually the county courthouse was closed too; the Sac and Fox casino shut its doors; public schools closed, optimistically planning to re-open in April, and instruction moved online; May graduation ceremonies were also held virtually, prompting the Journal to report on "a historic class thrust into adulthood much sooner than they had anticipated." Executive orders also came down from the governor, requesting restaurants and bars to voluntarily restrict occupancy to ten patrons. Most Falls City enterprises complied, relying on take-out services and generous tipping from a faithful clientele to keep them going. A few businesses would actually do well during the dark months of the pandemic: nurseries, serving those who wanted to sow life anew in a time of sickness and death, stores selling outdoors equipment like bicycles for the enjoyment of the relatively safe open air, and pet stores, where those seeking companionship at a time when human contacts were restricted.[93] But most businesses, like most people, just tried to get by.

Richardson County recorded its first case, a woman in her thirties, a week later. The first COVID-19 death came on June 22. The number of infections increased slowly at first, to 10 by July 17, and 33 on September 10, before rising rapidly to the late November peak. One of those infected at this stage of the pandemic, Sharon Walker, became ill at the end of October. Within a week she was in emergency care at Community Medical Center with double pneumonia, struggling to breathe. She was fortunate to get a bed in Bryan West hospital in Lincoln, which had the technology and trauma teams to deal with such a critical case. She spent a month there on oxygen, not far from death. She was sufficiently recovered to return home on December 3, but even by the following April she was weak and disoriented from the aftereffects of the disease.[94] Such are the individual stories behind the cold statistics of the COVID-19 pandemic.

As the first stage began to wane in December 2020, there was more good news. The welcome doses of the Pfizer vaccine reached Richardson County on December 21, where they were administered to the staff of the Community Medical Center. One of the doctors there commented that it was "exciting to finally have a light at the end of the tunnel." The assisted living homes, filled with vulnerable people, were vaccinated in January, and the general public aged 75 and over became eligible at the same time. As eligibility expanded, the percentage of those fully vaccinated increased: from 33 percent of the county's population over 16 in the last week of April to 42 percent on May 26, and 54 percent of all ages (and 78 percent of those 65 and older) by January 10, 2023. These are lower rates than in Nebraska's urban counties and in the nation as a whole, but much higher than in the rural counties in the western parts of the state. Part of the credit goes to the White Cloud Health Center, which was given the Indian Health Services Area Director's Award for its role in dispensing vaccinations to tribal members, and then to the community as a whole.[95]

Quentin Bowen, a forty-one-year-old farmer from Richardson County, is another story behind the statistics. He had been planning on getting vaccinated in the spring of 2021, but soybean planting got in the way. He started feeling ill on May 15, but, typically independent, he tried to handle it himself. Soon he had viral pneumonia and a massive blood clot in his lungs. He was taken by ambulance to Bryan East hospital in Lincoln, where he had to say goodbye to his family – in his own words the "hardest thing I'd done." He spent a week on oxygen there: his body was fighting off the Covid infection, but he still had the side effects. Back home in June he still struggled to breathe and was too tired to do his farm chores.[96]

The malicious disease, mutating to the more contagious, though less lethal, Omicron variant, surged again in October of 2021 in Richardson County and in the country as a whole, reaching new heights in terms of infections and hospitalizations, though not in deaths, due in large part to the protection given by vaccinations. This second surge peaked in February of 2022, then the number of cases fell rapidly and stayed relatively low through the year. At the beginning of 2023 Richardson County was seeing only one new case a day, compared to fifteen new cases a day at the crest of the surge. The disease became endemic, just a part of life, much as the influenza epidemic had done in 1919. Still, it took a heavy toll: as of January 9, 2023, Richardson County had seen 2,223 cases of Coronavirus (roughly one in four of the total population) and 33 of its residents had died from the disease.[97]

The last three momentous years are just the latest episode in the long history of this American corner of the world. They are a continuation of the protracted period of population decline that began in the early twentieth century. Before that came the days of growth in the second half the nineteenth century, when Richardson County was young and vibrant. And before that, in turn, for millennia when there were countless generations of Indians hunting bison, camping in the bluffs, forging trails across the prairie.

So much was lost as each new present was superimposed on what had gone before: gone is the dense rural population and the colorful mosaic of small, diverse farms; gone are the free-roaming bison, and the steamboats on the Missouri; gone are the one-room schools, filled with life; almost gone are small town newspapers like the *Falls City Journal*, the champions and conscience of their communities. But much of the past lives on and leaves its mark on the present: the grid laid down by the surveyors in 1855 is still the inescapable spatial framework of life; the towns founded by the railroads in the 1870s and 1880s are mostly still there, though diminished in population and only as husks of their former selves; the two reservations, older than the county itself, are still in place, and their futures perhaps look brighter than ever; some one-room schoolhouses, now empty and forlorn, still sit in the fields; the bullet-ridden sign on Half-Breed Creek brings back to mind the enigma that was the Half-Breed Tract; the five-thousand-year-old stone tools uncovered by the farmer's plow bring the distant past back into the light of day. Layer upon layer of life, repeatedly laid down in the same place.

Acknowledgments

Many people helped me bring this book to fruition. The expert staff on the front desk of the archives at the Nebraska State Historical Society aided me greatly in my research. Jessica Heck carefully turned my handwritten manuscript into a form suitable for submission. Ezra Zeitler skillfully completed the maps and graphs. Thanks also go to David Bristow of the Nebraska State Historical Society for his careful and considerate editing. Finally, I thank my wife, Sarah Disbrow, for commenting on the manuscript, for accompanying me on my trips down to Richardson County, and for so much more.

Notes

1. ANTECEDENTS, BEFORE 1854

1. There is also a "Half Breed Drive" in Auburn, the county seat of Nemaha County, just to the north of Richardson County. See Peter Salter, "History and Hurt on Half Breed Drive," *Lincoln Journal Star*, Dec.7, 2015; Nebraska State Historical Society, Archaeological Site Survey, Lincoln, Nebraska.

2. Gary E. Moulton, ed., *The Definitive Journals of the Lewis and Clark Expedition* (Lincoln and London: University of Nebraska Press, 1986) 2:366-71. The original spelling is kept.

3. A. T. Hill and Waldo R. Wedel, "Excavations at the Leary Indian Village and Burial Site, Richardson County, Nebraska," *Nebraska History Magazine*, XVII, No. 1 (Jan-March, 1936): 3-73.

4. Nebraska State Historical Society, Archaeological Site Survey.

5. Alfred E. Johnson, ed., *Archaic Prehistory on the Prairie-Plains Border*, University of Kansas Publications in Anthropology, No. 12 (Lawrence, KS, 1980).

6. Moulton, *The Definitive Journals of the Lewis and Clark Expedition*, 3:395.

7. John Bradbury, *Travels in the Interior of America, 1809-1811*, in Reuben G. Thwaites, ed. *Early Western Travels, 1748-1846* (Cleveland: Arthur H. Clark, 1904), 5:78-80.

8. William Whitman, *The Oto* (New York: Columbia University Press, 1937).

9. Christopher Steinke, "Leading the 'Father,' the Pawnee Homeland, Coureurs de Bois, and the Villasur Expedition of 1720," *Great Plains Quarterly*, 32 (Winter 2012): 43-62.

10. Colin G. Calloway, *One Vast Winter Count: The Native American West before Lewis and Clark* (Lincoln and London: University of Nebraska Press, 2003), 415-26.

11. Alexis de Tocqueville, *Democracy in America*, J. P. Meyer and Max Lerner, eds. (New York, Evanston, and London: Harper and Row, 1966), 298.

12. Tocqueville, *Democracy in America*, 300.

13. Basil B. Chapman, *The Otoes and Missourias: A Study of Indian Removal and Its Legal Aftermath* (Oklahoma City: Times Journal, 1965), 20; "Extracts from Minutes of a Treaty held at Prairie du Chien, July 7, 1830," in Documents Relating to the Negotiation of Ratified and Unratified Treaties with the Various Tribes of Indians, 1801-1869, National Archives, RG75, R2, 1827-33.

14. Charles J. Kappler, ed., *Indian Affairs: Laws and Treaties* (Washington D.C.: GPO, 1903-1938), 2:305-10; Charles C. Royce, *Indian Land Cessions in the United States*, Eighteenth Annual Report, Bureau of American Ethnology, 1896-1897 (Washington D.C.: GPO, 1899): 726-7 and Plate 24.

15. Gregory J. Johansen, "'To Make Some Provision For Their Half-Breeds,' The Nemaha Half-Breed Reserve, 1830-66," *Nebraska History* 67 (1986): 8-29.

16. Tocqueville, *Democracy in America*, 303.

17. Maximilian, Prince of Wied, *Travels in the Interior of North America, 1832-34*, in Reuben Gold Thwaites, ed., *Early Western Travels, 1748-1846* (Cleveland: Arthur H. Clark, 1904) 22:259; John Dougherty to William Clark, May 29, 1838. John Dougherty Papers, 1791-1860. Nebraska State Historical Society. RG3902.AM; Isaac McCoy, *History of Baptist Indian Missions* (Washington D.C: William H. Morrison, 1840), 525-26; Chapman, *Otoes and Missourias*, 51-63.

18. Chapman, *Otoes and Missourias*, 60; Half-Breed Tract (Nemaha and Richardson Counties Neb.) Nebraska State Historical Society. RG0726.AM, Series 1, Correspondence, 1857-1943; Johansen, "'To Make Some Provision For Their Half-Breeds'": 10-11.

19. McCoy, *History of Baptist Indian Missions*, 525-26; Chapman, *Otoes and Missourias*, 53-4; Johansen, "'To Make Some Provision For Their Half-Breeds'": 10-11.

20. Kappler, *Indian Affairs*, 2:22-5; David J. Wishart, "Compensation for Dispossession: Payments to the Indians for Their Lands on the Central and Northern Great Plains in the Nineteenth Century," *National Geographic Research* 6 (Winter 1990): 94-109.

21. Kappler, *Indian Affairs*, 2:400-01; David J. Wishart, *An Unspeakable Sadness: The Dispossession of the Nebraska Indians* (Lincoln and London: University of Nebraska Press, 1994), 71-100.

22. Kappler, *Indian Affairs*, 2:268-70.

23. Andrew Hughes to William Clark, May 12, 1837, June 29, 1837, Letters Received Office of Indian Affairs (LR 01A), 1824-1881, Great Nemaha Agency, 1837-1876, Emigration, 1837-38, Microcopy 234, Roll 314; Kappler, *Indian Affairs*, 2:468.

24. George A. Root, "Ferries in Kansas. Part 1. Missouri River," *The Kansas Historical Quarterly* 2.1 (1933): 3-28; 2.2 (1933): 115-38; Kappler, *Indian Affairs*, 2:469.

25. Greg Olson, *Ioway Life: Reservation and Reform, 1837-1860* (Norman: University of Oklahoma Press, 2016), 69-74; Martha Royce Blaine, *The Ioway Indians* (Norman: University of Oklahoma Press, 1979), 170.

26. Olson, *Ioway Life*, 76.

27. William Richardson, Census, Sept. 6, 1842, LR 01A, Great Nemaha Agency, Roll 307; Wishart, *Unspeakable Sadness*, 74.

28. Richardson, Census; Wishart, *Unspeakable Sadness*, 82, 90.

29. Hugh J. McClintock, Report, Sept. 13, 1845, LR 01A, Great Nemaha Agency, Roll 307; J. N. B. Hewitt, ed. *Journal of Rudolph Friederich Kurz* (Lincoln: University of Nebraska Press, 1970), 40.

30. Richardson, Report, Oct. 18, 1843, LR 01A, Great Nemaha Agency, Roll 207.

31. Richardson, Report, Annual Report of the Commissioner of Indian Affairs (ARCIA) 1851 (Washington D. C: 1851): 99-101.

32. Morris W. Werner, "St. Joseph: 1844 Gateway to Oregon," Pioneer Trails, www.kansasheritage.org.

33. Edward E. Hill, *The Office of Indian Affairs, 1824-1880: Historical Sketches* (New York: Clearwater Publishing Company, Inc. 1974): 69-71.

34. Richardson, Report, ARCIA, 1852 (Washington D. C: Robert Armstrong, 1852): 70-72; Vanderslice to Col. A. Cuming, Nov. 30, 1854, LR 01A, Great Nemaha Agency, Roll 308.

35. Olson, *Ioway Life*, 35.

36. George Catlin, *Adventures of the Ojibbeway and Iowa Indians* (London: Published by the Author, 1852): Vol. 2, 1-261.

37. A. B. Greenwood, Report, ARCIA, 1859 (Washington D.C: George W. Bowman, 1860): 142.

38. Vanderslice to Cuming, Dec. 30, 1854, LR 01A, Great Nemaha Agency, Roll 308.

39. Whitman, *The Oto,* 14.

40. B. A. James, Report, ARCIA, 1854 (Washington D.C: GPO, 1854): 104.

41. Blaine, *The Ioway Indians*, 170-94; 218-28. Mildred Mott Wedel, "Iowa," in Raymond J. DeMallie, *Plains*, Vol. 13, Part 1, *Handbook of North American Indians* (Washington D.C: Handbook of North American Indians, 2001), 43-46.

42. J. Clark Archer, Richard Edwards, Leslie M. Howard, Fred M. Shelley, Donald A. Wilhite, and David J. Wishart, *Atlas of Nebraska* (Lincoln and London: University of Nebraska Press, 2017): 50-1 and Figs. 2-10, 2-11, 2-12.

43. James C. Malin, *The Nebraska Question, 1852-1854* (Lawrence, KS: Published by the Author, 1953).

44. Wyatt Winton Belcher, *The Economic Rivalry between St. Louis and Chicago, 1850-1880* (New York: Columbia University Press, 1947), 55-95, 193-206.

45. Quoted in Malin, *The Nebraska Question*, 444.

46. *St. Joseph Gazette*, April 26, 1854, quoted in Malin, *The Nebraska Question*, 341.

47. Royce, *Indian Land Cessions*: Fig. 41.

48. Daniel Vanderslice, Report, ARCIA, 1854 (Washington D.C: 1854): 98.

49. Kappler, *Indian Affairs*, Vol. 2, 628-33; Royce, *Indian Land Cessions*, Figs. 27, 42.

50. Thomas Donaldson, *The Public Domain* (Washington D.C: GPO, 1884): 214-16.

51. Martha Caldwell, ed., "Records of the Squatter Association of Whitehead District, Doniphan County," *Kansas Historical Quarterly* 13 (February 1944): 16-35.

52. Caldwell, "Records of the Squatter Association," 18, 19, 20, 22, 25, 28.

53. Maps of Nebraska County Formations, 1854-1925, datausa.10|profile|-geo|richardson_county_ne.

2. BEGINNINGS, 1854-67

1. Nebraska Territorial Census, 1854, Vol. 1, RG513, Nebraska State Historical Society; Aieta, Nicholas J. "Frontier Settlement and Community Development in Richardson, Burt, and Platte Counties, Nebraska, 1854-1870," Diss. University of Nebraska-Lincoln, 2007: 106-16.

2. Kenneth E. Colton, "Stagecoach Travel in Iowa," *The Annals of Iowa* 22.3 (1940): 175-200. By 1850, a stagecoach route traversed Iowa from Davenport to Council Bluffs, roughly following the route of Interstate 80.

3. Lewis C. Edwards, *History of Richardson County, Nebraska* (Indianapolis: B. F. Bowen and Company, 1917), 296. This monumental history, filled with facts and reminiscences, is a valuable source.

4. Richardson County File, 0653; Supplement to the *Falls City Journal*, "Let us Show You Richardson County:" 6-8; Aieta, "Frontier Settlement and Community Development": 140-45.

5. Hiram Martin Chittenden, *History of Steamboat Navigation on the Missouri River* (New York: Francis P. Harper, 1903); William J. Peterson, "Steamboating on the Missouri River," *Nebraska History* 35 (1954): 255-75; *Rulo Western Guide*, Aug. 12, 1858.

6. *Broad Axe*, Nov. 20, 1860.

7. Edwards, *History of Richardson County*, 292-5; Peterson, "Steamboating on the Missouri": 265-6.

8. *Broad Axe*, Jan. 1, 1861; also "My Present Past," www.mypresentpast.com/home/railroads/hannibal-st-joseph-railroad. This early railroad did not result in St. Joseph becoming the main metropolis in the region, because in 1867 a cutoff was built to Kansas City, where the first bridge across the Missouri was built two-years later, securing its control of western development.

9. U.S. Bureau of the Census, Nebraska Territorial Census, 1860. Record Group 513, Series 1, Roll 1; Aieta, "Frontier Settlement and Community Development": 112-17; Edwards, *History of Richardson County*, 100-02.

10. Aieta, "Frontier Settlement and Community Development": 112; Edwards, *History of Richardson County*, 198-9, 207-10.

11. *Rulo Western Guide*, June 18, 1858. By this time, passenger liners, with new iron hulls and compound steam engines, could cross the Atlantic in ten days.

12. Edwards, *History of Richardson County*, 711-12; Vanderslice, "Reports," AR-CIA, 1854, 98-9; 1856, 119-11; 1858, 105; 1860, 99-100.

13. Charles D. Calomiris and Larry Schweikart, "The Panic of 1857: Origins, Transmission, and Containment," *Journal of Economic History* 51 (1991): 807-34.

14. James A. Rawley, "Bleeding Kansas," in David J. Wishart, ed., *Encyclopedia of the Great Plains* (Lincoln and London: University of Nebraska Press, 2004): 823-4; James E. Potter, *Standing Firmly by the Flag: Nebraska Territory and the Civil War, 1861-1867* (Lincoln and London: University of Nebraska Press, 2012); Edwards, *History of Richardson County*, 487-93; *Broad Axe*, Oct. 15, 1861; *Falls City Journal*, Oct. 19, 30, 2022; Paul Hammel, "Underground Railroad Site in Falls City Recognized by National Park Service," *Nebraska Examiner*, Nov. 22, 2022; US Census Bureau, Population of the United States, 1860, census.gov/library/publications/1864/dec/1860a.html, 281, 566.

15. Peterson, "Steamboating on the Missouri River": 266; "My Present Past." The Civil War did not significantly reduce the number of Europeans coming to the United States, some of whom undoubtedly found their way to Richardson County. See Eszter Szabó, "The Migration Factor in the American Civil War: the Impact of Voluntary Population Movements on the War Effort," *Americana E-Journal of American Studies in Hungary*, 12-1 (2016).

16. Charles O. Paullin, *Atlas of the Historical Geography of the United States* (Washington D. C.: Carnegie Institute and American Geographical Society, 1932), Plate 140.

17. Drake Hokanson's *Reflecting a Prairie Town: A Year in Peterson* (Iowa City: University of Iowa Press, 1994): 46-67, gives a particularly vivid description of the public land survey in Clay County, Northwest Iowa, which was surveyed at the same time as Richardson County.

18. Edwards, *History of Richardson County*, 128-32.

19. The mapped-out plats and field notes for Richardson County can be most easily accessed at Nebraska State Surveyor's Office: www.sso.nebraska.gov/maps/fieldbooks/county/richardson.html. The relevant books are numbered 117, 121, 124, 126, 128, and 129.

20. General Land Office, *To the Surveyors General of Public Lands of the United States for the Surveying Districts Established In and Since the Year 1850* (Washington D.C.: GPO, 1855). Also see the fine dissertation by Charles Howard

Richardson entitled "Early Settlement of Eastern Nebraska Territory: A Geographical Study Based on the Original Land Survey." Diss. University of Nebraska-Lincoln, 1968.

21. For information on the geology, soils, and water resources of Richardson County, see Philip A. Emery, *Geology and Ground-Water Resources of Richardson County, Nebraska.* Resource Atlas No. 10 (Lincoln: Conservation and Survey Division, UNL, 2017); and J. A. Elder, *Soils of Nebraska.* Resource Report No. 2 (Lincoln: Conservation and Survey Division, UNL, 1969).

22. Richardson, in "Early Settlement of Eastern Nebraska Territory": 17-23, discusses potential errors in the surveyors' accounts.

23. For a wealth of ideas on the emergence and functions of towns on the Great Plains, see John C. Hudson, *Plains Country Towns* (Minneapolis: University of Minnesota Press, 1985).

24. The dates of first sales are from the United States General Land Office Tract Books, 1860-1954. Series 3, vols. 148, 149. RG509.

25. Thomas Donaldson, *The Public Domain: Its History, with Statistics* (Washington D. C.: G. P. O., 1884); Roscoe L. Lokken, *Iowa Public Land Disposal* (Iowa City: The State Historical Society of Iowa, 1942), 76-96.

26. Lokken, *Iowa Public Land Disposal*, 131-53; Donaldson, *The Public Domain*, 232-7; James W. Oberly, *Sixty Million Acres: American Veterans and the Public Lands Before the Civil War* (Kent and London: The Kent State University Press, 1990).

27. Oberly, *Sixty Million Acres*, 92.

28. See the remarkable map of "Methods of Land Transfer," compiled by Russell Lang, in Archer, et al., *Atlas of Nebraska*, 66.

29. Numerical Index, Richardson County, Deed Record, Vol. 16, 35, 7, 362; Vol. 19, 527. County Courthouse, Falls City.

30. For example, Township 2 North Range 13 East. Nebraska State Surveyor's Office. Book 117.

31. Donaldson, *The Public Domain*, 349-50. The case for homesteads aiding settlement, rather than abetting speculation, is strongly made in Richard Edwards, Jacob J. Friefeld, and Rebecca S. Wingo, *Homesteading the Plains: Toward a New History* (Lincoln and London: University of Nebraska Press, 2017).

32. Johansen, "To Make Some Provision for Their Half-Breeds": 15-26; Chapman, *Otoes and Missourias*, 60-83; Half-Breed Tract, Correspondence, 1857-1943. Nebraska State Historical Society Archives.

33. Robert M. Kvasnicka, George W. Manypenny, 1853-57, in Robert M. Kvasnicka and Herman J. Viola, eds. *The Commissioners of Indian Affairs, 1824-1917* (Lincoln and London: University of Nebraska Press, 1979), 57-67; Wishart, *An Unspeakable Sadness*, 102-3, 111-12.

34. Chapman, *Otoes and Missourias*, 63-4.

35. Chapman, *Otoes and Missourias*, 77-8; Half-Breed Tract, Correspondence, 1857-1943.

36. Johansen, "To Make Some Provision for Their Half-Breeds": 21-6; Chapman, *Otoes and Missourias*, 77-8; Edwards, *History of Richardson County*, 125-8.

37. Edwards, *History of Richardson County*, 225-7, 578, 688-91.

38. Chapman, *Otoes and Missourias*, 80; Edwards, *History of Richardson County*, 226.

39. C. O. Snow, "History of the Half-Breed Tract," Half Breed Tract, Correspondence. Nebraska State Historical Society Archives; Donald Chaput, "James W. Denver, 1857, 1858-9," in Kvasnicka and Viola, *The Commissioners of Indian Affairs*, 69-75.

40. Vanderslice, "Report," ARCIA, 1854, 98-101; ARCIA, 1857, 157-60.

41. Vanderslice, "Report," ARCIA, 1857, 157-60; ARCIA, 1859, 141-43.

42. Vanderslice, "Report," ARCIA, 1860, 99-100.

43. See the treaty details in Kappler, *Indian Affairs*, Vol. 2, 811-14, and for the maps see Royce, *Indian Land Cessions*, Plates 27, 42. The land sold for an average of $1.60 an acre. Burbank, "Report," ARCIA, 1864, 374-5.

44. In 1867, according to their agent, there was "a great deal of anxiety" among the Iowa, who feared they would be forced to sell their lands and be shifted south. C. H. Norris, "Report," ARCIA, 1967, 273.

45. Nebraska Territorial Census, 1855, Vol. 2; Nebraska Territorial Census, 1860. Series 2, Vol. 2. Agriculture.

46. Richardson, "Early Settlement of Eastern Nebraska Territory", 180-214.

47. Edwards, *History of Richardson County*, 715-18.

48. Nebraska Territorial Census, 1860, Vol. 2. Agriculture.

49. Hiram M. Drache, "The Impact of John Deere's Plow." https://www.lib.niu.edu

50. *The Nebraskian*, Aug. 13, 1856; Nebraska Territorial Census, 1860. Vol. 2. Agriculture; Vol. 3. Social Statistics.

51. *Rulo Western Guide*, June 18, 1858.

52. Nebraska Territorial Census, 1860. Vol. 5. Social Statistics.

53. Nebraska Territorial Census, 1860. Roll 1. Rulo City and Township and Falls City and Township.

54. Nebraska Territorial Census, 1860. Vol. 5. Social Statistics.

55. Nebraska Territorial Census, 1860. Vol. 4. Series 2.

56. Edwards, *History of Richardson County*, 443-4, 575-6; Vanderslice, "Report," ARCIA, 1860, 99.

57. Edwards, *History of Richardson County*, 619; Blaine, *The Ioway Indians*, 255-6; Vanderslice, "Report," ARCIA, 1854, 99.

58. Burbank, "Report," ARCIA, 1865, 415; Edwards, *History of Richardson County*, 619-21.

59. Vanderslice, "Report," ARCIA, 1857, 106-8. Jurisdiction over crimes on reservations involving a non-Indian perpetrator and an Indian victim was a federal matter regulated by the General Crimes Act of 1817. See "General Guide To Criminal Jurisdiction in Indian Country," www.tribal-institute.org/lists/jurisdiction.html

60. Edwards, *History of Richardson County*, 575-86.

61. *Rulo Western Guide*, June 18, 1858. The *White Cloud Chief* from June 10, 1858 no longer exists, but its argument was reiterated in detail in the Rulo paper the following week.

62. The minutes of the various elections are compiled in Edwards, *History of Richardson County*, 154-9.

63. Edwards, *History of Richardson County*, 168-70, 650-1; for other "county seat wars," see James A. Schellenberg, *Conflict Between Communities: American County Seat Wars* (New York: Paragon House Publishers, 1987). See also,

Nikki McKim, "One of the most sensational, prolonged and bloodiest county seat fights in Nebraska history," *Falls City Journal*, April 19, 2023.

64. Edwards, *History of Richardson County*, 157, 164. Salem would make another futile attempt to get the county seat in 1871.

65. Edwards, *History of Richardson County*, 141-2, 355, 374; *Broad Axe*, Feb. 19, 1861.

3. EXPANSION, 1868-1930

1. Paullin, *Atlas of the Historical Geography of the United States*, Plates 139A, 140.

2. John C. Hudson, "Towns of the Western Railroads," *Great Plains Quarterly* 2 (Winter 1982): 41-54.

3. Edwards, *History of Richardson County*, 305-6.

4. Edwards, *History of Richardson County*, 302-3, 319-20.

5. *Nemaha Valley Journal*, July 6, 1871.

6. *Nemaha Valley Journal*, July 13, 1871.

7. Information on the extension of the network is from Edwards, *History of Richardson County*, 238-9, 319-21.

8. The seminal works on Plains railroads and the towns they created are by John C. Hudson, including, "Towns of the Western Railroads" and, especially, *Plains Country Towns*.

9. George O. Carney, "Grain Elevators in the United States and Canada: Functional or Symbolic?," *Material Culture* 27 (Spring 1995): 1-24.

10. *Nemaha Valley Journal*, July 6, 1871.

11. Edwards, *History of Richardson County*, 241-4; Hudson, *Plains Country Towns*, 48-70.

12. *Nebraska State Gazetteer and Business Directory* for 1886-7 (Lincoln: J. M. Wolfe,

1887); *Nebraska State Gazetteer and Business Directory for 1915*, Reel 11, Film 917.82/N27g, Nebraska State Historical Society. Population figures in the text and on the graphs come from the U.S. Census Bureau, "Census of Population and Housing." https://www.census.gov/prod/www/decennial.html.

13. Edwards, *History of Richardson County*, 321; *Falls City News*, Aug. 3, 1882; *Nebraska State Gazetteer and Business Directory for 1890-91* (Omaha: J. M. Wolfe, 1891); and *Nebraska State Gazetteer and Business Directory for 1915.*

14. Edwards, *History of Richardson County*, 538-61, 561-374; *Nebraska State Gazetteer and Business Directory for 1890.*

15. Edwards, *History of Richardson County*, 237-8, 240-1; *Nebraska State Gazetteer and Business Directory for 1915.*

16. *Nebraska State Gazetteer and Business Directory for 1915.*

17. Hudson, *Plains Country Towns*, 26-38.

18. Edwards, *History of Richardson County*, 583-4.

19. Edwards, *History of Richardson County*, 585-9, 656-7.

20. Edwards, *History of Richardson County*, 241; Jim McKee, "Rise and Fall of Nims City," *Lincoln Journal Star*, Feb. 16, 2010.

21. Edwards, *History of Richardson County*, 190-3; *Nebraska State Gazetteer and Business Directory for 1890.*

22. U.S. Census Bureau, "Census of Population and Housing."

23. *Falls City Tribune*, Feb. 5, 1904; Aug. 6, 1909; Dec. 10, 1910; April 14, 1911.

24. *Falls City Tribune*, Dec. 17., 1909; Jan. 27, 1910; Feb. 10, 1911.

25. *Falls City Tribune*, Jan. 27, 1910; March 24, 1911. Edwards, *History of Richardson County*, 503-4.

26. Edwards, *History of Richardson County*, 504; *Nebraska State Gazetteer and Business Directory for 1915.*

27. Edwards, *History of Richardson County*, 533-7; *Nebraska State Gazetteer and Business Directory for 1915*; *Falls City Tribune*, Dec. 16, 1910.

28. *Falls City Tribune*, June 24, 1904; Dec. 16, 1910; Edwards, *History of Richardson County*, 503-4.

29. The main sources of information for this section are the decennial censuses of agriculture from 1860 to 1935, most easily accessed at USDA, Census of Agriculture, Historical Archive, Albert R. Main Library, Cornell University, Mannlib.cornell.edu/usda/AgCensusimages. The 1910 census is particularly relied upon: *Thirteenth Census of the United States Taken in the Year 1910.* Vol. 7, Agriculture, Nebraska (Washington D. C.: 1913). There is also a useful chapter in Edwards, *History of Richardson County*, 252-91, which relies on the 1910 census, but also includes a survey of Richardson County agriculture in about 1917. Also, *Report on the Productions of Agriculture as Returned in the 1880 Census* (Washington D.C.: GPO, 1883), Table 7, 125; and *Twelfth Census of the United States Taken in the Year 1900.* Agriculture, Part 30.

30. Wayne D. Rasmussen, "The Mechanization of Agriculture," *Scientific American* 247.3 (Sept. 1982), 76-89; Edwards, *History of Richardson County*, 201; "Results of Horse and Tractor Survey," *The Nebraska Farmer* (May 6, 1922), 4; *Thirteenth Census of the United States Taken in the Year 1920,* Vol. 6, Part 1, *Agriculture* (Washington D.C.: GPO, 1922), Table 1, 694; *United States Census of Agriculture, 1925.* Part 1 (Washington D.C.: GPO, 1927), Table 3, 1158; Bureau of the Census, *United States Census of Agriculture, 1935.* Vol. 1, Part 1 (Washington D.C.: GPO, 1936), Table 2, 338.

31. *Thirteenth Census of the United States Taken in the Year 1910.* Vol. 7, *Agriculture.* Nebraska, Table 1, 37; Edwards, *History of Richardson County*, 262, 1328-30.

32. *Thirteenth Census of the United States Taken in the Year 1910.* Vol. 7, *Agriculture.* Nebraska. Table 1, 37; *Report on the Productions of Agriculture as Returned in the 1880 Census.* Table 5, 72.

33. *Thirteenth Census of the United States Taken in the Year 1910.* Vol. 7, Agriculture. Table 4, 54; Edwards, *History of Richardson County*, 254-6. These are also the main references for the following sections on crops.

34. See the series of maps in Archer et. al., *Atlas of Nebraska*, Figs. 4-24 and 4-25.

35. Edwards, *History of Richardson County*, 986-8.

36. *Thirteenth Census of the United States Taken in the Year 1910.* Vol. 7, *Agriculture.* Table 3, 46. This is also the reference for the following paragraphs on beef cattle, poultry, and hogs.

37. Edwards, *History of Richardson County*, 951-2.

38. Edwards, *History of Richardson County*, 986-7.

39. Edwards, *History of Richardson County*, 879-81, 933-5, 1125-7.

40. Edwards, *History of Richardson County*, 260-1, 265-72, 532-3; *Fourteenth Census of the United States Taken in the Year 1920*, Vol. 6, Part 1, *Agriculture*, Table 5, 719; Edwards, *History of Richardson County*, 1328-30.

41. Alfred Charles True, *A History of Agricultural Extension Work in the United States, 1785-1923*. USDA Miscellaneous Publications, No. 15 (Washington D.C.: GPO, 1928).

42. *Nebraska Farmer*, Feb. 4, March 4, and Dec. 9, 1922. A. J. Weaver, "Orcharding," Address Given at the Missouri Valley Industrial and Farmers' Congress, Dec. 1914.

43. Edwards, *History of Richardson County*, 262-4, 755-7, 1372-4.

44. Edwards, *History of Richardson County*, 286-7, 1288-9.

45. Edwards, *History of Richardson County*, 945-6, 1242-4. For example, *Nebraska Farmer*, Sept. 23, 1922.

46. Edwards, *History of Richardson County*, 287.

47. Edwards, *History of Richardson County*, 322-3, 503; George E. Koster, *A Story of Highway Development in Nebraska* (Lincoln: Nebraska Dept. of Roads, 1997).

48. See U.S.G.S. Rulo Quadrangle, 1965.

49. *Fourteenth Census of the United States Taken in the Year 1920*. Vol. 7. Irrigation and Drainage (Washington D.C.: GPO, 1922), 346; Edwards, *History of Richardson County*, 276-81; *Falls City Tribune*, Sept. 30, 1910.

50. John Blair, "Report," ARCIA, 1888, 140-3; M. B. Kent, "Report," ARCIA, 1890, 101.

51. J. A. Scott, "Report," ARCIA, 1892, 269-74; Scott, "Report," ARCIA, 1893, 156-64. Note there are discrepancies in the records concerning the size of the Iowa Reservation, with some sources giving 16,000 acres. The 11,400 acres adopted here is most commonly recognized in the records of the time.

52. Blair, "Report," ARCIA, 1889, 216-19.

53. George W. James, "Report," ARCIA 1897, 152; K. Nadau, "Report," ARCIA, 1901, Pt. 1, 242-6.

54. Nadau, "Report," ARCIA, 1901, Pt. 1, 242-6.

55. Nadau, "Report," ARCIA, 1904, 213.

56. J. H. Grover, "Report," ARCIA, 1887, 120-4.

57. Fifty-First Congress. Session II. Ch. 383. 1891; Nadau, "Report," ARCIA, 1901, 242-6.

58. Fifty-Ninth Congress. Session I. Ch. 2348. Eighty-Second Congress. Session II. House Report No. 790 (Washington D. C., 1952), Table VI, 722, 823. Trust lands, individual or tribal, are Indian lands whose title is held by the federal government.

59. Claude S. Fischer, "Changes in Leisure Activities, 1890-1940," *Journal of Social History*, Vol. 27, No. 3 (Spring 1994), 453-75.

60. *Falls City Tribune, 1904-11*. Chronicling America: Historical American Newspapers. Library of Congress. https://chroniclingamerica.loc.gov.

61. *Falls City Tribune*, Jan. 3, 1908.

62. For a recent analysis, see Justin Gage, *We Do Not Want the Gates Closed Between Us: Native Networks and the Spread of the Ghost Dance* (Norman: University of Oklahoma Press, 2020).

63. *Falls City Tribune*, Feb. 23, 1906; Feb. 14, 1908.

64. *Falls City Tribune*, May 13, 1904; Dec. 2, 1904; March 24, 1905; Feb. 12, 1901.

65. *Falls City Tribune*, Dec. 17, 1909.

66. *Falls City Tribune*, Jan. 15, 1904; Jan. 29, 1904; Dec. 17, 1909.

67. *Falls City Tribune*, March 31, 1905. Archer et al, *Atlas of Nebraska*, 200-2.

68. Edwards, *History of Richardson County*, 518-21; Lynn Dumeril. *Freemasonry and American Culture, 1880-1930* (Princeton: Princeton University Press, 1984).

69. *Falls City Tribune*, Aug. 7, 1904; June 15, 1906.

70. Edwards, *History of Richardson County*, 514-5.

71. *Falls City Tribune*, Feb. 23, 1904; April 22, 1904; Nov. 18, 1904; March 7, 1907. There were state restrictions on the hunting of deer and prairie chickens as early as 1873: see *Nemaha Valley Journal* (Falls City), July 21, 1873.

Also, Larkin Powell. *Great Plains Birds* (Lincoln: University of Nebraska Press, 2019), 97-104.

72. *Falls City Tribune*, Oct. 14, 1904; Oct. 21, 1904; Oct. 28, 1904; Nov. 4, 1904; Aug. 7, 1908.

73. *Falls City Tribune*, April 15, 1904; Oct. 28, 1904. Also, Robert Pruter, *The Rise of American High School Sports and the Search for Control, 1880-1930* (Syracuse: Syracuse University Press, 2013), 145-69.

74. *Falls City Tribune*, Oct. 21, 1904; Nov. 18, 1904; Dec. 2, 1904.

75. *Falls City Tribune*, Oct. 14, 1904; Oct. 28, 1904; Nov. 18, 1904.

76. *Falls City Tribune*, April 13, 1906; Sept. 14, 1906. Sanborn Fire Insurance Map, Falls City, 1908-09, https://www.loc.gov/collections/sanborn-maps/

77. *Falls City Tribune*, Dec. 16, 1904; Jan. 13, 1905; July 7, 1905; June 8, 1906. Almost every agent's report complained of the ongoing alcohol trade on the reservations. For example, Honnell, "Report," *ARCIA*, 1900, Part 1, 255.

78. *Falls City Tribune*, March 18, 1904; Dec. 9, 1904; Nov. 16, 1906.

79. *Falls City Tribune*, Oct. 14, 1904; Sept. 7, 1906; Dec. 21, 1906.

80. *Falls City Tribune*, Sept. 14, 1906.

81. Bureau of the Census, *Thirteenth Census of the United States Taken in the Year 1910*. Vol. 3. *Population* (Washington D.C.: GPO, 1913), 64-6. *Falls City Tribune*, March 16, 1906; Nov. 16, 1906.

82. *Falls City Tribune*, Jan. 3, 1908.

83. *Falls City Tribune*, Feb. 23, 1906; Dec. 15, 1905.

84. *Falls City Tribune*, Jan. 3, 1908; Dec. 18, 1908; July 7, 1911. Sanborn Fire Insurance Map, Falls City, 1908-09; D. Lane Ehlers, *National Register of Historic Places, Gehling Theater, Falls City*, Nomination, National Parks Service, 1988.

85. *Falls City Tribune*, Jan. 3, 1908; June 3, 1910.

86. *Falls City Tribune*, Oct. 30, 1908; March 17, 1911; May 5, 1911.

87. *Falls City Tribune*, April 22, 1904; May 6, 1904; Sept. 15, 1904; Sept. 7, 1905; June 16, 1911. See also Janet M. Davis, *The Circus Age: Culture and Society Under the American Big Top* (Chapel Hill: University of North Carolina Press,

2002); List of American Circuses, circusandsideshows.com/circuses.html; and Stephanie Decker, "Miller Brothers," in Wishart, ed. *Encyclopedia of the Great Plains*, 273.

88. *Falls City Tribune*, Sept, 16, 1904; July 7, 1905.

89. *Falls City Tribune*, May 6, 1904.

90. *Falls City Tribune*, June 3, 1910.

91. *Falls City Tribune*, May 6, 1904; May 13, 1904; May 30, 1904; June 24, 1904; July 27, 1904; Sept. 16, 1904.

92. *Falls City Tribune*, April 7, 1906; July 20, 1906; Sept. 21, 1906. Oct. 26, 1906.

93. *Falls City Tribune*, May 6, 1904; July 29, 1904; Oct. 14, 1904; Sept. 7, 1906. See also, Thomas Weiss, "Tourism in America Before World War II," *The Journal of Economic History* 64.2 (June 2006): 289-327.

94. *Falls City Tribune*, April 22, 1904; Sept. 16, 1904; Dec. 16, 1904; Dec. 21, 1906; Aug. 7, 1908.

95. *Falls City Tribune*, April 14, 1911; Archer et al, *Atlas of Nebraska*, Fig. 1-17, p. 23. Only twelve tornadoes were reported in Richardson County from 1950 (when records were first kept) to 2015, none of them severe.

96. U.S. Department of Agriculture, Weather Bureau, *Summaries of Climatological Data by Sections* (Washington D.C.: Weather Bureau, 1926), Section 37, Southern Nebraska, 3-4; *Falls City Tribune*, April 29, 1904; May 20, 1904.

97. Edwards, *History of Richardson County*, 630-3; Kansas State Board of Agriculture, *Third Annual Report* (Topeka: Geog. W. Martin, 1874), 13-38. See also, Jeffrey A. Lockwood, *Locust: The Devastating Rise and Mysterious Disappearance of the Insect that Shaped the American Frontier* (New York: Basic Books, 2004).

98. *Nemaha Valley Journal*, Aug. 6, 1874; Aug. 27, 1874; Edwards, *History of Richardson County*, 630-1; Kansas State Board of Agriculture, *Fourth Annual Report* (Topeka: Geog. W. Martin, 1875), 47.

99. *Nemaha Valley Journal*, Aug. 27, 1874; May 20, 1875; Edwards, *History of Richardson County*, 632-3; Lockwood, *Locust.*

100. *Nemaha Valley Journal*, Oct. 2, 1873; May 14, 1874; David Glasner, "Crisis of 1873," in David Glasner and Thomas F. Cooley, *Business Cycles and Depressions: An Encyclopedia* (New York: Garland Pub; 1997), 132-3.

101. *Nemaha Valley Journal*, Aug. 28, 1874; Oct. 2, 1873. See also, Pearl Louise Erickson, Destitution and Relief in Nebraska, 1874-1875. Thesis. University of Nebraska.

102. Edwards, *History of Richardson County*, 632-3; Alexandra M. Wagner, "Grasshoppered: America's Response to the 1874 Rocky Mountain Locust Invasion," *Nebraska History* 89 (2008): 154-67.

103. Julie Courtwright, "'When We First Come Here It All Looked Like Prairie Land Almost' : Prairie Fire and Plains Settlement," *Western Historical Quarterly* 38 (Summer 2007): 157-79; Edwards, *History of Richardson County*, 515.

104. *Falls City Press*, April 19, 1877.

105. *Falls City News*, May 6-9, 1919.

106. *The Humboldt Leader*, May 8, 1919; May 22, 1919; June 12, 1919; July 3, 1919; July 24, 1919; Sept. 11, 1919.

107. *Falls City News*, October 1, 1919; History Book Committee, *Richardson County Nebraska 1985* (Dallas: Taylor Publishing Co., 1985), 23.

108. History Book Committee, *Richardson County Nebraska 1985*, 58.

109. *Rulo Register*, May 4, 1904. For economic booms following fires, see also Hudson, *Plains Country Towns*, 108.

110. Richardson County, Ne. 1870 Mortality Census, http://ftp.us-census.org/pub/usgenweb/census/ne/richardson/1870/. See also, Alan C. Swedlund and Alison K. Donta, "Scarlet Fever Epidemics of the Nineteenth Century: A Case of Evolved Pathogenic Virulence," in D. Ann Herring and Alison K Donta, eds., *Human Biologists in the Archives: Demography, Health, Nutrition, and Genetics in Human Populations*. (Cambridge: Cambridge University Press, 2003), 159-77.

111. Nadau, "Report," ARCIA, 1901, Part 1, 243; *Falls City Tribune*, April 15, June 29, 1918.

112. John M. Barry. *The Great Influenza* (New York: Penguin Books, 2004). The reason Spain became linked to the pandemic was that, unlike most other European nations, Spain was not embroiled in the war and under strict censorship. The impact of the flu was reported more openly in neutral Spain; hence the association.

113. For example, *The Humboldt Leader*, Oct. 3, 1918; October 12, 1918.

114. *The Humboldt Leader*, Oct. 10, 1918; Nov. 23, 1918; *Falls City News*, Oct. 29, 1919. See also the in-depth reporting by Nikki McKim, "The 1918 'Flu' Pandemic in Richardson County," which appeared in eight episodes in the *Falls City Journal* from June 10, 2020 to Sept. 10, 2020.

115. *The Humboldt Leader*, Dec. 13, 1918; Barry, *The Great Influenza*, 370.

116. Kristin Watkins, *It Came Across the Plains: The 1918 Influenza Epidemic in Rural Nebraska*, Ph. D. Dissertation, University of Nebraska Medical Center, 2015; *The Humboldt Leader*, Oct. 17, 1918; Nov. 1, 1918; Nov. 28, 1918; *Falls City News*, Oct. 22, 1918; Nov. 26, 1918.

117. *The Humboldt Leader*, Nov. 28, 1918; Dec. 19, 1918.

118. *The Humboldt Leader*, Oct. 31, 1918; *Falls City News*, Dec. 11, 1918.

119. *The Humboldt Leader*, Dec. 5, 1918; Dec. 11, 1918; *Falls City News*, Dec. 11, 1918; Dec. 23, 1918.

120. *The Humboldt Leader*, Feb. 27, 1919.

4. CONTRACTION, 1931-2023

1. George C. Schottenhamel, "The Richardson County Oil Boom, 1938-1942," *Nebraska History* 60 (1979): 357-70.

2. State Historic Preservation Office, *Nebraska Historic Buildings Survey. Reconnaissance Survey Final Report of Richardson County, Nebraska* (Lincoln, 1993), 11, 16.

3. Bill Schock, "Falls City Railroading." *Falls City Journal*, Sept. 4, 2013.

4. USDA Census of Agriculture Historical Archive, agcensus.library.cornell.edu. 1930, Table 1; 1959, Table 1; 2017 Census of Agriculture, County Profile, Richardson County, Nebraska, nass.usda.gov/Publications/AgCensus/2017

5. Larkin Powell, "Hitler's Effect on Wildlife in Nebraska: World War II and Farmed Landscapes," *Great Plains Quarterly* 35 (Winter 2015): 1-26; Tim L.

Hiller, Larkin Powell, Tim D. McCoy, and Jeffery J. Lusk; "Long-Term Agricultural Land-Use Trends in Nebraska, 1866-2007," *Great Plains Research* 19 (Fall 2009): 225-37.

6. 2017 Census of Agriculture, County Profile, Richardson County, 2.

7. Powell, "Hitler's Effect on Wildlife," 9-15; 2017 Census of Agriculture, County Profile, Richardson County, 2.

8. James M. MacDonald, Robert A. Hoppie, Doris Newton, *Three Decades of Consolidation in U.S. Agriculture*, E1B-189, U.S. Department of Agriculture, Economic Research Service, March 2018: 320-41.

9. USDA Census of Agriculture, 1950, Table 3; 1959, Tables 4 and 6.

10. USDA Census of Agriculture, 1940, Table X; 1950, Table 3; Powell, "Hitler's Effect on Wildlife," 7; Ronald R. Kline, "Resisting Development, Reinventing Modernity: Rural Electrification in the United States before World War II," *Environmental Values* 11 (Aug. 2002): 327-44.

11. James Marten, "Agricultural Adjustment Acts," in Wishart, *Encyclopedia of the Great Plains*, 32-3; Report of the Great Plains Committee, *The Future of the Great Plains* (Washington D.C., 1936), 57.

12. Edward J. Deibert, "Soil Bank," in Wishart, *Encyclopedia of the Great Plains*, 50-1. Also Hiller, Powell, McCoy, and Lusk, "Long-Term Agricultural Land-Use Trends in Nebraska, 1866-2007," 229-34.

13. Unless otherwise noted, the specific data in this and the following two paragraphs are from the Environmental Working Group's Farm Subsidy Database and Conservation Database. farm.ewg.org.

14. In addition to the EWG data, see Chris Dunker, "694M. Bailouts Aid Farmers During Trade War," *Lincoln Journal Star*, Sept. 22, 2019, 1, 2.

15. Mike Dorning, "Farm Bailout Benefited Top 1%," *Lincoln Journal Star*, March 7, 2021, C1, 4; David Pitt, "Watchdog: USDA Overpaid Corn Farmers by $3B," *Lincoln Journal Star*, Dec. 22, 2021, 1, 2. See also, Census of Agriculture, 2007, 2012, 2017 County Profile, Richardson County. The average payment was calculated only for the farms receiving payments.

16. Miles T. Bryant, "School Consolidation and Reorganization," in Wishart (ed.), *Encyclopedia of the Great Plains*, 211-12. In 1924, there were 56,121 school districts in the Great Plains states. By 1968, only 4,822 districts

remained. See also, Daniel H. Weber, "Report," in Edwards, *History of Richardson County*, Vol. 1, 326-34.

17. Joan M. Blauwkamp, Peter J. Longo, and John Anderson, "School Consolidation in Nebraska: Economic Efficiency vs. Rural Community Life," *Online Journal of Rural Research and Policy*, Vol. 6.1 (2011): 1-20; Table Rock Historical Society, *Richardson County Comprehensive Plan* (Humboldt: Southeast Nebraska Council of Governments, 1977): 74; "Some of the Country Schools in Richardson County, Nebraska that were still standing in 2017," http://www.tablerockhistoricalsociety.com.

18. Jeanne L. Surface, "Losing a Way of Life: The Closing of a County School in Rural Nebraska," *Publications of the Rural Futures Institute* (University of Nebraska-Lincoln, 2016): 2, http://digitalcommons.unl.edu/rfipubs/2; Office of Data, Research, and Evaluation, Nebraska Department of Education, Richardson County School Districts, 1983-2022; Margaret Reist, "For Maple Grove School's Out…Forever," *Lincoln Journal Star*, May 31, 2009.

19. Jeanne Surface, in "Losing a Way of Life," emphasizes the alienation felt by residents in her study of the "Closing of a Country School." Surface also makes a strong case for the effectiveness of a small school education.

20. *Pages of History. Nebraska High Schools Present and Past, Public and Private* (Lincoln: Nebraska High School Historical Society, Inc.: 1994): 639, 640, 650.

21. *Pages of Nebraska History*: 647, 648; Nikki McKim, "SE Consolidated for a Night Roars Back to Life," *Falls City Journal*, June 6, 2017.

22. Bill Hafer, "Dawson-Verdon District Dissolving," *Beatrice Daily Sun*, Dec. 17, 2003.

23. Chris Dunker, "The End of an Era," *Beatrice Daily Sun*, March 11, 2009; Chris Dunker, "Final Class Graduates from Southeast Consolidated," *Beatrice Daily Sun*, May 18, 2009; Lori Gottula, "SE Consolidated for a Night Roars Back to Life," *Falls City Journal*, June 6, 2017.

24. Humboldt-Table Rock-Steinhauer School District, Annual Report, 2019-20, https://www.htrstitans.com.

25. Bruce E. Lang, "Southeast Nebraska 911 Center Is Mutually Beneficial for Several Counties," News Release, Aug. 27, 2021, https://www.beatrice.ne.gov/police/page/southeast-nebraska-911-center-mutually-beneficial-several-counties; John Nixon, "Richardson County Board Discussing Regional Dispatching," *RMG Online News*, May 25, 2021,

rmgonlinnews.com; Nikki McKim, "Richardson County Commissioners Vote to Join Southeast Communications 911 Center," *Falls City Journal*, June 15, 2021; Dan Swanson, "Richardson County Forges Ahead with Regional 911 Dispatching," *News Channel Nebraska*, June 22, 2021, newschannelnebraska.com.

26. Monica Birch, "Southeast Communications to Dispatch for Richardson County," *Beatrice Daily Sun*, July 7, 2021; Doug Kennedy, "Beatrice-Based 911 Center Adding Richardson County to Coverage Area," *News Channel Nebraska*, July 7, 2021.

27. John Nixon, "Richardson County Seeks to Terminate Dispatch Contract," *Many Signals Communications*, Jan. 26, 2022, msc.net; John Nixon, "Beatrice Sets Terms to Terminate Dispatch Agreement with Richardson County," *Many Signals Communications*, April 18, 2022; Nikki McKim, "County Rebuffs Falls City's Combined 911 Proposal," *Falls City Journal*, Feb. 7, 2024.

28. Francis Paul Prucha, *The Great Father: The United States Government and the American Indians* (Lincoln and London: University of Nebraska Press, 1986), 311-25.

29. United States Department of the Interior, Office of Indian Affairs, *Constitution and By-Laws for the Iowa Tribe of Indians of the Iowa Reservation in Kansas and Nebraska* (Washington D.C.: G.P.O., 1937); United States Department of the Interior, Office of Indian Affairs, *Constitution and By-Laws of the Sac and Fox Tribe of Missouri of the Sac and Fox Reservation in Kansas and Nebraska* (Washington D.C.: G.P.O., 1937).

30. Charles F. Wilkinson, *American Indians, Time, and the Law* (New Haven and London: Yale University Press, 1987), 68; *Constitution and By-Laws of Iowa Tribe of Kansas and Nebraska* (as amended Sept. 28, 2013), iowatribeofkansasandnebraska.com.

31. *Termination of Federal Supervision Over Certain Tribes of Indians.* Joint Hearing Before the Subcommittee of the Committees on Interior and Insular Affairs, Eighty-Third Congress, Second Session, S. 2743 and H.R. 7318 (Washington D.C.: GPO, 1954): 1320-26, 1404-12.

32. Prucha, *The Great Father*, 340-51.

33. *Termination of Federal Supervision*, 1313-30. Quote from p. 1317. See also, Joseph B. Herring, *The Enduring Indians of Kansas: A Century and a Half of Acculturation* (Lawrence: University Press of Kansas, 1990), 158-62.

34. *Termination of Federal Supervision*, 1350-2. Quote from p. 1385.

35. *Termination of Federal Supervision*, 1327-42; 1353.

36. Prucha, *The Great Father*, 346-51.

37. Indian Claims Commission, *Final Report* (Washington, D.C., G.P.O, 1978), 1-21. Quote from p. 14. See also, Imre Sutton, ed., *Irredeemable America: The Indians' Estate and Land Claims* (Albuquerque: University of New Mexico Press, 1985).

38. Indian Claims Commission Decisions, Oklahoma State University Library, Digital Collections, https://library.okstate.edu/. Iowa, Sac and Fox.

39. Docket 135. 6 ICC 464. Indian Claims Commission Decisions. Iowa; Docket 79-A. 20 ICC 308; 21 ICC 15. See also, ICC *Final Report*, 50-2.

40. John R. Wunder, *"Retained by the People:" A History of American Indians and the Bill of Rights* (New York and Oxford: Oxford University Press, 1994), 203-13.

41. Tribal State Compact Among the Iowa Tribe of Kansas and Nebraska and the State of Kansas, June 23, 1995, kansas.gov/ksga; Class III Gaming Compact Between the Sac and Fox Nation of Missouri and the State of Kansas and Nebraska and the State of Kansas, Oct. 17, 1995, sacandfoxks.com

42. Casino White Cloud, www.casinowhitecloud.org; "Casino White Cloud," 500 Nations, www.500nations.com/casinos/ksWhiteCloud.asp; Sac and Fox Casino, www.sacandfoxcasino.com; "Sac and Fox Casino," 500 Nations, https://www.500nations.com/casinos/ksSacFox.asp. The Bear Claw necklace was repatriated from the Detroit Institute of Arts.

43. Dave Ranney, "Tribes say casinos have transformed reservations," *Lawrence Journal World,* May 29, 2005, www2.ljworld.com. The Kickapoo casino opened in 1996, the Prairie Band Casino in 1998.

44. "Iowa Tribe of Kansas and Nebraska," AAA Native Arts, aaanativearts.com/iowa-tribe-of-kansas-and-nebraska-index; "Sac & Fox Nation of Missouri in Kansas and Nebraska," AAA Native Arts, aaanativearts.com/sac-fox-nation-of-missouri-index. See also Olson, *Ioway Life*, 123-5.

45. Iowa Tribe of Kansas and Nebraska, iowatribeofkansasandnebraska.com; Sac & Fox Nation of Missouri in Kansas and Nebraska, sacandfoxks.com;

Reconciliation Rising, "An Interview with Lance Foster," soundcloud.com/indianz/reconciliation-rising-an-interview-with-lance-foster

46. Institute for Tribal Environmental Professionals, Northern Arizona University, "Prairies Region: Sac and Fox of Missouri," farm.ewg.org

47. Institute for Tribal Environmental Professionals.

48. Iowa Tribe of Kansas and Nebraska, iowatribeofkansasandnebraska.com

49. Reconciliation Rising, "An Interview with Lance Foster;" Paul Hammel, "Iowa Tribe Creates 444-Acre Tribal National Park," *Lincoln Journal Star*, Nov. 27, 2020. The Rulo bluffs in turn had been gifted to the Nature Conservancy by environmentalist Ray Schulenberg in 1989.

50. "Iowa Tribe Awarded USDA Grant to Develop Trading Post," *Hiawatha World*, Aug. 17, 2022.

51. USDA Census of Agriculture Historical Archive, 1930, Nebraska, County Table VIII; Richardson County History Book Committee, *Richardson County*, 12; Hannesina Shafer, Lucia Ahem, Eleanor Shafer, *Shubert: The First 100 Years* (1983), 19.

52. High Plains Regional Climate Center, climod.unl.edu.

53. USDA Census of Agriculture Historical Archive, 1940: Nebraska, Table 14.

54. National Weather Service, "Armistice Day Blizzard Remembered," www.weather.gov

55. *Falls City Journal*, Nov. 11, Nov. 12, Nov. 13., Nov. 14., Nov. 15, 1940; Shafer, Ahem, and Shafer, *Shubert: The First 100 Years*, 97-8.

56. *Shubert Citizen*, Jan. 30, 1941; Shafer, Ahem, and Shafer, *Shubert: The First 100 Years*, 97-8.

57. The 2012 Census of Agriculture recorded four commercial orchards in Richardson County, one apple and three grape. Their acreages were not given, to avoid "disclosing data for individual farms." USDA Census of Agriculture Historical Archive, 2012, Nebraska, Table 30.

58. Historic Crests for the Missouri River at Rulo, https://water.weather.gov; "Historic Floods on the Missouri River: Fighting the Big Muddy in Nebraska," Nebraska Department of Natural Resources, www.dnr.ne.gov/floodplain/mitigation/mofloods.html

59. Pat Guinan, "March 2019 Weather and Its Impacts on Missouri," Missouri Climate Center, College of Agriculture, Food and Natural Resources, University of Missouri, climate.missouri.edu; Tyler J. Kelley, "The Fight to Tame a Swelling River With Dams That May Be Outmatched By Climate Change," *New York Times*, March 21, 2019.

60. April Simpson, "Midwest Farmers Suffer After Floods: 'I Got My Life in This Ground,'" The Pew Charitable Trusts, pewtrusts.org; "Nebraska, Missouri and Iowa Sees Historic Flooding," *Falls City Journal*, March 20, 2019; Nikki McKim, "Missouri Bridges Damaged in Spring 2019 Flooding Now Open to Traffic," *Falls City Journal*, Sept. 4, 2020; "Village of Rulo, Still on Path To Recovery From 2019 Flooding, Finds Help in Community Development Block Grant Program Emergent Threat Category," *Falls City Journal*, Nov. 18, 2020.

61. Martha Shulski, "Nebraska's Changing Climate – Highlights From the 4th National Climate Assessment," Cropwatch, Dec. 6, 2018, Institute of Agriculture and Natural Resources, University of Nebraska-Lincoln, cropwatch.unl.edu/2018/nebraska-changing-climate

62. Bill Schock, "42 Dead in Airliner Crash," *Falls City Journal*, Aug. 8, 1966; "Braniff Airways – Flight 250, 50th Anniversary Photos," nebraskaaircrash.com/civilian/braniff50anniversary.html; Claire Hurlbert, "Experience a Terrible Nightmare," *Falls City Journal*, Aug. 8, 1966; Peter Salter, "Fire in the Sky: Flight 250, 50 Years Later," *Lincoln Journal Star*, July 31, 2016.

63. *Aircraft Accident Report*, Braniff Airways, Inc, BAC 1-11, N1553, National Transportation Safety Board, U.S. Department of Transportation, April 18, 1968.

64. Schock, "42 Dead in Airliner Crash"; "Braniff Jetliner Falls into Field on Schwang Farm," *Falls City Journal*, Aug. 8, 1968.

65. Bill Schock, "Aug. 19, 1966 – Back to Normal After Hectic Days," *Falls City Journal*, Aug. 19, 1966.

66. John Oswald and Rudolph Unger, "Settlement Reached in AirCrash Suit," *Chicago Tribune*, Oct. 29,1968, in "Braniff Airways – Flight 250, 50th Anniversary Photographs."

67. Bill Schock, "A Day of Emotional Remembrance and Healing," *Falls City Journal*, Aug. 8, 2016.

68. Archer, et al, *Atlas of Nebraska*, Fig. 6-10.

69. Barry J. Barnett, "The U.S. Financial Crisis of the 1980s," *Agricultural History* 74.2 (Spring 2000): 366-80; Bill Ganzel, "Farm Bust of the 1980s," Wessels Living History Farm (York, NE: 2009), https://livinghistoryfarm.org

70. Southern Poverty Law Center, "Christian Identity"; "James Wickstrom"; "Hate Group Expert Daniel Levitas Discusses Posse Comitatus, Christian Identity Movement and More," www.spicenter.org

71. The main sources for the following pages are Rod Colvin, *Evil Harvest: A True Story of Cult Murder in the American Heartland* (New York: Bantam Books, 1992) and Supreme Court of Nebraska. State v. Ryan. 44 N.W. 2d 610 (1989), law.justice.com/cases/nebraska/supreme-court/1989. See also, James Coates, "Nightmare in Rulo," *Chicago Tribune*, Nov. 16, 1986; Robert Nelson, "Flush Him Down the Toilet," *Omaha Magazine*, May 26, 2015. The grotesque details of the two murders are given in Colvin, *Evil Harvest*, 236-308 and State v. Ryan (1989).

72. "In the end, State never does kill Michael Ryan," *Falls City Journal*, May 26, 2015.

73. Standing out in the vast literature on the Humboldt murders because of its insight and eloquence is John Gregory Dunne, "The Humboldt Murders," *The New Yorker*, Jan. 13, 1997. See also, State v. Lotter, Supreme Court of Nebraska, Decided: November 06, 1998, https://lp.findlaw.com. For local coverage of the murders, see *Falls City Journal*, Jan. 4, 1994.

74. Stephanie Fairyington, "Two Decades After Brandon Teena's Murder, a Look Back at Falls City," *The Atlantic*, Dec. 31, 2013.

75. Andrew Wegley, "Nebraska Supreme Court Rejects John Lotter's Latest Challenge To Death Sentence," *Lincoln Journal Star*, July 1, 2002.

76. Susan Muska and Greta Ólafsdóttir, *The Brandon Teena Story*, Zeitgeist Films, 1998; Kimberly Pierce, *Boys Don't Cry*, Hart-Sharp Entertainment, 1999. On the erasure of DeVine, see C. Riley Snorton, "DeVine's Cut: Public Memory and the Politics of Martyrdom," in Snorton, *Black on Both Sides: A Racial History of Trans Identity* (Minneapolis and London: University of Minnesota Press, 2017): 177-98. On how Teena's story was framed at the time, and subsequently, see Donna Minkowitz, "How I Broke and Botched the Brandon Teena Story," *The Village Voice*, June 20, 2018, www.villagevoice.com.

77. Brandon Estate of Brandon v. County of Richardson. Supreme Court of Nebraska, No. S-00-022. Decided: April 20, 2001, http://caselaw.findlaw.com/ne-supreme-court.1275811.html

78. "Village of Preston Officially Abolished as of June 2," *Falls City Journal*, June 8. 2022.

79. "Quick Facts: United States," United States Census, census.gov/quickfacts/fact/table/US/PST04521; "Quick Facts: Richardson County, Nebraska," census.gov/quickfacts/fact/table/richardsoncountynebraska/POPO 10220; "Richardson County, Nebraska Population," World Population Review, worldpopulationreview.com/us-counties/ne/Richardson-county-population.

80. Peter Salter, "He Broke Every Record," *Lincoln Journal Star*, March 24, 2021; Peter Salter, "Farm Sells for $27,400 an Acre," *Lincoln Journal Star*, Nov. 2, 2022.

81. Daniel Munch and Shelby Myers, "2022 Farm Profitability Outlook: Production Expenses Up, Net Farm Income Down," *Market Intel*, Feb. 15, 2022, American Farm Bureau Federation, fb.org; Michael Hirtzer, "Farmland Escapes Real Estate Slump," *Lincoln Journal Star*, Dec. 27, 2022.

82. J. Clark Archer, Stephen J. Lavin, Kenneth C. Martis, and Fred M. Shelley, *A Historical Atlas of U.S. Presidential Elections, 1788-2004* (Washington D.C.: CQ Press, 2006). The exceptions, when Richardson County voted Democrat in presidential elections, were 1896 and 1900 when farmers supported free coinage of silver, which they hoped would allow them to pay their debts more readily, and when William Jennings Bryan, a Nebraska favorite son, was the candidate; in 1912, when the Republican Party was divided, and 1916, when Richardson County voters backed Woodrow Wilson's platform of keeping the United States neutral in the war; in 1932 and 1936, when Franklin D. Roosevelt's New Deal brought in large amounts of federal aid; and in 1964 when Barry Goldwater's extremism turned voters to Lyndon B. Johnson.

83. "2020 General Election: Election Results," Richardson County, Nebraska, https://co.richardson.ne.us/

84. "Peaceful Protest Held in Falls City," *Falls City Journal*, Dec. 24, 2019.

85. "Falls City Hot Air Balloon Festival Returning For 2020," *Falls City Journal*, Dec. 24, 2019; "FC Balloon Festival Blown Away," *Falls City Journal*, June 22, 2022.

86. Nikki McKim, "New Drug Coalition Hopes to Slow the Spread of Meth in Nebraska, Starting with Richardson County," *Falls City Journal*, March, 9, 2022.

87. Nikki McKim, "The Kids Aren't All Right – Bullying Hits and All-Time High," *Falls City Journal*, Dec. 7, 2022.

88. Nikki McKim, "Parental Concerns Lead to Spillover FCPS Board Meeting," *Falls City Journal*, May 18, 2022.

89. "A Closer Look at the Six Falls City School Board #56 Candidates," *Falls City Journal*, Nov. 2022. For election results, see Dan Swanson, "Richardson County Election Results," News Channel Nebraska: River Country, Nov. 8, 2022, rivercountry.newschannelnebraska.com

90. Nikki McKim, "President Trump Makes Historical Stop in Omaha Prior to Election," and "Walk Don't Run," *Falls City Journal*, Nov. 4, 2020.

91. Statistics throughout this section are from the *Falls City Journal*, which reported numbers of cases and deaths weekly during the pandemic. Also see the *New York Times* online site, "Tracking Coronavirus in Richardson County, Neb," updated Jan. 10, 2023, https://www.nytimes.com/interactive/2021/us/richardson-nebraska-covid-cases.html

92. *Falls City Journal*, Feb. 20, 2020.

93. Nikki McKim contributed five revealing articles to the *Falls City Journal* in the spring of 2021, entitled "The Covid-19 Pandemic," detailing local residents' experiences with the disease. See *Falls City Journal*, March 10, March 17, March 24, March 31, April 14. Also, McKim, "Graduating During a Pandemic: The FCPS Class of 2020 Shares Their Thoughts," *Falls City Journal*, May 13, 2020.

94. *Falls City Journal*, May 22, 28; also McKim, "The COVID-19 Pandemic: One Year Later; It Lingers With You For a Long Time," *Falls City Journal*, April 14, 2021.

95. Nikki McKim, "COVID Vaccine Reaches Richardson County," *Falls City Journal*, Dec. 30, 2020; Henry J. Cordes and Julie Anderson, "Nebraska Has Widest Vaccination Gap," *Lincoln Journal Star*, June 30, 2020; "White Cloud Health Center's Impressive COVID-19 Response," *Falls City Journal*, July 21, 2021.

96. Matt Olberding, "I Thought I Had Time," *Lincoln Journal Star*, June 27, 2021.

97. "Tracking Coronavirus in Richardson County, Neb.," *New York Times*, updated Jan. 9, 2023.

Index